Banking Governance, Performance and Risk-Taking

Series Editor
Chantal Ammi

Banking Governance, Performance and Risk-Taking

Conventional Banks Vs Islamic Banks

Faten Ben Bouheni
Chantal Ammi
Aldo Levy

iSTE

WILEY

First published 2016 in Great Britain and the United States by ISTE Ltd and John Wiley & Sons, Inc.

ISTE Ltd
27-37 St George's Road
London SW19 4EU
UK

www.iste.co.uk

John Wiley & Sons, Inc.
111 River Street
Hoboken, NJ 07030
USA

www.wiley.com

Library of Congress Control Number: 2016944314

British Library Cataloguing-in-Publication Data
A CIP record for this book is available from the British Library
ISBN 978-1-78630-082-9

Contents

Preface

The global financial crisis and sovereign debt have a close relationship with the governance, performance and risk taking of banks. Therefore, to reduce financial turmoil, mechanisms of banking governance must be reviewed in order to increase performance and reduce risk-taking.

In this book, we review and compare banking corporate governance, performance and risk-taking by conventional banks and Islamic banks. We note that Islamic banks may use the same governance mechanisms as a conventional bank in addition to the Shariah Supervisory Boards (SSB), the Shariah review unit, the Islamic International Rating Agency (IIRA) and the Islamic Financial Services Board (IFSB) as the main mechanisms of monitoring the Islamic banking system. However, unlike conventional systems, Islamic banking is based on the active participation of public policy institutions, regulatory and supervisory authorities and Shariah authorities, which ensures consistency with Islamic law (*Shariah*) principles and guided by Islamic economics. It is worth recalling that banking governance affects performance and risk-taking. Therefore, performance measurement is an assessment of an organization's performance, including the measures of productivity, effectiveness, quality and timeliness. Hence, traditional methods (e.g. ratio analysis, income statement analysis, market value added, cash flow statement, variance analysis, standard costing, etc.) and modern methods, mainly economic value added, are bestowed.

Performance is the outcome of many interlinking factors where corporate governance is the only one possible element within the whole set of performance drivers. Good banking governance has long been considered a crucial role for stakeholders in the business environment. Moreover, risk-taking has been widely debated in the financial literature. Further to financial scandals, managerial risk-taking has been specifically emphasized. Indeed, it is worth pointing out the different banking risk exposure – market risk, liquidity risk, credit risk and operational risk. We conclude that all banks are exposed to the same risks. In addition, Islamic banks are exposed to Shariah risk or operational risk, which is related to the structure and functioning of Shariah boards at the institutional and systemic level. Regarding risk management, many tools are used to reduce risk-taking (e.g. asset–liability management, financial derivatives, Basle principles, risk adjusted return on capital, market value at risk (VAR), Monte Carlo method, beta method, minimizing credit risk, assessing the default risk and the credit VAR). For operational risk management, quantitative and qualitative methods are proposed. Moreover, the IFSB has issued many guiding principles and technical note for the Islamic financial services industry in order to reduce risk-taking.

We conclude that there are similar determinants of performance and risk-taking for both conventional banks and Islamic banks. This similarity is due to the fact that all banks operate in the same institutional environment, they are exposed to same risks – except operational issues generated by Shariah SupervisionBoards (SSB) – and they use the same tools in managing their assets and liabilities. However, there are significant differences between conventional and Islamic banks governance because the latter provide Shariah compliant finance and have Shariah Supervision Boards (SSB) as a key feature of their banking governance.

Faten BEN BOUHENI
Chantal AMMI
Aldo LEVY
June 2016

Introduction

International scandals and recent financial and economic crises, especially the European sovereign debt crisis, have led to renewed interest in corporate governance, in particular banking governance. As such, in recent years banking governance has become one of the most debated subjects [BEN 10, BEN 13a]. As a fundamental economic concept, corporate governance has come to the attention of media and of academics [BEN 15, LEV 15]. Corporate governance is a set of mechanisms that affect how a corporation is operated. It deals with goals and welfare of all the stakeholders, including shareholders, management, board of directors and the economy as a whole. Adams *et al.* [ADA 10] argue that the firm is confronted by a myriad of governance-related problems and that its governance structure emerges as its best response to those problems. Hence, given the heterogeneity of governance issues faced by firms, it is unlikely that a unique governance policy is in the best interest.

In contrast to the failures in the conventional banking sector, Islamic banks did not announce substantial write-offs during the financial crisis but have been rather resilient [CHA 09, CHA 10, GRE 10]. While conventional banks have faced significant difficulties, Islamic banks seem to have fared better during the global financial crisis [MOL 15]. We must note that Islamic finance represents only 1% of global finance [LEV 16].

In this book, we review the theoretical and empirical research of banking corporate governance and its main mechanisms, especially in comparative banking governance between conventional banks and Islamic banks, and thus present the different tools used in banking performance and risk-taking. We highlight banks because they are the engine of the economy and their bankruptcy disrupts the whole economic system. These strong externalities on the economy make the corporate governance of banks a fundamental issue. Well-governed banks will be more efficient in their functions than those governed poorly [LEV 04].

Seeing the phenomenal growth of Islamic finance and the supply of Islamic financial products and services around the world by many banks, including well-known institutions, may be crucial to understand the features of Islamic banking and Islamic banking governance. Not only the good governance of banks is important; the question arises as to whether they are different from other corporations. Banks appear with new questions to the corporate governance problem due to their specific characteristics and their regulated condition.

Recently, Mollah and Zaman [MOL 15] examined whether Shariah supervision helps Islamic banks perform better and create shareholder value during the period 2005–2011. In particular, they focused on exploring the effect of (1) Shariah boards, (2) board structure and (3) CEO power on the performance of Islamic banks vis-à-vis conventional banks. Their analysis of bank performance and governance shows that boards of Islamic banks are more independent compared with their conventional counterparts and that conventional banks recruit more internal CEOs than Islamic banks. The small boards in Islamic banks and Shariah boards seem to be profit driven, but independent directors are associated with a decline in the performance of Islamic banks. They find different results between Islamic and conventional banks. Therefore, they conclude that the "multilayer" corporate governance model instituted in Islamic banks helps them to perform better than conventional banks, but this is due to inbuilt Shariah mechanisms in Islamic banking. Despite concerns about their independence and limited monitoring ability, they find that Shariah boards play a significant role in protecting shareholder interest and affect the performance of Islamic banks. They also find that board structure and CEO power are also an important influence on the performance of Islamic banks.

Our reflection can be briefly summarized around the following questions:

1) why has corporate governance become more important?

2) what is special about the banking governance of Islamic banks?

3) what are the different measures of banking performance?

4) what is the impact of banking governance on performance?

5) how can we analyze and manage banking risks?

6) what is the impact of banking governance on risk-taking?

Corporate governance relates to the manner in which the business of the bank is governed, including setting corporate objectives and the bank's risk profile, aligning corporate activities and behaviors with the expectation that the management will operate in a safe and sound manner, running day-to-day operations within an established risk profile, while protecting the interests of depositors and other stakeholders. It is defined by a set of relationships between the bank's management, its board, its shareholders and other stakeholders[1]. La Porta *et al.* [LA 00] pointed out that corporate governance has an important influence on the development of financial markets and corporate values, and that, as a whole, financial markets are developed in order to protect the rights of investors. They find that firms in countries that provided better protection to shareholders, on average, had a higher Tobin's Q. However, Johnson *et al.* [JON 00] indicate that corporate governance mechanisms could explain the depreciation of the currency and the extent of the decline in the stock market more than macroeconomic factors during the Asian financial crisis. They also found that those countries that provided better protection to minority shareholders suffered less severely than those that only provided weak protection to minority shareholders during the Asian financial crisis. Claessens *et al.* [CLA 02], using a sample of nine countries in Asia, showed that corporate value would be greater in firms with higher cash flow rights held by controlling shareholders.

Mitton [MIT 02], by using the five countries, the most affected by the Asian financial crisis as his sample (Indonesia, South Korea, Malaysia, the Philippines and Thailand), noted that firms with better corporate governance had smaller declines in their stock prices during the financial crisis. The major findings of Mitton [MIT 02] also state that the stock price would

1 See, for instance, [VAN 08].

perform better when the firm had a higher quality of information disclosure or a greater concentration of external shareholdings, where a higher quality of information disclosure meant that the firm had an American depositary receipts offering, or that its financial statements had been audited by a Big-Six accounting firm. Mitton [MIT 02] also find that the decline in the stock price was smaller for firms whose activities were concentrated than for diversified firms. In addition, Lemmon and Lins [LEM 03] indicate that the stock price decline during a financial crisis was greater when a firm's controlling shareholders had greater control rights and smaller cash flow rights. Joh [JOH 00] indicates that corporate profitability would be lower if the firm had lower ownership concentration, or if there was a high disparity between control rights and ownership rights, which suggests that corporate governance impacts accounting performance.

Using data for a sample of South Korean firms during the Asian financial crisis, Baek *et al.* [BAE 04] find that corporate governance had an influence on the decline of stock prices. They indicated that the decline in a firm's stock price during a financial crisis was smaller when that firm's unaffiliated foreign investors accounted for a larger shareholding within the firm or a better quality of information disclosure, and that the decline in the stock price during this period was larger when the controlling family in the firm had a larger shareholding or when the voting rights of the controlling shareholders were greater than their cash flow rights. Moreover, Klapper and Love [KLA 04] pointed out that better corporate governance helps improve operating performance and raises the firm's market value, and so corporate governance is more valuable when the minority shareholders are not protected enough by the legal environment.

Beltratti and Stulz [BEL 12] and Fahlenbrach and Stulz [FAH 11] analyze the influence of corporate governance on bank performance during the credit crisis: by analyzing the influence of CEO incentives and share ownership on bank performance Fahlenbrach and Stulz [FAH 11] find no evidence for a better performance of banks in which the incentives provided by the CEO's pay package are stronger. In fact, their evidence points to banks providing stronger incentives to CEOs performing worse in the crisis. A possible explanation for this finding is that CEOs may have focused on the interests of shareholders in the build-up to the crisis and took actions that they believed the market would welcome. However, these actions were costly to their banks and their shareholders when the results turned out to be poor. Moreover, their results indicate that bank CEOs did not reduce their stock holdings in anticipation of the crisis and CEOs did not hedge their holdings. Hence, their results suggest that bank CEOs did not anticipate the crisis and thus the resulting poor performance of the banks as they suffered huge losses themselves. Beltratti and Stulz [BEL 12] investigated the relationship between corporate governance and bank performance during the credit crisis in an international sample of 98 banks. Most importantly, they find that banks with more shareholder-friendly boards as measured by the "corporate governance quotient" obtained from Risk Metrics performed worse during the crisis, which indicates that the generally shared understanding of "good governance" does not necessarily have to be in the best interest of shareholders. They argue that "banks that were pushed by their boards to maximize shareholder wealth before the crisis took risks that were understood to create shareholder wealth, but were costly ex-post because of outcomes that were not expected when the risks were taken".

Moreover, Erkens *et al.* [ERK 10] investigated the relationship between corporate governance and performance of financial firms during the credit crisis of 2007/2008 using an international sample of 296 financial firms from 30 countries. Consistent with Beltratti and Stulz [BEL 12], they find that firms with more independent boards and higher institutional ownership experienced worse stock returns during the crisis. They argue that firms with higher institutional ownership took more risks prior to the crisis, which resulted in larger shareholder losses during the crisis period. Moreover, firms with more independent boards raised more equity capital during the crisis, which led to a wealth transfer from existing shareholders to debt holders. Minton *et al.* [MIN 10] investigated how risk-taking and U.S. banks' performance in the crisis relate to board independence and financial expertise of the board. Their results show that the financial expertise of the board is positively related to risk taking and bank performance before the crisis but is negatively related to bank performance in the crisis. Finally, Cornett *et al.* [COR 11] investigate the relation between various corporate governance mechanisms and bank performance in the crisis in a sample of approximately 300 publicly traded U.S. banks. In contrast to Erkens *et al.* [ERK 10], Beltratti and Stulz [BEL 12] and Fahlenbrach and Stulz [FAH 11], they find better corporate governance, for example a more independent board, a higher pay-for-performance sensitivity and an increase in insider ownership to be positively related to the banks' crisis performance.

This book is organized as follows:

– *Part 1: From Corporate Governance to Banking Governance*: in this part, we review the academic literature trying to understand the special features of the corporate governance, the banking governance and the Islamic banking governance, and the different mechanisms of corporate governance;

– *Part 2: Banking Performance*: this part is divided into three chapters, the first chapter deals with the different performance measurement tools, which vary among traditional and modern methods, the second chapter is about the relationship between corporate governance and performance and the third chapter presents banking governance and performance;

– *Part 3: Banking Risk-Taking*: this part is divided into three chapters; in the first two chapters, the banking risk analysis and management are discussed, and in the last chapter, we expose the relationship between corporate governance and risk taking by banks.

PART 1

From Corporate Governance to Banking Governance

In this first part we review the academic literature in trying to understand the special features of the corporate governance, the banking governance and the Islamic banking governance and the different mechanisms of corporate governance. We touch on research points of many characteristics, such as nature of activities, regulation, supervision, capital structure, risk and ownership, that would make banks unique and thereby influence their corporate governance.

This part is composed of four sections. Section 1.1 broadly defines corporate governance and their features. Section 1.2 explains the special characteristics of banks and banking governance. Section 1.3. deals with Islamic banking governance and their singularity compared to conventional banks. Section 1.4 focuses on the different mechanisms of corporate governance, banking governance and Islamic banking governance.

1

Corporate Governance: A Brief Literature Review

1.1. The features of corporate governance

1.1.1. *Definitions of corporate governance*

Corporate governance in the academic literature seems to have been first used by Eells [EEL 60] to denote "the structure and functioning of the corporate polity". The most quoted definition of corporate governance is the one given by Shleifer and Vishny [SHL 97]: "Corporate governance deals with the ways in which suppliers of finance to corporations assure themselves of getting a return on their investment. Corporate governance deals with the agency problem: the separation of management and finance, the fundamental question of corporate governance is how to assure financiers that they get a return on their financial investment".

In their survey, Shleifer and Vishny [SHL 97] account for different governance models, especially those of the United States, UK, Germany and Japan. They conclude that the United States and the United Kingdom have a governance system characterized by a strong legal protection of investors and a lack of large investors, except when ownership is concentrated temporarily during the takeover process. However, in continental Europe as well as in Japan, the system is characterized by a weak legal protection of minorities and the presence of large investors.

According to Braendle and Kostyuk [BRA 07], the term "corporate governance" is susceptible to both narrow and broad definitions, related to the two perspectives of shareholder and stakeholder orientation. It therefore revolves around the debate on whether management should run the corporation solely in the interests of shareholders (shareholder perspective) or whether it should take account of other constituencies (stakeholder perspective).

Narrowly defined corporate governance concerns the relationships between corporate managers, the board of directors and shareholders, but it might as well encompass the relationship of the corporation to stakeholders and society. More broadly defined, corporate governance can encompass the combination of laws, regulations, listing rules and practices that enable the corporation to attract capital, perform efficiently, generate profit and meet both, legal obligations and general societal expectations.

Lipton and Lorsch [LIP 92] give a definition in favor of a shareholder perspective as follows: the approach of corporate governance that social, moral and political questions are proper concerns of corporate governance is fundamentally misconceived. If we expand corporate governance to encompass society, as a whole it benefits neither corporations nor society, because management is ill-equipped to deal with questions of general public interest.

Hess [HES 96] mentioned that "corporate governance is the process of control and administration of the company's capital and human resources in the interest of the owners of a company". In the same sense, Sternberg [STE 98] considered that "corporate governance describes ways of ensuring that corporate actions, assets and agents are directed at achieving the corporate objectives established by the corporation's shareholders".

The OECD[1] principles of corporate governance (2004, 2015[2]) tried to give a very broad definition, as it should serve as a basis for all OECD countries:

1 The Organization for Economic Co-operation and Development (OECD) is an international economic organization of 34 countries founded in 1961 to promote policies that will improve the economic and social well-being of people around the world.

2 "The G20/OECD principles of corporate governance help policy makers evaluate and improve the legal, regulatory and institutional framework for corporate governance. They also

"Corporate governance defines a set of relationships between a company's management, its board, its shareholders and other stakeholders". An even broader definition is to define a governance system as "the complex set of constraints that shape the ex post bargaining over the quasi rents generated by the firm" [ZIN 98].

This definition focuses on the division of claims and can be somewhat expanded to define corporate governance as "the complex set of constraints that determine the quasi-rents (profits) generated by the firm in the course of relationships and shape the ex-post bargaining over them". This definition refers to both the determination of value added by firms and the allocation of it among stakeholders that have relationships with the firm. It can be referred to a set of rules and principles, as well as to institutions.

Du Plessis *et al.* [DU 05] define corporate governance as: "The process of controlling management and of balancing the interests of all internal stakeholders and other parties (external stakeholders, governments and local communities, etc.) who can be affected by the corporation's conduct in order to ensure responsible behavior by corporations and to achieve the maximum level of efficiency and profitability for a corporation". Under a definition more specific to corporate governance, the focus would be on how outside investors protect themselves against expropriation by the insiders (large investors). This would include minorities' protection and the strength of creditor rights, as reflected in collateral and bankruptcy laws, and their enforcement. It could also include such issues as requirements on the composition and the rights of the executive directors and the ability to pursue class-action suits [CLA 12].

Although there are a myriad of definitions on corporate governance and they vary between narrow and broad perspectives, governance may be defined as a set of internal and external mechanisms working together to obtain an efficient and an optimal alignment of all parties' interests, and

---

provide guidance for stock exchanges, investors, corporations and others that have a role in the process of developing good corporate governance. First issued in 1999, the principles have become the international benchmark in corporate governance. They have been adopted as one of the Financial Stability Board's Key Standards for Sound Financial Systems and endorsed by the G20. This 2015 edition takes into account developments in both the financial and corporate sectors that may influence the efficiency and relevance of corporate governance policies and practices" http://www.amazon.fr/G20-Oecd-Principles-Corporate-Governance/dp/9264236872/ref=sr_1_4?s=books&ie=UTF8&qid=1459015809&sr=1-4&keywords= governance.

getting a win–win relationship. In a subjective conception of the term *corporate governance*, "banking governance is defined as a set of internal and external mechanisms, which aims optimal harmonization between shareholders, directors and stakeholders. It is based on the safe cooperation between management and control in order to obtain a win–win relationship in which interests are aligned and goals are achieved".

1.1.2. *Nature of the agency problem*

The problem of corporate governance is rooted in the Berle–Means [BER 32] paradigm of the separation of shareholders' ownership and management's control in the modern corporation. The agency problem occurs when the principal (shareholders) lacks the necessary power or information to monitor and control the agent (managers) and when the compensation of the principal and the agent is not aligned. The separation of ownership and control results in information asymmetry, thus potentially leading to two types of agency problems: (1) one agency problem is between outside investors and managers ("principal-agent" agency problem) and (2) the other one is between controlling shareholders and minority shareholders ("principal–principal" agency problem) [JEN 76]. Moreover, La Porta *et al.'s* [LA 99] research of corporate governance patterns in 27 countries concludes that "the principal agency problem in large corporations around the world is that of restricting expropriation of minority shareholders by the controlling shareholders".

Shleifer and Veshny [SHL 97] consider that contracts between financiers and manager are the source of the first agency problem because they lead to management discretion. Then, the existence of large investors, which causes expropriation of minorities, is the second source of the agency problem. Hence, to mitigate the conflict between all the parties (managers and shareholders, large and minority shareholders), the literature offers several solutions, such as monitoring by the board of directors, incentive contracts and protection of minorities.

1.1.3. *Origins of the agency problem*

1.1.3.1. *Contracts*

The substratum of the agency problem is the separation of management and finance, or ownership and control. A manager raises funds from investors either to put them to productive use or to cash out his holdings in the firm. The financiers need the manager's specialized human capital to generate returns on their funds [SHL 97].

As Hart [HAR 89] observes, every business organization, including the corporation, "represents nothing more than a particular 'standard form' contract". The very justification for having different types of business organizations is to permit investors, entrepreneurs and other participants in the corporate enterprise to select the organizational design they prefer from a menu of standard-form contracts.

So there is a contract signed between owners (financiers) and managers that specifies what the manager does with the funds, and how the returns are divided between him and the financiers. The problem is that the manager is motivated to raise as much funds as he can, and so tries hard to accommodate the financiers by developing a complete contract. And the manager and the financier have to allocate residual control rights not fully foreseen by the contract [GRO 86, HAR 90].

The effect of this is that managers end up with significant control rights (discretion) over how to allocate investors' funds. To begin, they can expropriate them, which Shleifer and Vishny [SHI 97] refer to as management discretion.

A vast amount of literature explains how managers use their effective control rights to pursue projects that benefit them rather than investors[3]. Grossman and Hart [GRO 88] describe these benefits as the private benefits of control.

Moreover, managers can expropriate shareholders by entrenching themselves and staying on the job even if they are no longer competent or qualified to run the firm [SHL 89]. As argued in [JEN 83], poor managers who resist being replaced might be the costliest manifestation of the agency problem.

1.1.3.2. *Large investors*

When control rights are concentrated in the hands of a small number of investors, this can lead to the expropriation of minorities. In their survey,

---

3 See, for example, [BAU 59], [MAR 64], [WIL 64] and [JEN 86].

Shleifer and Vishny [SHL 97] discussed the forms of concentrating ownership, and how they address the agency problem. Hence, they subdivided large investors as follows:

– Large shareholders:

Their control rights give them the power to put pressure on the management, or in some cases to oust the management through a proxy fight or a takeover [SHL 86b].

In the United States, large share holdings, and especially majority ownership, are relatively uncommon probably because of legal restrictions on high ownership and exercise of control by banks, mutual funds, insurance companies and other institutions [ROE 94]. Even in the United States, however, ownership is not completely dispersed, and concentrated holdings by families and wealthy investors are more common than is often believed[4].

In Germany, large commercial banks often control over a quarter of the votes in major companies through proxy voting arrangements, and also have smaller but significant cash stakes as direct shareholders or creditors[5]. In addition, one study estimates that about 80% of the large German companies have an over 25% non-bank large shareholder [GOR 98]. In smaller German companies, the principle is family control through majority ownership or pyramids, in which the owner controls 51% of a company, which in turn controls 51% of its subsidiaries and so on [FRA 94]. In France, cross-ownership and the so-called core investors are common [OEC 95].

In Britain and the United States, two of the countries where large shareholders are less common, a particular mechanism for consolidating ownership has emerged, namely the hostile takeover [JEN 83, FRA 90].

– Large creditors:

Like the large shareholders, they have large investments and want to see the returns on their investments materialize. The effectiveness of large creditors, such as the effectiveness of large shareholders, depends on the legal rights they have. In Germany and Japan, the powers of the banks

4 See [EIS 76, DEM 83, SHL 86b].
5 See [FRA 94, OEC 95].

vis-à-vis companies are very significant because banks vote on significant blocks of shares, sit on boards of directors, play a dominant role in lending and operate in a legal environment favorable to creditors. In other countries, especially where procedures for turning control over to the banks are not well established, bank governance is likely to be less effective.

1.1.4. *Solutions*

1.1.4.1. *Incentive contracts*

The agency problem arises when contracts are incomplete and managers possess more expertise than shareholders, such that managers typically end up with the residual rights of control, giving them enormous latitude for self-interested behavior. So the better solution is the "incentive contract" to align his interests with those of investors. In this way, incentive contracts can induce the manager to act in investors' interest without encouraging blackmail [SHL 97].

Incentive contracts can take a variety of forms, including share ownership, stock options or a threat of dismissal if income is low [JEN 76, FAM 80]. The optimal incentive contract is determined by the manager's risk aversion, the importance of his/her decisions and his/her ability to pay for the cash flow ownership up front[6].

1.1.4.2. *Monitoring by board of directors*

The board of directors is presumed to carry out the monitoring function on behalf of shareholders, because the shareholders themselves would find it difficult to exercise control due to wide dispersion of ownership of common stocks. Therefore, the board's effectiveness in its monitoring function is determined by its independence, size and composition. The bulk of the literature is empirical, which takes as given the current structure of board governance and studies its impact on firm performance [JOH 98].

However, monitoring by the board of directors is not the best option for minimizing the agency problem, because the agency problem, sometimes, can come from the directors themselves.

---

6 See, for instance, [ROS 73, STI 75, MIR 76, HOL 79, HOL 82].

Adams [ADA 01] focuses on the conflict between the monitoring and advisory functions of the board of directors: the board's monitoring role can restrict its ability to extract information from management that is needed for its advisory role. Thus, the model gives insight into the possible benefits of instituting a dual-board system, as in Germany.

The literature has mainly focused on issues relating to board composition, board size and the selection of directors. However, issues relating to the functioning of the board, their dependence from what and from who and how board meetings can be structured to ensure more effective monitoring of management, are equally important. This is a particularly fruitful area for future research.

1.1.4.3. *Minority protection*

The minority shareholder problem maintains that both the controlling shareholders [SHL 88, GAD 06] and managers [JEN 86, LAN 89, PEA 03] have the power to extract private benefits at the cost of minority shareholders. However, legal regimes, if such exist, may give minority shareholders enough power to extract cash dividends [LA 00].

Corporate and other law gives outside investors, including shareholders, certain powers to protect their investments against expropriation by insiders. For shareholders, these powers range from the right to receive the same per share dividend as the insiders, to the right to vote on important matters, including the election of directors, and to the right to sue the company for damages. The very fact that legal protection exists probably explains why becoming a minority shareholder is a viable investment strategy, as opposed to just being an outright gift of money to strangers who are under few, if any, obligations to give it back [LA 00]. The extent of legal protection of outside investors differs enormously across countries and according to La Porta *et al.* [LA 98] in common law countries compared to civil law countries, there is better minority protection.

Djankov *et al.* [DJA 08] discuss and reject two extreme approaches to resolve the principal–principal agency problem. First, they argue that the exclusive reliance on market forces will not solve the problem because, in the absence of regulations, and thus of risks, the temptation for controlling shareholders to engage in opportunistic behavior is too high. Second, because certain related-party transactions, such as propping, may benefit a firm and all its shareholders, governments or regulators cannot legally restrict all of them. Hence, most countries adopt a middle of the road approach, enacting laws that do offer minority shareholders any rights to monitor controlling shareholders and that provide governance mechanisms that restrict private control rights. Accordingly, in countries with better legal protection, investors believe that they are more likely to receive their fair share of their investment's profits as controlling shareholders are less likely to divert corporate resources away.

1.1.4.4. *General actions*

Becht *et al.* [BEC 02] proposed five main ways to mitigate shareholders' collective action problems:

1) election of a board of directors representing shareholders' interests, to which the chief executive officer (CEO) is accountable;

2) when the need arises, a takeover or proxy fight launched by a corporate raider who temporarily concentrates voting power (and/or ownership) in his/her hands to resolve a crisis, reach an important decision or remove an inefficient manager;

3) active and continuous monitoring by a large blockholder, who could be a wealthy investor or a financial intermediary, such as a bank, a holding company or a pension fund;

4) alignment of managerial interests with investors through executive compensation contracts;

5) clearly defined fiduciary duties for CEOs and the threat of class-action suits that either blocks corporate decisions that go against investors' interests, or seek compensation for past actions that have harmed their interests.

They explained that there is potential difficulty with the first three approaches, which is the old problem of who monitors the monitor and the risk of collusion between management (the agent) and the delegated monitor (director, raider, blockholder). It might appear that corporate raiders, who concentrate ownership directly in their hands, are not susceptible to this delegated monitoring problem. This is only partially true since the raiders themselves have to raise funds to finance the takeover. Typically, firms that are taken over through a hostile bid end up being substantially more highly levered. They may have resolved the shareholder collective action problem, but at the cost of significantly increasing the expected cost of financial distress.

1.2. Fundamental theories of corporate governance

1.2.1. *Transaction cost theory*

Transaction cost theory was first initiated in Coase's [COA 37] paper and later theoretical described and exposed by Williamson [WIL 96]. Transaction cost theory was an interdisciplinary alliance of law, economics and organizations. This theory attempts to view the firm as an organization comprising people with different views and objectives. The underlying assumption of transaction theory is that firms have become so large they in effect substitute for the market in determining the allocation of resources. In other words, the organization and structure of a firm can determine price and production. The unit of analysis in transaction cost theory is the transaction. Therefore, the combination of people with transaction suggests that transaction cost theory managers are opportunists and arrange firms' transactions to their interests [WIL 96].

The essential element of transaction costs, that property rights must be protected, is found in most fields of economics and throughout the discipline's history. Adam Smith, in discussing foreign trade, endowments, corporate ownership structure and non-profit organizations, repeatedly exploits concepts of costly information and the ability of individuals to exploit others' ignorance to their own advantage [WES 90].

In his study about "the transaction costs", Allen [ALL 99] mentioned that in macroeconomics the notion of costly information lead to the rational expectations revolution and subsequent real business cycle models based on search and the disincentives found in unemployment insurance programs. Public choice models are founded on the premise that individuals can use the state as a mechanism to transfer wealth to themselves. In game theory, the prisoner's dilemma and other non-cooperative games are essentially transaction cost problems. And other fields like industrial organization, international trade, development and labor, all contain ideas that hinge on the protection of property rights.

This connection between transaction costs and property rights is summarized in the Coase theorem, which is defined as:

> *In the absence of transaction costs, the allocation of resources is independent of the distribution of property rights.*

There are many attacks and defenses of the Coase theorem, none of which are dealt with here[7]. The point is that for all property right approaches to transaction costs, the two concepts of property rights and transaction costs are fundamentally interlinked. The neoclassical literature on transaction costs begins in the early 1950s; this literature defines transaction costs more narrowly and models them more explicitly. The definition of transaction costs found in the neoclassical approaches is as follows:

> "In general, transaction costs are ubiquitous in market economies and can arise from the transfer of any property right because parties to exchanges must find one another, communicate and exchange information. There may be a necessity to inspect and measure goods to be transferred, draw up contracts, consult with lawyers or other experts and transfer title. Depending upon who provides these services, transaction costs can take one of two forms, inputs or resources – including time – by a buyer and/or a seller or a margin between the buying and selling price of a commodity in a given market" [STA 95].

1.2.2. *Agency theory*

The phenomena of corporate governance are linked directly to the agency theory, or agency relationships, which focuses on the relationship and goal incongruence between managers and stockholders [JEN 86, JEN 76]. Managers are considered as shareholder agents. There are potential conflicts of interest between the management, ownerships and shareholders due to the delegation of decision-making authority from shareholders to managers. Shareholders and ownerships cannot perfectly and costlessly, monitor the

7 See [SHA 74, ALL 97, ZER 80].

managers, but they are in a position to monitor and acquire the available information possessed by managers otherwise risk information asymmetry.

Agency theory was exposited by Alchian and Demsetz [ALC 72] and further developed by Jensen and Meckling [JEN 76]. Agency theory is defined as "the relationship between the principals, such as shareholders and agents, and the company executives and managers". In this theory, shareholders, who are the owners or principals of the company, hire agents. Principals delegate the running of business to the directors or managers, who are the shareholder's agents [CLA 04].

Daily *et al.* [DAI 03] argued that two factors could influence the prominence of agency theory. First, that the theory is conceptual and simple, reducing the corporation to two participants of managers and shareholders. Second, agency theory suggests that employees or managers in organizations can be self-interested. Agency theory shareholders expect the agents to act and make decisions in the principal's interest. On the contrary, the agent may not necessarily make decisions in the best interests of the principals. Such a problem was first highlighted by Adam Smith in the 18th Century and subsequently explored by Ross [ROS 73] and the first detailed description of agency theory was presented by Jensen and Meckling [JEN 76]. Indeed, the notion of problems arising from the separation of ownership and control in agency theory has been confirmed by Davis *et al.* [DAV 97].

In agency theory, the agent may succumb to self-interest, opportunistic behavior and thus fall short of congruence between the aspirations of the principal and the agent's pursuits. Even the understanding of risk defers in its approach. Although with such setbacks, agency theory was introduced simply as a separation of ownership and control [BHI 08]. Holmstrom and Milgrom [HOL 94] argued that instead of providing fluctuating incentive payments, the agents should only focus on projects that have a high return and have a fixed wage without any incentive component. Although this will provide a fair assessment, it does not eradicate or even minimize corporate misconduct. Here, the positivist approach is used where the agents are controlled by principal-made rules, with the aim of maximizing shareholder value, hence a more individualistic view is applied [CLA 04]. Indeed, agency theory can be employed to explore the relationship between the ownership and management structure.

Where there is a separation, however, the agency model can be applied to align the goals of the management with that of the owners. Due to the fact that in a family-run firm the management comprises family members, the agency cost would be minimal as any firm's performance does not really affect the firm performance. The model of an employee portrayed in agency theory is more of a self-interested individual with bounded rationality where rewards and punishments seem to take priority [JEN 76]. This theory prescribes that people or employees are held accountable in their tasks and responsibilities. Employees must constitute a good governance structure rather than just providing the need of shareholders, which maybe challenging the governance structure.

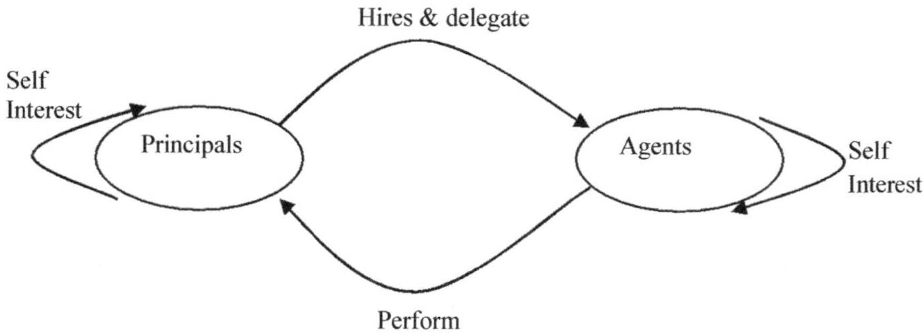

Figure 1.1. *The agency model*

The goal of corporate governance is to engender the successful operation of organizations [KEA 93], to minimize agency problem related costs and to create harmony and synchronization between all parties. Corporate governance includes employing thorough contracts that specifically and in detail denote managements' duties and freedom as well as the profit sharing [SHL 97].

1.2.3. *Stewardship theory*

Stewardship theory has its roots in psychology and sociology and is defined by Davis *et al.* [DAV 97]: "A steward protects and maximizes shareholders wealth through firm performance, because by so doing, the steward's utility functions are maximized". In this perspective, stewards are company executives and managers working, protecting and making money for the shareholders. Unlike agency theory, stewardship theory stresses not on the perspective of individualism [DON 91], but rather on the role of top management as stewards, integrating their goals as part of the organization. The stewardship perspective suggests that stewards are satisfied and motivated when organizational success is attained.

Agyris [AGY 73] argues that agency theory looks at an employee or people as an economic being, which suppresses an individual's own aspirations. However, stewardship theory recognizes the importance of structures that empower the steward and offers maximum autonomy built on trust [DON 91]. It stresses on the position of employees or executives to act more autonomously so that the shareholders' returns are maximized. Indeed, this can minimize the costs aimed at monitoring and controlling behaviors.

On the other end, Daly *et al.* [DAL] argue that in order to protect their reputations as decision makers in organizations, executives and directors are inclined to operate the firm to maximize financial performance as well as shareholders' profits. In this sense, it is believed that the firm's performance can directly impact perceptions of their individual performance. Indeed, Fama [FAM 80] contends that executives and directors are also managing their careers in order to be seen as effective stewards of their organization, while Shleifer and Vishny [SHL 97] insist that managers return finance to investors to establish a good reputation so that they can re-enter the market for future finance. Stewardship model can have linking or resemblance in countries like Japan, where the Japanese worker assumes the role of stewards and takes ownership of their jobs and work diligently.

Moreover, stewardship theory suggests unifying the role of the CEO and the chairman so as to reduce agency costs and to have a greater role as stewards in the organization. It was evident that there would be better safeguarding of the interest of the shareholders. It was empirically found that the returns have improved by having both these theories combined rather than applied separately [DON 91].

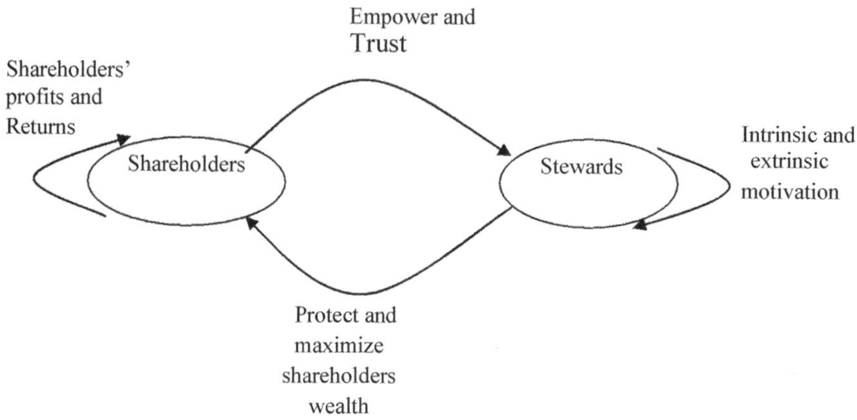

Figure 1.2. *The stewardship model*

1.2.4. *Stakeholder theory*

Stakeholder theory was embedded in the discipline of management in 1970 and gradually developed by Freeman [FRE 84] incorporating corporate accountability to a broad range of stakeholders. Wheeler *et al.* [WHE 03] argued that stakeholder theory derived from a combination of the sociological and organizational disciplines.

Indeed, stakeholder theory is less of a formal unified theory and more of a broad research tradition, incorporating philosophy, ethics, political theory, economics, law and organizational science. Stakeholder theory can be defined as "any group or individual who can affect or is affected by the achievement of the organization's objectives". Unlike agency theory in which the managers are working and serving for the stakeholders, stakeholder theorists suggest that managers in organizations have a network of relationships to serve – this includes the suppliers, employees and business partners. It has been argued that this group is more important than other owner–manager–employee relationships as in agency theory [FRE 99].

On the other end, Sundaram and Inkpen [SUN 04] contend that stakeholder theory attempts to address the group of stakeholders deserving and requiring management's attention, while Donaldson and Preston [DON 95] claimed that all groups participate in a business to obtain benefits.

Nevertheless, Clarkson [CLA 95] suggested that the firm is a system, where there are stakeholders and the purpose of the organization is to create wealth for its stakeholders.

Freeman [FRE 84] contends that the network of relationships with many groups can affect decision-making processes as stakeholder theory is concerned with the nature of these relationships in terms of both processes and outcomes for the firm and its stakeholders. Donaldson and Preston [DON 95] argued that this theory focuses on managerial decision-making and interests of all stakeholders have intrinsic value, and no set of interests is assumed to overpower the others.

We should note immediately that in the context of Islamic banks, depositors are the main financiers of the bank and that these stakeholders have a notable and notorious influence on profitability (return on equity) and the risks of these banks (Bale II) [LEV 12].

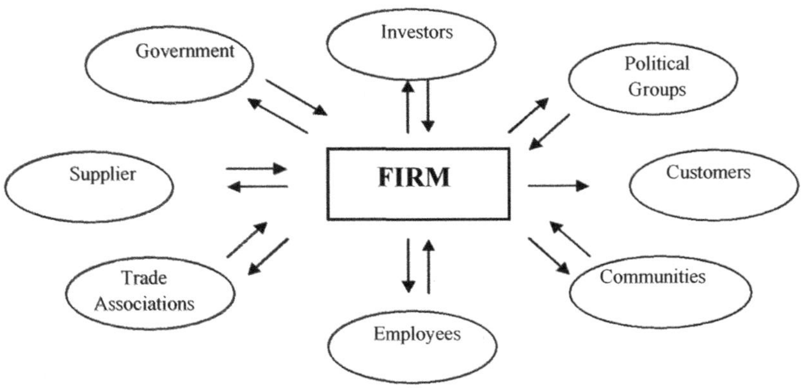

Figure 1.3. *The stakeholder model [DON 95]*

1.2.5. *Resource dependency theory*

While stakeholder theory focuses on relationships with many groups for individual benefits, resource dependency theory concentrates on the role of board directors in providing access to resources needed by the firm. Hillman *et al.* [HIL 00] contend that resource dependency theory focuses on the role that directors play in providing or securing essential resources to an organization through their links with the external environment. Indeed,

Johnson *et al.* [JOH 96] concur that resource dependency theorists provide focus on the appointment of representatives of independent organizations as a means for gaining access in resources critical to firm success. For example, outside directors who are partners to a law firm provide legal advice, either in board meetings or in private communications with firm executives that may otherwise be more costly for the firm to secure. It has been argued that the provision of resources enhances organizational functioning, firm's performance and its survival.

According to Hillman *et al.* [HIL 00], directors bring resources to the firm, such as information, skills and access to key constituents such as suppliers, buyers, public policy makers, social groups, and legitimacy. Directors can be classified into four categories of insiders, business experts, support specialists and community influential. First, the insiders are current and former executives of the firm and they provide expertise in specific areas such as finance and law on the firm itself as well as general strategy and direction. Second, the business experts are current or former senior executives and directors of other large for-profit firms and they provide expertise on business strategy, decision making and problem solving. Third, the support specialists are lawyers, bankers, insurance company representatives and public relations experts and these specialists provide support in their individual specialized field. Finally, the community influential are the political leaders, university faculty, members of clergy and leaders of social or community organizations.

1.2.6. *Political theory*

Political theory considers the approach of developing voting support from shareholders, rather by purchasing voting power. Hence having a political influence in corporate governance may direct corporate governance within the organization. Public interest is much reserved as the government participates in corporate decision-making, taking into consideration cultural challenges [POU 93]. The political model highlights the allocation of corporate power; profits and privileges are determined via the governments' favor. The political model of corporate governance can have an immense influence on governance developments. Over the past decades, the government of a country has been seen to have a strong political influence on firms. As a result, there is an entrance of politics into the governance structure or firms' mechanism [HAW 96].

1.3. Corporate governance and ethics

Corporate governance is not only the process of control and administration of a company's capital and human resources in the interest of the owners of a company, but also the whole system of rights where social, moral and political questions are legitimate concerns. It deals with questions of general public interest.

Under this definition, corporate governance would include the relationship between shareholders, creditors and corporations, between financial markets, institutions and corporations and between employees and corporations. Corporate governance would also encompass the issue of corporate social responsibility, including such aspects as the dealings of the firm with respect to culture and the environment. Giving the example of the loyalty that is an important virtue, many works in empirical social psychology suggests that loyalty is hardwired into human behavior. Milgram [MIL 63, MIL 74] shows that a human subject suppresses internal ethical standards surprisingly readily if these conflict with loyalty to an authority figure. This accords well with officers and directors' stalwart loyalty to misguided or errant CEOs, even under clear signs of impending financial doom. Milgram argues that loyal behavior stimulates feelings of well-being, and that this reflects evolutionary pressure on early human societies, when obedience to authority wrought social organization that raised survival odds [HOB 52].

Milgram [MIL 74] posits what he calls an *agentic shift*, whereby individuals forsake rational reasoning for loyalty. Milgram [MIL 74] states, "the most far-reaching consequence of the agentic shift is that a man feels responsibility to the authority directing him, but feels no responsibility for the content of the actions that the authority prescribes". Directors enchanted by a powerful CEO feel a profound duty to live up to the CEO's expectations, but none at all for how their actions affect shareholders, or other stakeholders for that matter.

Human nature changes slowly, if at all, and terms like *loyalty* and *duty* are laden with moral charge. Milgram [MIL 74] despairs that "the virtues of loyalty, discipline, and self-sacrifice that we value so highly in the individual are the very properties that create destructive engines of war and bind men to malevolent systems of authority". Corporate governance scandals seem anticlimactic to this, but arise from the same weakness in human nature.

One hope whenever behavioral biases induce irrational or unethical behavior is that informing people about those biases can help them correct their errors and induce appropriate behavior. Gergen [GER 73] argues that sophistication as to psychological principles liberates one from their behavioral implications.

There is far more to a job than just showing up and completing your work. You need to understand very well your social environment. Employers expect you to show up every day on time, looking good, enthused and focused on the job at hand. As basic as these expectations sound, it is not easy for many people to show up consistently in this manner. The people who do, however, have an advantage which is basically their knowledge of others and their behaviors.

We have never heard of anyone criticized for being too positive or too professional, but we have heard a lot of criticism about people who are negative, unreliable and difficult to get along with. You will have an advantage in the workplace and in life if you are dependable, professional, flexible and likeable. Doing a job well is a key factor for success, but your ability to succeed encompasses much more. Do not overlook the importance of your attitude and demeanor; picking up after yourself, pitching in without being asked, and being consistent in all of your behaviors toward other people.

1.3.1. *Ethics in Islamic finance*

Islam as a way of life has, in some verses of the Koran [LEV 13], promoted good ethics, strong morals, unshakeable integrity and honesty of the highest order positive values and high ethical conduct should be integrated and inherent in the Muslim community. Therefore, the issue of corporate governance is not foreign to Islamic financial institutions. As organizations governed by the principles laid out in the Koran, Islamic financial institutions must strictly observe and fulfill their obligations as prescribed by the Islamic Law of Shariah [DUS 06].

Hence, Islamic finance has to put Islamic principles about the economy into practice. Attempts have been undertaken specifically to develop an

Islamic type of economy, based upon the precepts of the holy book of Muslims, the Koran, and on Islamic religious law, the principles of Shariah. The tenets of Islamic finance are the avoidance of riba (fixed and predetermined interest), gharar (uncertainty, risk and speculation), and haram (religiously prohibited) activities. Therefore, Islamic finance strictly prohibits fixed and predetermined interest-based transactions, but it embraces the sharing of profit and loss or, in other words, sharing of the risk in the real economy by the provider and the user of the funds invested. The ownership and trading of a physical good or service is a critical element in structuring Islamic financial products. Islamic finance encourages, but without obligation, active participation of financial institutions and investors in achieving the goals and objectives of an Islamic economy. It merges the ethical teachings of Islam with finance as a means to meet the needs of society and encourage socioeconomic justice.

According to McMillen [MCM 08], the Shariah which is the Islamic finance law is composed of and embodies religion, ethics, morality and behavioral admonitions as well as those that are more customarily recognized as legal requirements: it is the Whole Duty of Man's moral and pastoral theology and ethics, high spiritual aspiration and the detailed ritualistic and formal observance which to some minds is a vehicle for such aspiration and to others a substitute for it in all aspects of law.

The prohibition of interest plays a key role in Islamic finance. But this ban is not the Koran. It was not born with Islam but dates back to the Jewish worship which passages from Deuteronomy and Exode5 mention that a Jew cannot lend with interest to a non-Jew:

> "From abroad you may charge interest, but to your brother you shall lend on the point, that the Lord thy God may bless you in all that you undertake in the land where you'll regain possession [...]. If you lend money to my people that is poor by thee, thou shalt not behave with him in usurer; you put over him wear"[8].

In Ancient Greece, there are also traces of a disdain for any form of remuneration of the money lent. Indeed, Aristotle (Greek philosopher who lived in the fifth Century before Christ) already evokes in its policies:

8 Deuteronomy, 23 :19, 20; Exodus, 22:25.

> "It is quite normal to hate the profession of usurer that his wealth comes from his money himself and that it was not invented for it. It was made for the exchange, while the interest only multiplies. And this is where it got its name: small, in fact, are similar to their parents, and the interest is money born of money. So this is the way to gain more unnatural"[9].

Christianity, through the Gospels, also prohibited interest, but this time implicitly:

> "If you lend to those from whom you hope to receive, what credit is that for you? Even sinners lend to sinners so that they may receive back an equal amount. But love your enemies, and do good, and lend, do not despair nobody"[10].

It was not until 1515 that the Catholic religion allowed interest through Concil Lateran V10. At this time, reformers such as Calvin authorized interest, without allowing wear. Calvin opposed the loan resulting in a depletion of the debtor, but was favorable to the enrichment of the latter. He defended the loan to non-usury when applied to the rich.

The following passage is taken from the Koran and is the basis of the interpretation of the prohibition of interest in Islam:

> "Those who feed on usury shall rise up in the judgment that stands as one the demon violently struck. This will be so because they say the sale is like usury. But God allowed the sales and forbid usury. He who renounces the benefit of wear, from an admonition from his Lord will keep reaches him what he has earned. His case comes from God. But those returning to wear the Fire will host where they will remain immortal. (...) O you who believe! Fear God! Give up if you believe in what you have profits from wear. If you do not expect to war from God and his prophet"[11].

In fact, money is only potential capital and becomes capital only after its association with another tangible resource to undertake a productive activity.

9 Aristotle, Politics, Book 1, Chapter 3.
10 Gospels, Luke 6: 34, 65.
11 Sura II, verse 275 to verse 281.

1.4. Corporate governance and psychological biases

Behavioral finance is a very important field, because it has explained the behavior of managers and shareholders in their decision-making relying on psychological biases, such as the over confidence kink. A vast amount of literature shows that people tend to be overconfident. De Bondt and Thaler [DE 95] said that the most robust finding in the psychology of judgment is that people are overconfident. People tend to be too optimistic about outcomes they believe they control and to take too much credit for success while blaming other factors for failure or underperformance. Not surprisingly, people tend to believe that they exert more control over results than they actually do, discounting the role of luck and chance.

Shiller [SHI 03] mentions that "the collaboration between finance and other social sciences that has become known as behavioral finance has led to a profound deepening of our knowledge of financial markets". Moreover, "behavioral finance is the study of the influence of psychology on the behavior of financial practitioners and the subsequent effect on markets" [SEW 05].

Shleifer and Vishny [SHL 97] argue that corporate governance problems often involve corporate insiders failing to act as agents of the firm's shareholders and other providers of capital. This view derives from the agency problem model of Jensen and Meckling [JEN 76], in which corporate officers and directors have a duty as agents of shareholders, but act for themselves.

Adams *et al.* [ADA 05] argue that the CEO can manipulate agendas to frame issues most easily if he is the only insider on the board, and that boards entirely composed of independent directors actually strengthen the CEO's power. Ocasio [OCA 94] argues that other corporate insiders on boards can emerge as alternative "leaders" if they feel they can usurp the CEO's position.

In a recent study, Hirshleifer *et al.* [HIR 12] investigate how managers' psychological biases, especially overconfidence, affect firm decisions. They note that Steve Jobs, former CEO of Apple Computers, was ranked by Business Week as one of the greatest innovators of the last 75 years in a 2004 article written before Apple's introduction of the path-breaking iPhone and iPad, because "more than anyone else, Apple's co-founder has brought digital technology to the masses". They confirm that Jobs is almost as famous for his self-confidence.

This study also found that over the 1993–2003 period, firms with overconfident CEOs have greater return volatility, invest more in innovation, obtain more patents and patent citations, and achieve greater innovative success for given research and development expenditures. However, overconfident managers achieve greater innovation only in innovative industries. Their findings suggest that overconfidence helps CEOs exploit innovative growth opportunities.

Recent empirical studies document the presence of managerial overconfidence and its effects on corporate policies. For example, Malmendier and Tate [MAL 05, MAL 08] use the tendency of CEOs to delay the exercise of their stock options to proxy for overconfidence, and show that this measure correlates with the intensity of firm investments.

Liu and Taffler [LIU 08] use formal content analysis of CEO statements to measure CEO overconfidence, and find that high ratings of this measure correlate with investment activity

For instance, Gervais *et al.* [GER 11] studied overconfidence, compensation contracts and capital budgeting. They investigated the effects that overconfident managers have on corporate policies and firm value. How does overconfidence affect the investment decisions that managers make on behalf of shareholders? Do firms benefit from managerial overconfidence? Thus, they studied the interaction of managerial overconfidence and compensation in the context of a firm's investment policy. To do so, they developed a simple capital budgeting problem in which a manager, using his information about the prospects of a *risky project*, must decide whether his firm should undertake the project or drop it in favor of *a safer investment* alternative. Their model shows that a manager's overconfidence creates two potential sources of value for him and the firm. First, the manager's overconfidence commits him to follow an optimal risky investment policy with a flatter compensation schedule. Second, the manager's overconfidence commits him to exert effort to gather information that improves the success rate and value of the firm's investment policy. They conclude that overconfident managers are also more attractive to firms than their rational counterparts because overconfidence commits them to exert effort to learn about projects. But too much overconfidence is detrimental to the manager since it leads him to accept highly convex compensation contracts that expose him to excessive risk.

In a world where agents make decisions based on their subjective probabilities, psychological factors can play an important role in explaining investor behavior. Different experimental settings can lead to under- or overreliance on new signals; people seem to make judgments differently in different situations. A large amount of literature shows that real-world decision makers do not predict outcomes as well as mechanical decision rules based on simple linear combinations of objective input measures [BEN 15].

Overall, the structure of corporate boards creates strong pressures on directors to fall into line behind the CEO. Fama [FAM 80] and Fama and Jensen [FAM 83] argue that directors seek to build reputations as effective monitors. However, such reputations may not be the key to successful careers as directors. A reputation as a "loose cannon" or a "troublemaker" may be a bigger impediment than a reputation as a "yes man" [MAC 71, WES 06, WES 07].

De Waal [DE 05] describes apes as organized into hierarchical social structures under alpha males (e.g. chimpanzees) or alpha females (e.g. bonobos), who command the obedience of other apes in the troop.

In corporate governance, obedience in corporate boardrooms might thus reflect behavioral biases, rational information cascades or some interaction of the two. Regardless, popular attention to recent corporate governance scandals is inducing major institutional reforms aimed at altering the dynamics of board decision making. Adams *et al.* [ADA 05] show that powerful CEOs raise the variance in firm performance: some firms with powerful CEOs do much better than firms with constrained CEOs, others do much worse. Simply constraining the CEO thus probably confers no clear advantage. Good corporate governance requires constraints that fall into place when the CEO is making an obvious mistake, but not when he is enacting a visionary strategy. In practice, this distinction may be difficult for independent observers to draw.

As Aristotle famously noted, humans are social animals, so perhaps fund managers also trade stocks that they learn about from other managers [POO 15]. Informing people about behavioral biases can help them correct their errors and induce appropriate and rational behavior. Gergen [GER 73] argues in this vein that sophistication as to psychological principles liberates one from their behavioral implications. Corporate governance reforms and director education programs are now providing a natural experiment that holds the promise of greatly advancing our understanding of these issues [MOR 07]. To summarize, behavioral arguments, up to now restricted within finance to explaining asset-pricing anomalies[12], may shed light on issues in other branches of financial economics, such as corporate governance.

1.4.1. *Transnational governance*

Transnational governance suggests that territorial grounds and national autonomy or sovereignty cannot be taken for granted. It also implies, however, that governance activity is embedded in particular geopolitical structures and hence enveloped in multiple and interacting institutional webs. Kobrin [KOB 02] saw parallels between present governance structures and medieval states:

> "Although medieval 'states' occupied geographic space, politics was not organized in terms of unambiguous geography… Borders were diffuse, representing a projection of power rather than a limit of sovereignty. In the context, power and authority could not be based on mutually exclusive geography".

With reference to Ruggie [RUG 83], Kobrin [KOB 02] characterized such political structures as "patchwork", meaning interdependence and entanglement. Interdependence and entanglement reflect in part regulation while driving it even further. Greater interdependence and entanglement foster the need for systematic comparisons and benchmarks and thus make it necessary to increase coordination across countries and regions. This in turn generates even more regulatory activity.

12 See [SHL 99, BAK 07].

Transnational regulation is not new but has changed and expanded, with diffusing logic moving from economic to social spheres [JOR 04]. Transnational regulation is a mode of governance in the sense that it structures, guides and controls human and social activities and interactions beyond, across and within national territories. As is shown throughout this book, however, transnational regulations are embedded in and supported by other modes of governance. As a concept, therefore, governance captures the re-ordering patterns of our contemporary world better than regulation [DJE 06].

2

Banking Governance

The corporate governance of banks, or banking governance, is an important factor in developing economies for several reasons. First, banks have a dominant position in developing economy financial systems and are extremely important engines of economic growth[1]. Second, as financial markets are usually underdeveloped, banks in developing economies are typically the most important source of finance for the majority of firms. Third, as well as providing a generally accepted means of payment, banks in developing countries are usually the main depository for the economy's savings. Fourth, many developing economies have recently liberalized their banking systems through privatization/disinvestments and by reducing the role of economic regulation. Consequently, the managers of banks in these economies have obtained greater freedom in how they run their banks.

This chapter provides an overview of banking and the role played by banks in an increasingly complex financial world. It begins with a review of the meaning of banking, the roles of central banks and the special features of banks that distinguish them from other financial institutions. Moreover, we will discuss the special features of banking governance that differentiates it from corporations.

1 See [KIN 93, LEV 97].

2.1. Banking

2.1.1. *What is banking?*

Collins [COL 06] described the origin of banking as "beyond the range of authentic history". According to Collins, banking may be assumed to have emerged as a necessary outgrowth of commerce. The notion of a medium of exchange was born because of the inconvenience of meeting and matching in barter trade, which commenced as civilizations evolved, and because people's needs increased and self-sufficiency declined. Because the mighty institution of banking arose after the establishment of an appropriate medium of exchange, the next logical and sequential step in the process was the development of the activities of lending and borrowing [SHA 09].

A bank's main source of income is interest paid on loans. A bank pays out at a lower interest rate on deposits and receives a higher interest rate on loans. The difference between these rates represents the bank's net income. The provision of deposit and loan products normally distinguishes banks from other types of financial firms. Deposit products pay out money on demand or after some notice. Deposits are liabilities for banks, which must be managed if the bank is to maximize profit. Likewise, they manage the assets created by lending. Thus, the core activity is to act as intermediaries between depositors and borrowers. Other financial institutions, such as stockbrokers, are also intermediaries between buyers and sellers of shares, but it is the taking of deposits and the granting of loans that singles out a bank, though many offer other financial services.

2.1.2. *Banking structure*

The structure of banking varies widely from country to country. Often, a country's banking structure is a consequence of the regulatory regime to which it is subject. In the following, different types of banking structures are defined. These different banking structures do not alter the core functions of banks, the provision of intermediation and liquidity and, indirectly, the payment services, which are the defining features of banks.

2.1.3. *Universal banking*

Universal banks offer the full range of banking services, together with non-banking financial services, under one legal entity. In addition, banks have direct links between banking and commerce through cross-shareholdings and shared directorships.

Following Danthine *et al.* [DAN 90], we can understand that universal banking is divided into three groups performing different functions: retail banking, investment banking and asset management. *Retail banking* can be subdivided into commercial banking or bank of deposit (in charge of lending to firms and consumers, collecting deposits and managing the accounts and transactions associated with the deposits) and private banking (responsible for the management of portfolios of wealthy individuals). *Investment banking* (merchant bank) comprises the underwriting of securities, market making and mergers and acquisitions, while the category of *asset management* takes care of the management of institutional assets, pension funds and other large-scale savings instruments.

Germany is the home of universal banking (the German hausbank), with banks such as Deutsche Bank and Dresdner offering virtually all of the services listed above.

Although German banks may own commercial concerns, the sum of a bank's equity investments (in excess of 10% of the commercial firm's capital), plus other fixed investments, may not exceed the bank's total capital. In addition to a German bank lending to commercial firms, it will also exert influence through the supervisory board. Seats on a supervisory board are for employees and shareholders. Most of the shareholder seats are held by bank executives because the bank normally has a large shareholding. The influence of the bank is increased because smaller shareholders nominate the bank to represent them when they deposit their shares at the bank for safekeeping.

2.1.4. *Bank holding companies*

The term "bank holding company" (BHC) originated in the United States. Japanese banks may also be a Financial Holding Company (FHC), though FHCs may not own insurance subsidiaries. However, cross-shareholdings and shared directorships are an integral part of the Japanese financial and commercial structure grew from 15% in the 1960s to over 90% by the 1990s. Each BHC owns banking (and in some countries, non-banking financial) subsidiaries, which are legally separate and individually capitalized.

In the United States, BHCs were used to circumvent laws that placed restrictions on interstate branching the act of having branches in more than one state. Through BHC, a bank might own several bank subsidiaries in a number of states.

2.1.5. *Offshore banks*

An offshore bank is a financial institution located in a country which typically accepts depositor funds from non-residents. Offshore banks are typically located in a low tax jurisdiction, also known as a "tax haven", that often provides legal or fiscal advantages. Getting an offshore bank account means opening an account outside of your home country. Offshore bank accounts are commonly available in more than one currency. This makes them extremely valuable to those who work in many countries or travel frequently. It is also very helpful to your average investor as a hedge against dramatic currency movements. The most important one is the fact that they are tax efficient. Offshore accounts have less restrictive legal regulation, allow for easy access to deposits and protect against local or financial instability.

Table 2.1 shows the largest 30 conventional banks in the world in 2015 in ranking order. According to SNL [SNL 15], China has four of the five largest banks in the world after weakening currencies pushed French and Japanese companies out of the top five in 2015. SNL ranks the largest banks in the world by converting their total assets into U.S. dollars using the exchange rate as of the end of the period measured. Most banks were ranked by total assets for the quarter ended March 31, 2015. The changes in the rankings since 2014 are due to fluctuations in the companies' reported currencies against the U.S. dollar. Paris-based BNP Paribas SA fell to rank 7 from rank 4 in SNL's 2014 ranking, as its assets declined to an equivalent of \$2.568 trillion as of March 31, 2015 from \$2.595 trillion in assets as of March 31, 2014. Currency conversion helped drive the decline, as the company's assets actually rose when measuring in euros to €2.392 trillion from €1.883 trillion. In addition, departing the top five, Tokyo-based Mitsubishi UFJ Financial Group Inc. fell to rank 8 from rank 5, partly based on a lower valuation of its assets in U.S. dollars. There is only one bank in the top five that is not headquartered in China, which is London-based HSBC Holdings Plc. Its rank is 4, with \$2.670 trillion in assets, down from its ranking of 2 in 2014, with \$2.758 trillion in assets.

Ranking the world's 100 largest banks

Current rank	Previous rank[#]	Current vs. previous	Company (ticker-exchange)	Headquarters	Accounting principle	Total assets (US$B)
1	1	NC	Industrial & Commercial Bank of China Ltd. (1398-HKG)	China	IFRS	3,452.02
2	3	▲	China Construction Bank Corp. (0939-HKG)	China	IFRS	2,819.47
3	7	▲	Agricultural Bank of China Ltd. (1288-HKG)	China	IFRS	2,716.31
4	2	▼	HSBC Holdings Plc (HSBA-LON)	U.K.	IFRS	2,669.72
5	8	▲	Bank of China Ltd. (3988-HKG)	China	IFRS	2,584.45
6	6	NC	JPMorgan Chase & Co. (JPM-NYSE)	U.S.	U.S. GAAP	2,577.15
7	4	▼	BNP Paribas SA (BNP-PAR)	France	IFRS	2,567.82
8	5	▼	Mitsubishi UFJ Financial Group Inc. (8306-TKS)	Japan	Japanese GAAP	2,385.15
9	12	▲	Bank of America Corp. (BAC-NYSE)	U.S.	U.S. GAAP	2,143.55
10	10	NC	Barclays Plc (BARC-LON)	U.K.	IFRS	2,102.74
11	11	NC	Deutsche Bank AG (DBK-ETR)	Germany	IFRS	2,099.04
12	9	▼	Crédit Agricole Group	France	IFRS	1,935.70
13	14	▲	Citigroup Inc. (C-NYSE)	U.S.	U.S. GAAP	1,831.80
14	21	▲	Wells Fargo & Co. (WFC-NYSE)	U.S.	U.S. GAAP	1,737.74
15	13	▼	Japan Post Bank Co. Ltd.	Japan	Japanese GAAP	1,735.24
16	17	▲	Royal Bank of Scotland Group Plc (RBS-LON)	U.K.	IFRS	1,639.86
17	16	▼	Mizuho Financial Group Inc. (8411-TKS)	Japan	Japanese GAAP	1,581.08
18	15	▼	Société Générale SA (GLE-PAR)	France	IFRS	1,533.71
19	20	▲	Sumitomo Mitsui Financial Group Inc. (8316-TKS)	Japan	Japanese GAAP	1,529.05
20	18	▼	Banco Santander SA (SAN-MAD)	Spain	IFRS	1,470.25
21	19	▼	Groupe BPCE	France	IFRS	1,329.51
22	22	NC	Lloyds Banking Group Plc (LLOY-LON)	U.K.	IFRS	1,260.80
23	NR	NR	ING Groep NV (INGA-AMS)	Netherlands	IFRS	1,130.72
24	24	NC	UBS Group AG (UBSG-SWX) ~	Switzerland	IFRS	1,079.40
25	27	▲	Bank of Communications Co. Ltd. (3328-HKG)	China	IFRS	1,069.20
26	29	▲	Postal Savings Bank of China Co. Ltd.[3]	China	IFRS	1,014.29
27	23	▼	UniCredit SpA (UCG-MIL)	Italy	IFRS	966.78
28	26	▼	Credit Suisse Group AG (CSGN-SWX)	Switzerland	U.S. GAAP	930.73
29	30	▲	Goldman Sachs Group Inc. (GS-NYSE)	U.S.	U.S. GAAP	865.46
30	33	▲	Crédit Mutuel Group[3]	France	IFRS	855.49

Table 2.1. *Largest 30 conventional banks [SNL 15]*

2.2. Central banks

A central bank is a government institution and does not compete with banks operating in the private banking sector. It is also called the bank of banks. It has specific functions and self-governing principles. Central banks are normally responsible for monetary control and, in addition, may be involved in prudential regulation and placing government debt on the most favorable terms possible.

2.2.1. *Monetary control or price stability*

A country's money supply is defined as currency in circulation outside the banking system plus deposits held at banks. Banks play an important role in creating money, but so does the central bank. Banks create money by lending out deposits, hence their activities can affect the central bank. The traditional methods for controlling the supply of money include open market operations, the buying or selling of securities in the financial market, the reserve ratios and the discount rate. Thus, a central bank can stabilize the price level by the exercise of monetary policy, through control of the money supply and/or the use of interest rates. By the late 1970s and early 1980s, many governments singled out price stability as the key objective of central banks. Some central banks were given a zero inflation target, or more commonly a range of acceptable inflation rates. For example, in the UK, the Bank of England, through its powerful Monetary Policy Committee, is required to exercise monetary control to meet an inflation rate target of 2.5% plus or minus 1%. Some bank governors (e.g. New Zealand) have their salaries and even job renewal dependent upon their success in meeting targets. In its place, most central banks have a committee that meets on a regular basis and decides what interest rate should be set to ensure the country's inflation rate meets the government target. Any change in the interest rate should affect aggregate demand, which in turn will keep inflation in check.

2.2.2. *Prudential control*

The central bank is expected to protect the economy from suffering the effects of a financial crisis. It is widely accepted that the banking system has a unique position in the national economy. A widespread collapse can lead to a decline in the intermediation, money transmission and liquidity services supplied by banks, which will, in turn, contribute to an inefficient allocation of resources in the economy. There are additional macroeconomic ramifications if there is a continuous reduction in the money supply growth rate or rise in interest rates.

A bank run begins when customers withdraw their deposits because they fear the bank will fail. Immediately, the bank finds it is unable to supply one of its key services: liquidity.

The banking system is particularly vulnerable to contagion effects: a lack of confidence associated with one poorly performing bank spreads to other healthy banks (case of the recent subprime crisis in the United States), because agents know that once a run on deposits begins, liquidated bank assets will decline in value, so everyone will want to withdraw their deposits before the run gains any momentum. In the absence of perfect information about the quality of each bank, the sudden collapse of one bank often prompts runs on other wholesome banks. The vulnerability of banks to contagion creates systemic risk: the risk that the economic system will break down as a result of problems in the banking sector. To expand on this theme, disturbances in a financial institution or market could spread across the financial system, leading to widespread bank runs by wholesale and retail depositors, and possibly the collapse of the banking system. This will severely hamper money transmission which, in the extreme case, could cause a breakdown in the economy as it reverts to barter exchange.

The threat of contagion and systemic risk has meant governments are inclined to treat banks as special and to provide, through the central bank, lender of last resort or lifeboat facilities. By acting as a lender of last resort, a central bank can supply liquidity to solvent banks threatened by contagion effects. Increasingly, central banks have pressured healthy banks to assist the bailout of troubled banks – known as a lifeboat rescue operation. If the central bank intervenes to assist weak or failing banks, it will be concerned as to how these banks are regulated and supervised because of the moral hazard that inevitably arises when private institutions know they have a chance of being bailed out by government funds if they encounter difficulties.

2.2.3. *Government debt placement*

The government can instruct the central bank to raise seigniorage income[2] through a variety of methods, which include a reserve ratio (requiring banks to set aside a certain percentage of their deposits as non-interest-earning reserves held at the central bank – an implicit tax), interest ceilings, issuing new currency at a rate of exchange that effectively lowers the value of old notes, subsidizing loans to state-owned enterprises and/or allowing bankrupt state firms that have defaulted (or failed to make interest payments) on their loans to continue operating. Otherwise, the inflationary consequences of an ongoing liberal monetary policy will reduce the real value of government debt.

This third function is important in emerging markets, but by the close of the 20th Century it has become less critical than the other two functions in the industrialized world, where policies to control government spending means there is less government debt to place. In emerging markets, central banks are usually expected to fulfill all three functions; ensuring financial and price stability, and assisting the government in the management of a sizeable government debt. While all three are critical for the development of an efficient financial system, the central banks of these countries face an immense task, which they are normally poorly equipped to complete because of inferior technology and chronic shortages of well-trained staff.

The Bank of England had a long tradition of assuming responsibility for all three functions, but in 1997 the Chancellor of the Exchequer announced the imminent separation of the three functions, leaving the Bank of England with the responsibility over monetary policy with which the Financial Supervisory Agency (FSA) regulates financial institutions, including consumer protection and prudential control of the banking sector. The Japanese government created the FSA in 1997 to supervise banks and other financial institutions. Part of the Prime Minister's office, this agency has taken over the job previously undertaken by the Ministry of Finance and Banking of Japan.

The U.S. authorities assign responsibility for prudential regulation to several organizations including the Federal Reserve, Comptroller of the

2 Income earned through, for example, printing money.

Currency and the Federal Deposit Insurance Corporation. The Federal Reserve also sets an independent monetary policy. Until France became part of Euroland, 20,000 plus employees of the Bank of France played a dual role: implementing monetary policy and regulating/supervising the banking system.

There are potential conflicts if one institution is responsible for the three objectives of price stability, prudential regulation and government debt placement. Given the inverse relationship between the price of bonds and interest rates, a central bank with control over government debt policy might be tempted to avoid raising interest rates (to control inflation) because it would reduce the value of the bank's debt portfolio. Or, it might increase liquidity to ease the placement of government debt, which might put it at odds with an inflation policy. Consider a country experiencing a number of bank failures, which, in turn, threaten the viability of the financial system. If the central bank is responsible for the maintenance of financial stability in the economy, it may decide to inject liquidity to try and stem the tide of bank failures. It does this by increasing the money supply and/or reducing interest rates, so stimulating demand. The policy should reduce the number of bankruptcies (personal and corporate), thereby relieving the pressure on the banking system.

However, if the central bank's efforts to shore up the banking system are prolonged, this may undermine the objective of achieving price stability. Continuous expansionary monetary policy may cause inflation if the rate of growth in the money supply exceeds the rate of growth of national output. A study by Goodhart and Schoenmaker [GOO 95] looked at the arguments for and against the separation of monetary policy from supervision. They could not find overwhelming support for either approach, consistent with their finding that of the 26 countries examined; about 50% assign the functions to separate bodies. Since the research was published, several countries have changed policy and the computations would show the majority separate the two responsibilities. Nonetheless, given the current trends, it is interesting that neither model was found to be superior.

Independence of central bank is an issue if a country is committed to a regime of fixed, managed or targeted exchange rates. It is the central bank that buys or sells foreign currency on behalf of a government committed to, say, a quasi-fixed exchange rate, only allowing fluctuation within a narrow band. In this situation, the central bank (or banks) will be trading against the market – trying to restore the value of a currency threatened with depreciation or appreciation. While the central bank or the efforts of several central banks might be able to stabilize a currency in the short term, the position cannot be sustained indefinitely.

Today major central banks are seen as the most powerful players in the global economy. Yet in 2015, monetary policy reached its limits in its traditional forms. With key interest rates close to zero, central bankers now have more leeway to stimulate economic activity. Moreover, the danger is not inflation, defined as their top priority, but the risk of deflation increases the real burden of debt and against which central bankers are helpless, as shown in the case of Japan. Finally, the massive creation of liquidity by central banks as part of the "quantitative easing" could fuel asset bubbles rather than economic recovery. Since monetary policy has become ineffective, it is necessary to resort to fiscal policy, much more appropriate than monetary policy to emerge from the current period of recession and low inflation.

We find ourselves in a paradoxical situation where, on the one hand, monetary policy has lost its effectiveness to overcome the crisis and, on the other hand, central banks have kept a strong legitimacy in the eyes of most economic and political actors. Under the influence of monetarist orthodoxy, which was widely imposed for several decades, it was decided to give preponderance to the monetary policy on the other instruments of economic policy, particularly fiscal policy. Behind this choice is the belief that inflation is a monetary phenomenon that must be fought by the instruments of monetary policy.

However, today we see that the relationship between money supply and inflation is not verified since the massive liquidity injections by central banks have no effect on the evolution of prices of goods and services, which remain in historically low levels.

Most economists recognize in hindsight that the dominant model of "central banking" based on inflation targeting, gave undue weight to monetary stability, and led central banks to underestimate the risk taken on markets that fueled the bubble and led to the 2007 crisis.

Central bankers have to admit their mistake and reform their model to abolish the separation prior to the crisis between the objectives of monetary stability and financial stability. In total, the theoretical and ideological framework that was the basis for the legitimacy of the central banks has been seriously undermined by the crisis. But the main source of power and legitimacy of the central banks is related to the exorbitant weight of finance and financial markets. The primary role of central bankers is to govern the markets, which are suspended at their least statements. The international financial crisis has accentuated this trend by central banks, the main bulwark against financial instability, particularly through their role as lenders of last resort for troubled banks [PLI 15][3].

2.3. Special features of banks

2.3.1. *Special activities of banks*

Before moving on to banking governance, our key topic, it is important to summarize the main reasons why banks are special. Foremost, unlike other financial firms, they act as intermediaries between borrowers and lenders and, in so doing, offer a unique form of asset transformation. Moreover, liquidity is an important service offered to customers. A by-product of intermediation is participation in the payments system. Finally, banks play an important role in the macroeconomic and have a special relationship with the central bank because the process of lending creates money. Following Gorton and Winton [GOR 02], the major theories on this issue point at five main roles of banks.

2.3.1.1. *Banks as delegated monitors*

Diamond [DIA 84] was the first to suggest that financial intermediaries exist because they "monitor" borrowers. In a contract between a borrower and a lender, there is an ex-post information asymmetry in that only the borrower knows the realized output of his/her project, and therefore he/she would not pay the lender back unless he/she has an incentive to do so (a moral hazard problem). If the lender could produce information about the borrower's realized output, he/she would overcome his/she disadvantage and

3 http://www.lemonde.fr/idees/article/2015/06/18/la-legitimite-paradoxale-des-banques-centrales_4657491_3232.html.

reduce the agency costs. This production of information about the borrower's output is what Diamond denominates as "monitoring". Given that monitoring borrowers is costly, it will be efficient for investors to lend to a specialized agent (the intermediary) who will be monitoring borrowers on behalf of them, as long as the costs of monitoring the intermediary (known as the "monitoring the monitor" problem) are lower than the costs of lenders lending directly to borrowers and directly incurring the monitoring costs.

As Diamond shows, this centralization of the task of monitoring is an efficient solution because, as banks grow large, only if they have monitored as promised, will they be able to satisfy their commitment to pay depositors back. Otherwise, they would incur non-pecuniary penalties, such as bankruptcy costs or loss of reputation. Diversification among different investment projects is crucial in explaining why delegating monitoring to an intermediary is a lower cost solution to the ex-post information asymmetry between borrowers and lenders than the securities market because diversification is critical to reducing the monitoring the monitor problem.

2.3.1.2. *Banks as information producers*

In addition, banks may also be in charge of producing information about investment opportunities and then sell the information to uninformed economic agents (see, among others, [BOY 86]). In this connection, a rich strand of literature has emerged that focuses on "relationship banking" and relies on the idea that banks acquire this private information through repeated interaction over time in what is known as "customer relationship" (see [HAU 89, RAJ 92], and for an extensive review of this topic, see [GOR 02]).

2.3.1.3. *Banks as consumption smoothers*

The Diamond and Dybvig model [DIA 83] looks at the liability side of banking, where demand deposits offer consumers the right to withdraw from the bank and prematurely end investments in order to satisfy their desired consumption paths. Banks act this way as vehicles for consumption smoothing, in the sense that consumers that save via intermediation get insurance against the consumption shocks derived by their random consumption needs.

2.3.1.4. *Banks as liquidity providers*

A fourth characteristic of banks is related to the fact that bank liabilities can function as a medium of exchange and may even dominate government-supplied money, which explains the central role banks have in payment systems as liquidity providers [FRE 96].

2.3.1.5. *Banks as commitment mechanisms*

Banks are very fragile institutions. Their above-mentioned liquidity production function (the mismatch in the term structure and liquidity of their assets and liabilities) together with high debt ratios makes bank runs a serious risk to be considered and, according to some, creates the need for the deposit insurance fund [MAC 03]. However, looking at it from a different perspective, fragility can also be seen as a positive attribute of banks. Some authors argue that capital structures are designed to be fragile, so that they function as a commitment mechanism, as a device to discipline bankers and prevent them to engaging in risky activities [CAL 91, FLA 94]. Nevertheless, as Diamond and Rajan [DIA 01] point out, moral hazard may not be the only reason behind bank runs, and in a situation of high liquidity demand very fragile structures might not be the most desirable, but the maintenance of an optimal level of bank equity capital would be a safer option. Banking is the activity of risk-taking and the degree of risk appetite varies between the different decision makers.

2.3.2. *Special problems of banks*

After reviewing the structure of banks and their special activities, it is now easy to explain the specific problems of banks and attempt to address why the scope of the duties and obligations of corporate officers and directors should be expanded in the case of banks. Referring to the study of Macey and O'Hara [MAC 03], the special corporate governance problems of banks weaken the case for making shareholders the exclusive beneficiaries of fiduciary duties. They tried to explain why banks are not like other firms, and thus why they should be treated differently, and presented the main problems that can deal banks.

2.3.2.1. *The liquidity production function*

What distinguishes banks from other firms is their capital structure, which is unique in two ways. First, banks tend to have very little equity relative to other firms. Although it is not uncommon for typical manufacturing firms to finance themselves with more equity than debt, banks typically receive 90% or more of their funding from debt. Second, banks' liabilities are largely in the form of deposits, which are available to their creditors/depositors on demand, while their assets often take the form of loans that have longer maturities. Thus, the principal attribute that makes banks as financial intermediaries "special" is their liquidity production function. By holding illiquid assets and issuing liquid liabilities, banks create liquidity for the economy.

The liquidity production function causes a collective action problem among depositors because banks keep only a fraction of deposits on reserve at any one time. Depositors cannot obtain repayment of their deposits simultaneously because the bank will not have sufficient funds on hand to satisfy all depositors at once. This dissonance between deposits and liabilities becomes a problem in the unusual situation of a bank run. Bank runs are essentially a collective action problem among depositors. Thus, in a classic prisoner's dilemma, depositors may collectively be better off if they refrain from withdrawing their money, but their inability to coordinate their response to the problem can lead to a seemingly irrational response, depositors rush to be among the first to withdraw their funds so that they can obtain their money before the bank's cash reserves are drained.

2.3.2.2. *The deposit insurance fund*

With the mass failure of depository institutions, Congress passed the Banking Act of 1933, establishing the Federal Deposit Insurance Corporation (FDIC) and giving the federal government the power to insure deposits in qualified banks. The creation of federal deposit insurance has been tremendously effective in preventing bank runs and keeping the failure of individual banks from affecting the larger economy. Deposit insurance has succeeded in achieving what had been a major objective of banking reform for at least a century, namely the prevention of banking panics. Despite the positive effect of FDIC insurance on preventing bank panics, the implementation of deposit insurance poses a regulatory cost of its own; it gives the shareholders and managers of insured banks incentives to engage in excessive risk-taking.

The problem of moral hazard is attenuated in situations where a bank is at or near insolvency. In such a situation, the shareholders have a strong incentive to increase risk because they can allocate their losses to third parties while still receiving any gains that might result from the risky behavior. Companies outside the banking industry that are close to insolvency also have an incentive to take added risks. However, their ability to do so is limited by normal market forces and contractual obligations. Non-financial firms that are in financial distress usually have significant liquidity problems. Nearly insolvent banks, however, can continue to attract liquidity in the form of (government-insured) deposits. Federal insurance eliminates the market forces that starve non-financial firms of cash. The federal government has attempted to replace these market forces with regulatory requirements such as capital requirements. Higher capital requirements force shareholders to put more of their money at risk, and this reduces moral hazard.

2.3.2.3. *The conflict between fixed claimants and shareholders*

A conflict between the interests of debt holders and the interests of shareholders exists in every corporation. Among any particular set of asset allocation decisions, any investment strategy that increases risk will transfer wealth from the fixed claimants to the residual claimants. This problem is raised to a new dimension in the banking context because of the high debt–equity ratio and the existence of deposit insurance.

In publicly held corporation, the problem of excessive risk-taking is mitigated by two factors. First, various devices serve to protect fixed claimants against excessive risk-taking. Corporate lenders typically insist on protection against actions by corporate managers that threaten their fixed claims. Second, risk-taking is reduced to some extent because managers are not perfect agents of risk-preferring shareholders. Managers are fixed claimants to that portion of their compensation designated as salary. In addition, managerial incentives for risk-taking are reduced, since managers have invested their no diversifiable human capital in their jobs. This capital would depreciate significantly in value if their firms were to fail.

In a world without deposit insurance, depositors would demand that banks refrain from engaging in risky investment strategies or else demand that they be compensated in the form of a higher interest rate for the extra risk. Thus, depositors of insured financial institutions cannot be expected to exert the same degree of restraint on excessive risk-taking as other fixed claimants, and this enhances the degree of influence exerted by shareholders, whose preference is to assume high levels of risk. The adverse incentive for risk-taking caused by federal insurance is one reason to have stricter accountability requirements for directors of banks.

	US (Dodd-Frank Act–Title II)	EU (BRRD)	Comparative
Goal	i) To resolve failing financial institutions quickly, ensuring the stability of the financial system ii) To minimize taxpayer contributions to resolution episodes		Yes
Scope	Only large and complex banks	All credit Institutions and investment firms	No
Resolution Authority	Existing Federal Deposit Insurance Corporation created by the Congress to, among other things, insure deposits	New Resolution Board composed by national and European authorities	Yes
Trigger for Resolution	i) Failing or likely to fail institutions i) To protect public interest iii) No private alternatives to prevent the default of the institution.		No
Recovery Plan	No requirement	Annual review, update and submission to the resolution authority and supervisor	No
Resolution Plan	Annual review, update and submission to the resolution authority (FDIC); bank ownership	Annual review and update; resolution authority ownership	No
Resolution Strategy	Single-Point-of-Entry in the US. No specific reference to global resolution scheme	Multiple-Point-of-Entry or Single-Point-of-Entry with a global perspective	No
Bail-in – *Hierarchy of claims*	Four layers: Capital + senior debt + uncovered deposits + covered deposits	Four layers: Capital + senior debt *paripassu* with uncovered corporate deposits + uncovered deposits of SME & households + covered deposits	No
Resolution Fund –*Usage*	Liquidity support	Liquidity and capital support	No
Resolution Fund – *Funding*	*Ex-post* funding by the financial sector contributions (if needed)	*Ex-ante* funding by the financial sector contributions	No
Public support	Not allowed	Limited to "a very extraordinary situation and systemic crisis"	No

Table 2.2. *Comparative analysis between U.S. and EU resolution regimes*

In Europe, the Bank Recovery and Resolution Directive (BRRD) is a centerpiece of the banking union. It aims to restructure banks on the verge of bankruptcy without the taxpayer paying to preserve financial stability. Indeed, so far, bankrupt banks have always turned to shareholders and creditors. They now have a third option: depositors:

> "We will first use internal resources, capital and obligations of the bank to cover the deficit of the bank and bank deposits of more than 100,000 euros".
>
> "Resolution frameworks should always seek two objectives. First, resolving banks should be a quick process and must avoid negative spillover effects to the rest of the financial system. Second, resolution regimes must be designed to protect taxpayers' money. Besides common principles, there are major differences on how countries design the resolution regimes to achieve those two goals. A clear example of those divergences is the EU and US resolution frameworks"[4].

2.3.2.4. *Asset structure and loyalty problems*

The presence of a federal insurance fund also increases the risk of fraud and self-dealing in the banking industry by reducing incentives for monitoring. In the 1980s, it was estimated that fraud and self-dealing transactions were "apparent" in as many as one-third of today's bank failures. A similar statistic shows that between 1990 and 1991, insider lending contributed to 175 of 286 bank failures. Such behavior, of course, is a possibility in any large firm, since it is inefficient for owners to monitor all employees at all times. These sorts of problems are particularly acute in financial institutions. However, because of the large portion of their assets held in highly liquid form [BEN 12], the same regulatory structure that creates a problem of excessive risk-taking by banks also leads to a reduction in the normal levels of monitoring within the firm, resulting in a higher incidence of bank failures due to fraud. Not only does the protection afforded by the FDIC remove any incentive for insured depositors to control excessive risk-taking, it also removes their incentive to monitor in order to reduce the incidence of fraud and self-dealing.

4 For further information, see https://www.bbvaresearch.com/wp-content/uploads/2014/06/Regulation-Outlook.pdf.

Shareholders have an incentive to monitor to prevent fraud and self-dealing in banks, but such monitoring is notoriously ineffective in many cases because individual shareholders rarely have sufficient incentives to engage in monitoring because of collective-action problems. Under the Federal Deposit Insurance Corporation Improvement Act, regulatory agencies were required to issue guidelines or regulations creating standards for safety and soundness. Regulators have five main enforcement tools: cease and desist powers, removal powers, civil money penalty powers, withdrawal or suspension of federal deposit insurance powers and prompt corrective-action powers. Cease and desist powers generally address both unsafe and unsound banking as well as violations of the law or regulations governing depository institutions. These powers allow regulators to issue injunctions as well as to take corrective actions against banks. Bank regulators may also remove officers and directors from their posts, or ban them from ever working for a depository institution in the United States, if they can show that the individual acted unlawfully, received a personal benefit, or acted in a manner detrimental to the bank or its depositors. Federal banking agencies also have the power to impose civil monetary penalties against a banking institution and its affiliates.

Thus, the problem with the current system, which substitutes government regulators for private sector creditors as the primary monitors of bank activity, is not that the regulators lack the administrative authority to do an effective job. Nevertheless, replacing private sector creditors with public sector regulators is the first line of defense against bank fraud.

2.4. Special features of banking governance

2.4.1. *Banking governance*

It is easy now, after reviewing the special features in banking, to understand the debate about the banking governance, and founding answer to this request. Does banking governance differ greatly from corporate governance? Corporate governance in banks plays a special role due to the special nature of these institutions. Studies on bank corporate governance[5] acknowledge the existence of difficulties, such as opacity or complexity and regulation, in the corporate governance of these institutions. Furthermore, such difficulties interfere with the way in which the usual corporate governance

5 For example, [BAR 13, BEN 13b, BEC 11, CIA 01, LEV 04, MAC 03, PRO 97].

mechanisms are applied to the governance of financial institutions. Adams and Mehran [ADA 03] and Macey and O'Hara [MAC 03] find systematic differences between the governance of banking and manufacturing firms and highlight the point that governance structures are industry specific.

However, Zingales [ZIN 98] defined corporate governance as a group of mechanisms used by stakeholders to ensure that directors efficiently manage corporate resources, a task that includes the manner in which quasi-rents are developed and distributed. Thus, the problem of bank governance does not differ greatly from the governance problem of any organization whose business involves an exchange of goods. The corporate governance of banks affects the value of banks, their cost of capital, their performance and their risk management [BEN 15]. Formal econometric studies show that banks exert a strong impact on economic development [LEV 97, LEV 05]. When banks efficiently mobilize and allocate funds, this lowers the cost of capital to firms, boosts capital formation and stimulates productivity growth [LEV 04]. Ben Bouheni and Ammi [BEN 15] note that banks exert corporate governance on firms; as creditors of firms and as equity holders, the corporate governance of banks becomes crucial for financial growth and economic development.

2.4.2. *Information asymmetries*

Since the study of Berle and Means [BER 32], the conflict between insiders and minority shareholders has been an object of research for scholars and a challenge for regulators. The separation of ownership and control results in information asymmetry, thus potentially leading to two types of agency problems – one between managers and outside investors (principal–agent) and another between controlling shareholders and minority shareholders (principal–principal) [JEN 76]. In general, agency theory predicts that ownership and control divergence negatively affects corporate value. The control divergence, as well as its informational advantage, motivates managers or controlling shareholders to expropriate corporate resources through their private control rights.

Information asymmetries exist in all sectors, yet the problems arising for financial intermediaries may be aggravated by the complexity of the bank business[6]. Bank opacity or complexity reflects the particular nature of the banking business and the difficulties outside stakeholders face when

6 See, for instance, [FUR 01, LEV 04, MOR 02].

monitoring bank transactions. Issues concerning complexity are common in banking, making it difficult for stakeholders to monitor their bank. Complexity can take the form of the quality of loans not being clearly perceived, financial engineering not being transparent, financial statements proving complicated, investment risk that can be easily modified or perquisites that are easier for managers or insiders to obtain [LEV 04]. In this way, complexity greatly aggravates the governance problem. The management of complexity requires a board that not only monitors managers efficiently, but also gives managers access to independent and valuable advice to run the bank.

Caprio and Levine [CAP 02] point out two interrelated features of financial intermediaries, which affect corporate governance. First, because of greater information asymmetries between inside and outside investors, the agency problem intensifies because banks are more opaque; in banking, it is more difficult for shareholders and ownerships to monitor managers and use incentive contracts, and easier for managers and large investors to exploit the private benefits of control, rather than maximize value. Second, banks are heavily regulated and this frequently impedes natural corporate governance mechanisms. Thus, the problem of information asymmetry between parties has a direct effect on the value of the firm and by consequence it affects the performance because the paucity of information in financial institutions led to great problems in corporate governance, which can directly affect the performance of the institution.

The literature has studied information asymmetries, but it has largely focused on portfolio choice and asset pricing. The difference in this study is that the concept of information asymmetry is used to explain the broadcasting of information's between all parties in banks under the phenomenon of corporate governance and his/her contribution in the rise of the return and the value of bank. Informational asymmetries between the providers of capital and the controllers of capital lie at the core of corporate governance problems. All firms suffer from some degree of information asymmetry between inside and outside investors.

According to Flannery *et al.* [FLA 04], loan illiquidity and private information about specific borrowers need not necessarily make banks more difficult to value than non-financial firms. Just as many loans do not trade in active secondary markets, neither do many assets of non-financial firms, e.g. plant and equipment, patents, managers' human capital or accounts receivable. How can outside investors accurately value the public securities issues by these firms?

Heffernan [HEF 05] mentioned that asymmetric information, or differences in information held by inside and outside agent, is the reason why banks face the problem of adverse selection because the bank normally has less information about the probability of default on a loan than the firm or individual, the agent. The presence of adverse selection may mean the supply of loans curve is discontinuous at some point. Adverse selection is the reason why the supply curve is discontinuous or even backward-bending, and shows that bankers are more reluctant to supply loans at very high rates because as interest rates rise, a greater proportion of riskier borrowers apply for loans. The problem of adverse incentives (higher interest rates encouraging borrowers to undertake riskier activities) is another reason why banks will reduce the size of a loan or even refuse loans to some individuals or firms.

2.4.3. *Moral hazard*

Hazard would come from the verb "yaçara", which means precisely "roll the dice". Moreover, when the Koran condemns gambling, he calls them "Mayçir", a noun from the same Arab radical "y.ç.r".

Banks as financial intermediaries exist generally to solve a number of market failures due to information asymmetry, economies of scale and liquidity mismatches. Providers of funds may find it prohibitively expensive to collect information on investors seeking funds, thus adverse selection and moral hazard problems prevent those investors from acquiring funds directly through financial markets. Banks solve this market failure due to information asymmetry by specializing in rating the credit worthiness of various investors. The cost of hiring and retaining skilled loan officers can be significantly reduced due to economies of scale. Banks also help to convert the funds of savers who demand high degrees of liquidity into longer term investments with entrepreneurs who need the funds for extended periods of time. Of course, while banks solve the adverse selection and moral hazard problems between savers and investors, they create multiple other moral hazard problems. There is a moral hazard problem between the bank and the entities that it helps finance, another moral hazard problem between banks and the providers of funds, and a third potential moral hazard problem between banks and any deposit insurance scheme that might be put in place. The liquidity transformation function of banking interacts with those information asymmetries to magnify the risk of bank failure.

Moral hazard arises whenever, as a result of entering into a contract, the incentives of the two parties change, such that the riskiness of the contract is altered. Depositors may not monitor bank activities closely enough for several reasons. First, the depositor's cost of monitoring the bank becomes very small, as the portfolio of loans becomes larger and more diversified. Though there will always be loan losses, the pooling of loans will mean that the variability of losses approaches zero. Second, deposit insurance reduces depositors' incentives to monitor the bank. If a bank can be reasonably certain that a depositor either cannot or chooses not to monitor the bank's activities once the deposit is made, then the nature of the contract is altered and the bank may undertake to invest in more risky assets than it would in the presence of close monitoring.

Shareholders do have an incentive to monitor the bank's behavior, to ensure an acceptable rate of return on the investment. Depositors may benefit from this monitoring. However, even shareholders face agency problems if managers maximize their own utility functions, causing managerial behavior to be at odds with shareholder interest. There are many cases of bank managers boosting lending to increase bank size (measured by assets) because of the positive correlation between firm size and executive compensation. These actions are not in the interests of shareholders if growth is at the expense of profitability.

Moral hazard justifies capital regulation, monitoring and supervision of banks' operations. In general, the highly regulated nature of banking empowers the regulatory authorities to influence, or even dominate, the corporate governance of banks. This has an impact on the incentives faced by private sector providers of bank corporate governance. Prowse [PRO 97] has even argued that the most important corporate control mechanism in banking is regulatory intervention. However, Ben Bouheni [BEN 13a] found that strengthening regulatory and supervisory policies in Greece, Spain and Italy during 2005–2011 encouraged moral hazard; thus, it encourages risk-taking by European banks.

3

Islamic Banking Governance

Unlike conventional banks, Islamic banks are not allowed to charge interest (returned to preestablished fixed rate) by lending money to their customers because, under Islamic law (Shariah), making money from money (riba) is strictly prohibited. In contrast, conventional banks charge interest on loans made to customers and pay interest on customers' deposits [BEN 12], which prohibits Islamic banks to finance on the interbank market [LEV 12]. The bank charges a higher rate of interest on loans made than it pays on deposits, and thus earns a profit from the spread between the interest rate on its assets and the rate on its liabilities [BEN 15].

Islamic banking refers to a system of banking or banking activity that is consistent with Islamic law (*Shariah*) principles and guided by Islamic economics. In particular, Islamic law prohibits usury, the collection and payment of interest, also commonly called riba in Islamic discourse. In addition, Islamic law prohibits investing in businesses that are considered unlawful or haram (such as businesses that sell alcohol or pork, or businesses that produce media which are contrary to Islamic values).

3.1. Specific products of Islamic banking

In his book, Levy [LEV 12] considers the basis of Islamic finance, in which the main sources are the following:

– Koran with 6219 verses, the main source of Islamic law; but only 10 verses relate to economics and finance, less than 0.2%;

– Hadith that form the Sunna allows interpretations, comments, details, digressions, etc.

Then, secondary sources are as follows:

– Ijtihad to interpret the founding texts of Islam and answer questions that are not explicitly considered;

– Ijmaa consensus is the main source of Sharia and Islamic jurisprudence;

– Fiqh Islamic jurisprudence;

– Qiyas to move from tacit knowledge to explicit knowledge (analogy allows similarities between two or more different elements, metaphor often used in religions, aims to convey meaning. But every metaphor is inaccurate, and besides, does not claim authenticity). Many other sources exist such as personal opinion; *ray'*, possibility to take context into account *istihsan*; consideration of the practice *istihsâb*; the consideration of general interest, *istislah*; the effort of personal reflection based on the general principles of Islam, *ijtihad*; pre-Islamic customs were incorporated into Muslim law; Sharia committees belong to governance are numerous and exegetes *fatwa* sometimes opposed the perimeter of Islamic finance in Islam (in white):

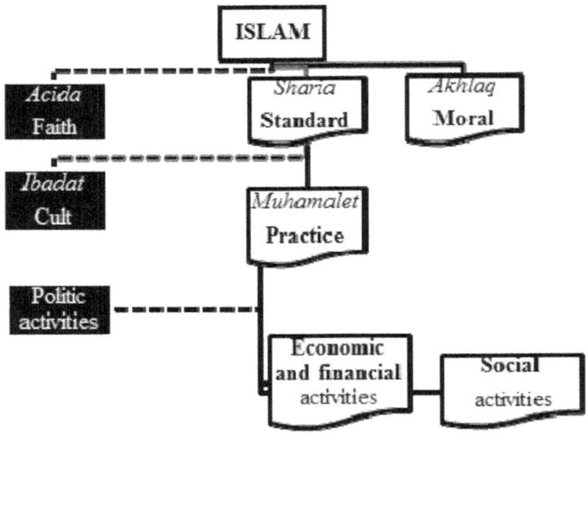

3.2. Financial transactions of Islamic banks with the bank's participation

Some of the most common Islamic financial products are described in the following sections.

<table>
<tr><td colspan="3">Financial Transactions of Islamic Banks</td></tr>
<tr><td rowspan="5">WITH
the bank's
participation</td><td rowspan="2">Mudarbah
Profit sharing</td><td>Limited = specific</td></tr>
<tr><td>Unlimited = inaccurate</td></tr>
<tr><td rowspan="3">Musharkah
Profits and losses
Participation
Joint venture</td><td>Simple = pooled</td></tr>
<tr><td>Decreasing = redemption invested shares</td></tr>
<tr><td>Securitization = pharaonic projects</td></tr>
<tr><td rowspan="8">WITHOUT
the bank's
participation</td><td>Murabahah
Cost Plus</td><td>Financing (owner and holder)</td></tr>
<tr><td>Ijarah</td><td>Simple = rental with rents</td></tr>
<tr><td>Ijarah wa Ictinah</td><td>Leasing</td></tr>
<tr><td>Istinah</td><td>Financing future or unfinished projects</td></tr>
<tr><td rowspan="2">Salam</td><td>Single</td></tr>
<tr><td>Mutual</td></tr>
<tr><td>Qard Hassan
Good loan</td><td></td></tr>
<tr><td>Tawarruq</td><td></td></tr>
<tr><td colspan="2" rowspan="3">Islamic Bank Financing operations</td><td>Sukuk</td></tr>
<tr><td>Investment Funds</td></tr>
<tr><td>Deposits</td></tr>
</table>

Table 3.1. *Principles of the most common Islamic financial products*

3.2.1. *Mudarbah (profit sharing)*

Mudarbah is an arrangement between the financial institutions (provider of capital), wherein an institution provides funds that are utilized by the entrepreneur for the production/or creation of wealth [HAS 86]. Labor, management skills and expertise are arranged by the entrepreneur for production. The predetermined or contracted ratio of the profit share is fixed between the banks and the entrepreneur before the start of the project. If the loss occurs, both parties bear the losses, banks in the shape of capital and labor, the entrepreneur in the form of management skill and expertise [HAS 01]. As a bank invests its money in an entrepreneur project, the financial risk taken by the banks entitles them to claim the profit share. Until the loan is repaid, the profit sharing system continues.

3.2.1.1. *Mechanism of a Mudarbah contract*

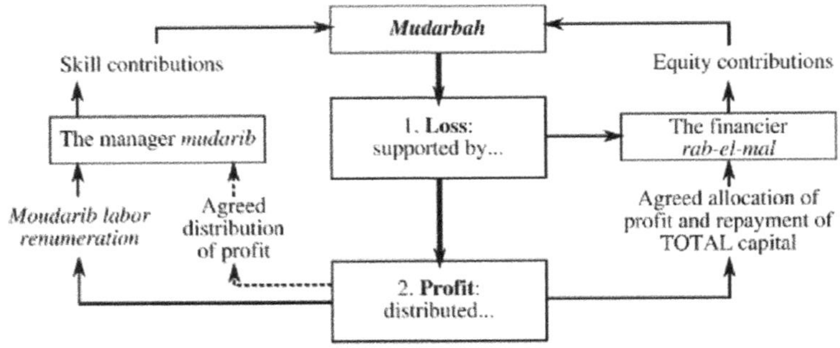

Specifically for the food industry, the *Murabaha* contract is appointed *Mousaraha.*

EXAMPLE 3.1.–

A developer wants to build an office building to sell in full. The project has a cost price of $1,000 million and the contractor is for an Islamic bank to finance the project.

The top N *Mudaraba* contract is signed on the following terms: one year project with the responsible *Mudarib*, gains will be distributed in the following proportion: 20% for the *Rab-el-mal* and the rest for *Mudarib*. Suppose the loan is 100% of the project. In December, the project is completed.

If the *Mudarib* sells all for € 1,280 million in *Rab-el-mal*, he gives:

– + $1,000 million of the loan;

– + 20% of the rightful profit = 20% × ($1,280 m – $1,000 m) was $56 m

– = $1.056 m

– ➔The *Mudarib* earning 80% × ($1,280 m – $1,000 m) was $224 m.

If the project is sold at a loss, when it is supported entirely by the *Rab-el-mal*.

3.2.2. *Musharkah (joint venture)*

Musharkah comes from Chirka, the term commonly used in Islamic jurisprudence (fiqh), which would mean sharing participation. As all sharing modes are called Chirka in the terminology of Fiqh, the term *Musharkah* does not explicitly exist in the books of Fiqh; the term Moucharaka is recent [LEV 12]. It is the agreement between the two parties, mainly the bank and the investor, who contribute their money in any business for making profit and divide it accordingly with respect to their investment or agreement. Musharkah is primarily used for three main purposes or projects, like a letter of credit, investment in a big project or purchase or renting of the real estate, which was at its boom during the last 4 years. In purchasing the real estate or property, the banker and the investor calculate its future rental earnings and divide the share accordingly in advance [MON 02]. The participation in the management by both parties is not mandatory but they are entitled to participate in the activities. As the earnings of the project are predetermined and profit is shared on the preagreed ratio, similarly the loss will be borne by the partners according to their proportion of capital investment or contributions [IWE 96].

Example 1 of pooled (simple) *Musharkah sabita*:

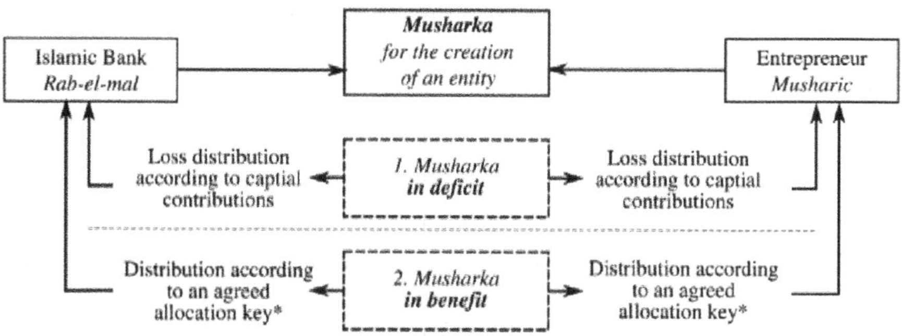

*For a capital of $100 m, an investor A provided 50%, B provided 10% and C provided 40%. If losses are incurred, they will be distributed proportionally to the contribution of each contributor. The bank would contribute to total equity for losses

3.2.2.1. *Decreasing Musharka (Mutanakissa)*

The participation of the contributor *Rab-el-mal* funds is acquired gradually by the other partners. For example, in the case of a *Mutanakissa* between an Islamic bank and its client, the two parties are receiving a percentage of profits but the client gives back all or part of his earnings to the bank to repay the amount it had originally invested. Therefore, in this *Mutanakissa* association, after enabling the project, the bank is disengaged once it has recovered its funds and the share of profit it deserves. Thus, the customer will come at the end of one contract project owner. This approaches a port operation of conventional finance.

Example 2: *Musharka Mutanakissa* mechanism with gradual redemption of the bank's shares

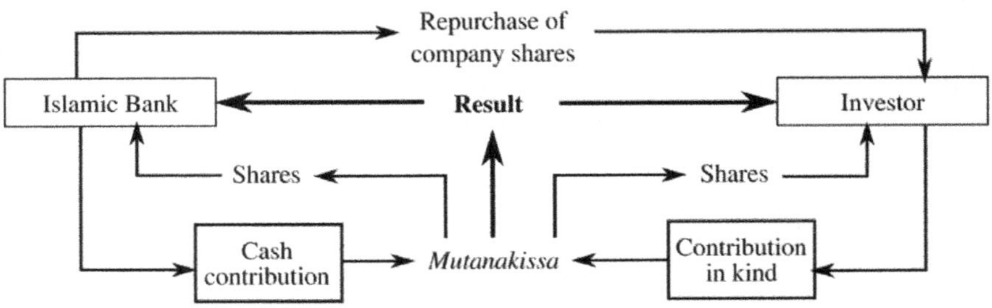

The surplus obtained by the Islamic bank corresponds to the remuneration of risk.

In all these financial products, operations can be with or without participation.

Example 3: using the *Mudarbah* contracts and *Musharka*: If the funder fully finances the project, *Mudarbah* is most effective. If it is a joint venture, then *Musharka* is best suited. But we can combine the two. P to $1,000 to N in a *Mudarbah* contract. N $500 added with the consent of the P. N the *Mudarib* can assign 1% as partner (*Charic*) and 2% for his work as manager *Mudarib*. N will win one-third of the profit + half of the remaining = 1/3. So in total N will win 1/3 + 1/3 = 2/3 of the profit. But N is limited to two-thirds of the benefit since it has not invested more than two-thirds of the capital.

	Musharkah	*Mudarbah*
Investment	Comes from all partners	Comes from the investor *Rab-el-mal*
Partners	Can contribute to the management and work; Share losses in proportion to their investment	The investor *Rab-al-mal* has no right to participate in managing the contractor manager *Mudarib* The loss is borne solely by the *Rab-al-mal* since *Mudarib* is not investing. His loss is established by its ultimately unnecessary work. Finally one loses capital and the other work (honest management under condition of its part)
Liabilities	If the liabilities exceed the assets and the *Musharka* is dissolved, the gap is supported by all the partners according to their contribution	The responsibility of the investor, *Rab-al-mal* is limited to its investment (except in the case of personal debts)
The goodwill	Is shared by all in proportion to contributions	The contractor is not entitled to a share of goodwill. Indeed, property acquired by the *Mudarib* entrepreneur, are exclusively the property of the *Rab-al-mal* investor. The only part played by *Mudarib* is that the profit from the sale of property.

Table 3.2. *Differences following Levy [LEV 12]*

3.3. Financial transactions of Islamic banks without the bank's participation

3.3.1. *Murabahah (cost plus)*

Derived from the word Rib, meaning profit, Murabahah means "profit taking" in a commercial sense. Murabahah is the purchase agreement between the banker and the client in which the good is sold to the client at a particular price, which also includes the profit margin agreed by both parties. In the agreement, everything is mentioned including the profit margin, cost and selling price when the sale is made [IMR 97]. The bank/financer charges or compensates the client in the form of profit for the time value of money. It might be referred to as a fixed income loan by the customer for the purchase of assets like real estate or a tangible asset on which the profit is charged with the fix rate calculated by profit margin. For example, if the original price of the car is 20,000 euros, the bank will purchase that car with 20,000 euros and sell it to the customer at 28,000, and will make the profit of 8,000 euros. The banks are not allowed to make extra profit by charging the time value of money on late payments [GAF 98]. The banks remain the owner of the asset until it receives the full amount of the asset.

To avoid falling into forbidden Sharia, Murabaha is subject to specific conditions in:

– Islamic finance;

- the seller must own and be in possession of the object at the time of resale,

- the price cannot be modified in the case of delay or anticipation of regulations,

- the profit margin must be determined accurately;

– Conventional finance;

- the free consent of the parties is an essential clause,

- the sale price must be clearly stated.

If the cost price is not stipulated clearly, that is not a Murabahah contract but Musawamah.

3.3.2. *Musawamah*

The sale made by the seller with the bargaining of the price of the product by its buyer, whereas no reference is made to the price paid by the buyer to how much it cost the seller while buying that product [SID 04]. Thus, in Musawamah the seller does not need to reveal the cost of its product, which is the main difference between the Musawamah and Murabahah with respect to its pricing. The rest of the conditions between the Musawamah and Murabahah are the same. The condition of the Musawamah is applied when the seller is not sure or not in the position to reveal or ascertain the cost of its products in front of the seller while offering his products.

3.3.3. *Ijarah*

Ijarah, which means "to rent", is a term that comes from the *Fiqh.*

It is essentially leasing, renting or a wage. The banks give the service or the right to use its asset, property, plant, office, motor vehicle, automation or equipment for a long period of fixed time and price. So the concept of Ijarah is to sell the benefits or the use of the assets of the other party on the basis of a fixed price and period [HAM 01].

Murabaha and Ijara divergence following Levy [LEV 12]:

– Ijara finance as well as movable property assets. Regarding the latter, the Ijara shares common factors with Murabaha, but is slightly different;

– for the Murabaha, there is the transfer of title to the buyer;

– for Ijara, the object in question is the property of the lessor, only the usufruct Manfa, that is to say the right to use is transferred to the lessee;

– in a Murabaha contract, the first sale is effective after the client has received the supply of goods by the financial institution and the other, the promise to purchase is not sufficient for the sale to become effective;

– in the case of Ijara, the contractors do not need to enter into force on the lease after the delivery was made, if the financial institution is designated by the client as his/her representative. The leasing contract will start automatically as soon as the customer uses the property.

In conventional finance, a financial institution may acquire property and sublet to professional rental companies. Thus, the subrenter and the financial institution share the rents. In Islamic finance, this type of contract is to be avoided because the owner has not the goods, but only the right to benefit from the usufruct. The financial institution eventually gives only part of his right to other entities. But this right cannot be sold because it amounts to a debt sale to collect possibly with a discount equivalent to a form of *Riba*.

In Islamic finance, leasing and credit-leasing are differentiated. Credit-leasing is *Ijarah wa ictina*.

3.3.3.1. *Ijarah wa ictina*

EXAMPLE 3.2.–

A person wishes to rent a flat, then at the end to buy it. This person targets an Islamic bank, who provides him cash, according to the precise specifications of the customer, but the customer and the bank must sign two parallel contracts:

1) a lease that provides for the amount of rent, including charges for the bank and its margin;

2) an offer to purchase the flat at a specified date for a specified price.

The margin may correspond to the interest rates that are conventional banks.

3.3.3.2. *Ijarah wa ictina mechanism*

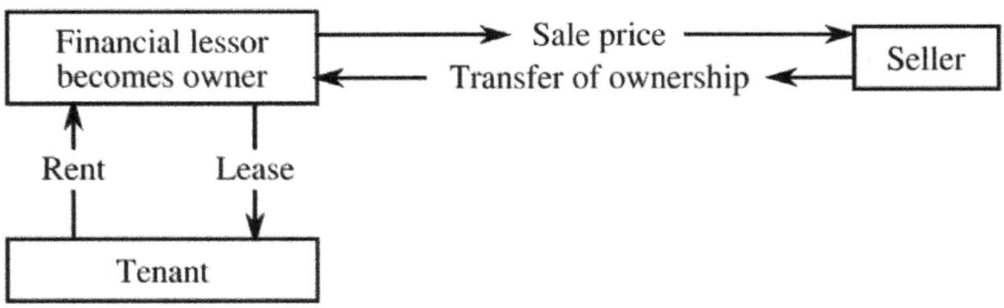

3.3.3.3. *Ijara with Musharaka*

A third option, offered in addition to the Ijara and Ijarah wa ictina, is the Ijarah with mouchracah.

In this case, if the tenant wants to buy the property out of contract (to build aircraft, infrastructure, etc.), it will pay the rental payments plus a part of the property purchase price. These additions will be invested by the Islamic bank in an investment account and the profits earned will go to the tenant. The goal is the complete transfer of ownership.

3.3.4. *Bai al-inah (sale and buy back agreement)*

In Baial-inah, the bank or financial institution sells the asset to the buyer, followed by buying back agreement of same asset. This means that the asset is sold on the deferred payments to the buyer and bought back or repurchased immediately on the discounted price, which keeps the ownership of the asset with the financier, bank or financial institution. It is designed for the protection of the financier against the default without explicitly charging interest [CHI 93].

3.3.5. *Bai' Bithaman Ajil (deferred payment sale)*

Mudarbah and Bai' Bithaman Ajil are the same concepts but include the deferred payments in the sale on goods, which also includes the profit margin on the agreement by both parties [HAM 01]. The main difference is that in Bai' Bithaman Ajil, the clients, customers or debtors make the full payments on the maturity instead of paying the monthly equal installments. As in other modes of finance, the high price is charged to the debtor for the use of an asset to make profit, which is more than or equal to the market interest rate at that time.

3.3.6. *Bai Muajjal (credit sale)*

The credit sale of any product is called a Bai Muajjal. In this contract, the bank buys the product at the market price with the intention to sell it at a higher price with a profit margin, and ask the buyer to pay the amount in a lump sum or instalments at future dates. As in other contracts, the cost and the profit are mentioned in the contract where both parties mutually agreed to proceed with the agreement. In such a transaction, the price can be fixed as the spot price or higher/lower than the market price or spot price.

3.3.7. *Bai Salam*

Salam is an abnormal financial package, with Istinah, specifically authorized by the Koran. Indeed, we are dealing with an exception to the rule of Islamic control, which is not selling anything, if the seller does not own it.

Bai Salam is a mode of finance in which the buyer makes advance payments for the goods that will be delivered at the future dates by the seller. For making the contract accordingly, the buyer has to pay the full amount in advance and the seller has to deliver the goods on the specific date agreed. The transaction will not be counted as successful until and unless the payment is made in full, and the transaction will be defeated if the payment is made in installments. If the buyer does not make the payment in full, it will be treated as the sale of debt, against debt, which is prohibited according to Islamic rules. In Bai Salam, the entire jurist agreed on the lump sum payment of the product in advance by the seller to fulfill the terms and conditions of contract. According to Malik [MAL 95], concession may be given by the seller in terms of payment days, for example two or three extra days may be given for the full payment by the seller to the buyer that is not included in the agreement. However, the quality of goods that need to be delivered should be same as written in the agreement; if not then it will lead to dispute between two parties. In Bai Salam, the buyer and seller can trade anything except gold, silver or any currency, which is barred from being traded. The quality, quantity and workmanship should clearly be defined in the contract. Salam says that the seller cannot sell the product without the specification of its quality and quantity.

The Salam contract of sale is now used to replace the derivatives of conventional finance, which nevertheless contain a large element of chance, Garar prohibited Salam principles.

If goods exist in a market, then:

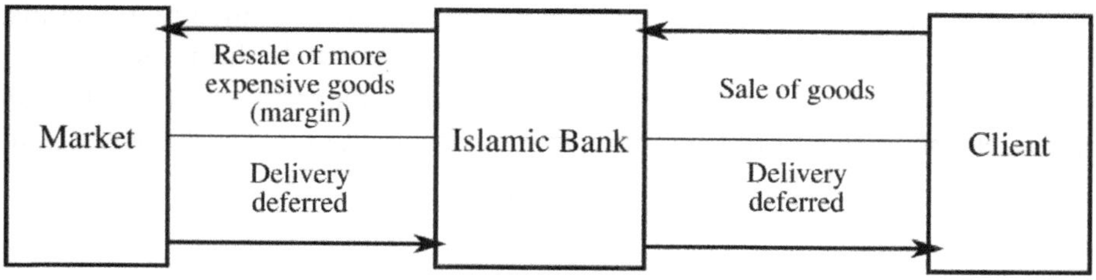

If goods do not exist, then:

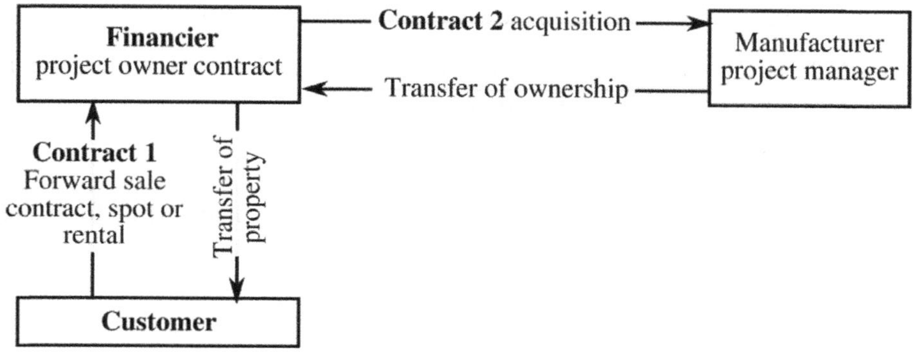

Istinah is a variant of a Salam contract. In:

– Salam, the subject is the delivery of goods (tradable items without processing elements);

– Istinah, the materials have undergone a transformation process, including the costs of raw materials, consumables, labor and other costs, etc., to the finished product ordered.

It is not necessary that the delivery date has been fixed in the contract, but a reasonable maximum delivery time may be mentioned, after which the buyer can consider themself released from the contract. The buyer can also ask for penalties [LEV 16].

Istinah is used to finance working capital and tangible goods such as gas, electricity, etc., that cannot inherently benefit from an Ijara contract, which funds movable and immovable property.

3.3.7.1. *Differences between Istinah and Ijarah*

A true Istinah contract requires that the contractor buys the raw materials, then add all the costs necessary to produce the good. If the project owner contract (applicant) provides the raw material, then it is not an Istinah contract but an Ijarah. Indeed this Ijarah contract is to pay for the services of a person as noted in the paragraph on Ijarah.

3.3.7.2. *Differences between Istinah and Salam contracts*

The contract:

– Istinah always relates specifically to property produced;

– Salam can be applied to any product, whether it has undergone a transformation process or is merely merchandise.

Regulation:

– For Salam, it is essential that the price has been paid in full from the start;

– For Istinah, this is not the case.

The withdrawal:

– Salam, once it has been signed, it is not possible to retract;

– For Istinah, while feasibility studies have not yet been commenced, it is always possible to cancel the contract.

Delivery:

– For Salam, the delivery period is an essential part of the sales contract;

– For Istinah, it is not necessary to set the delivery period in the contract.

3.3.8. *Hibah (gift)*

Instead of interest, the concept of Hibah was introduced in Islamic banking. Hibah means the gift offered voluntarily to the debtor by the creditor for the loan, which he took form creditor. The banks pay their customer in form of Hibah on fixed amount on their saving accounts [BUA 08].

3.3.9. *Qard Hassan (good loan)*

This is the interest-free loan for the debtors, in which case the creditors only receive the principle amount of the loan, which he/she forward to the debtor for the sake or development of his/her business. No compensation is made to the creditor for the time value of money. According to some scholars, this is the only type of loan that is lawful as Riba is not included in the loan and does not violate the Islamic principles. The debtor sometimes pays the extra amount on the return of Qard Hassan as an appreciation to the creditor, but this is not mandatory [LEW 01].

It is a loan of benevolence, which is repaid the principal at maturity but without interest, profit or loss. It is given in limited quantities for short periods and responsibility of a more social type of financing: microbusiness, occasional personal problems, etc. In fact, by not paying the capital, it amounts to a subsidy; nevertheless, all operations on Islamic deposit bank accounts are covered by the Qard Hassan [LEV 16].

3.3.10. *Wadiah (safekeeping)*

The bank acts as the Wadiah or trustee of the funds for its customers. The customer deposits their money in the bank, and banks acting as a trustee must refund the full amount on demand. The banks sometimes give the Hibah to its customer as an appreciation because of the funds deposited by the customers is used by the bank, which is at the discretion of bank. However, mainly this Hibah (gift) is the interest called as time value of money to compensate the depositors. As it is not guaranteed to be rewarded every time, it is thus called as Hibah.

3.3.11. *Sukuk (Islamic bonds)*

Sukuk is an Islamic financial certificate to interest bearing bonds. It works in the same way as the other bonds but prohibits the charging of any kind of interest according to Islamic law and investment principles. They are classified in secondary market with respect to their tradability and non-tradability. In accordance with Islamic investment principles, US $500 million of assets are managed.

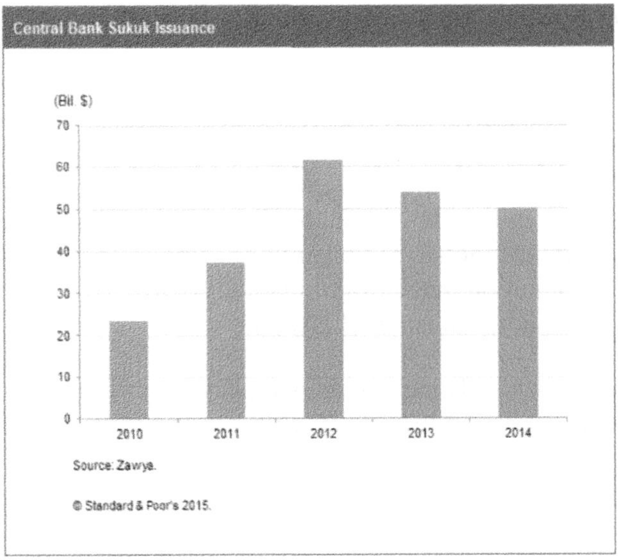

Figure 3.1. *Total Sukuk issuance (Source: S&P [2015])*

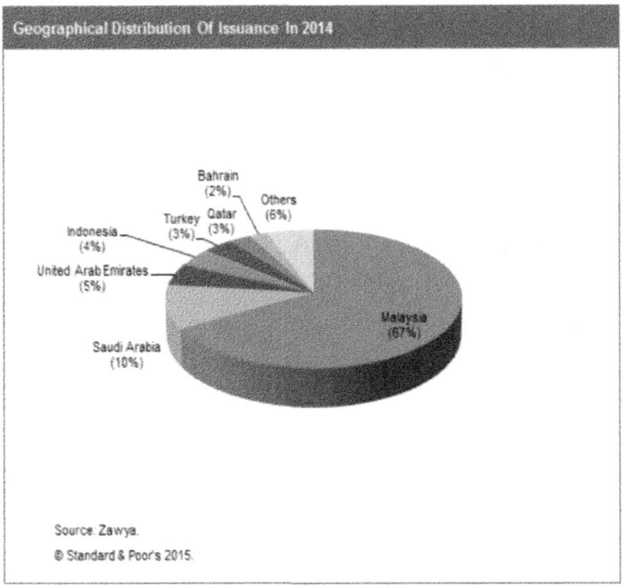

Figure 3.2. *Geographical distribution of issuance in 2014 (source: S&P 2015). For a color version of this figure, see www.iste.co.uk/benbouheni/banking.zip*

The main differences between Sukuk and bonds as follows:

– Sukuk generates income either through the securitization of real estate assets, Mudarabah, or through finance lease (leasing), Ijara;

– bonds are entitled to a predetermined fixed interest;

– Sukuk investors finance tangible assets (listed or not) by securities, participation, investment certificates, etc., with stable income over a period. The Sukuk can lean against all types of non-equity funding, if guaranteed Sharia;

– assets are divided equally as bonds, each Sukuk gives the investor a share of the underlying property and income is attached;

– bonds are not functions of an underlying asset;

– the bonds are due in accordance with a draw not related to the end of the funded project;

– the Sukuk have the same term as the funded project.

In 2015, Standard and Poor's published its updated criteria for rating Sukuk to further enhance its transparency. "Fundamentally our approach remains unchanged, and focuses on the contractual obligations of Sukuk sponsors to make certain payments. However, we have identified cases where a Sukuk rating could be lower than the sponsor's rating because the Sukuk may entail risks that do not exist in conventional bonds. Due to their Islamic nature and specifically to the principles of asset-backing and profit-and-loss-sharing, a total loss event of the Sukuk's underlying assets may result in an unpredictable resolution of the transaction. In most cases, the sponsor offers mechanisms to ensure that the ultimate risk investors take remains the sponsor's counterparty credit risk. Nevertheless, in a few instances, Sharia scholars request higher loss-sharing features, which imply residual asset risk. To rate such transactions, Standard & Poor's looks at the remoteness of the total loss event and the extent to which it affects the overall performance of the transaction. If the total loss event is not remote, we may cap our rating. Our view is underpinned by the lack of standardization in the Sukuk market and the lack of predictability regarding resolution, which could make Sukuk ratings considerations different from those of conventional bonds ratings"[1].

---

1 For further information see: file:///C:/Users/Aldol/Downloads/for_sukuk_issuance_emerging_headwinds_may_cause_turbulence_in_2015.pdf.

3.3.12. *Takaful (Islamic insurance)*

Takaful is kind of insurance that covers the risk of loss against uncertainty. The basis of Takaful is the principle that something which is uncertain for an individual will be uncertain for a very large number of individuals at the same time. So it provides ease to the individual by combining the risks of many people, which is provided by the law of large numbers. According to the Islamic financial system, it is not against the concept of insurance where the resources are pooled to help the needy. Islamic financing is not same as conventional insurance, as they have the element of uncertainty and gambling.

The Tacafuls are insurance companies that can make profits and are split into two separate entities:

1) a fund to pay claims and receive contributions;

2) a management company to handle the accounting of receipts and disbursements.

The investments of these funds are made in development projects and Islamic financing modes such as Muchraca and Mudrabah. In case of loss, it is through a loan without interest, paid by the management company, pending future surpluses will reimburse.

The classic insurance offers contracts based on a probable future, as Sharia prohibits betting, games, chance, Maysir, etc. The Islamic argument evokes:

– that if the disaster does not occur, the insurance company has unfairly profited by charging underlying tangible assets without insurance contributions;

– in case of claim, the insured receives compensation exceeding the allocation paid as conventional insurance pay small instalments with contributors, the major claims of victims, which seem fair.

The above is a Sharia mutual insurance system, but that already exists. However, the fundamentals of Islamic insurance require insurance policy clauses to be both precise and clear, without tedious interpretations.

3.3.13. *Wakalah (agency)*

The kind of agreement or arrangement whereby an agent becomes the third party and takes on the responsibility to undertake the transactions on behalf of the first person or principal person. All the Islamic banks offer those services that are instigated from Shariah. Islamic banking products are not only offered by fully Islamic firms, but also by non-Islamic banks. Western banks, such as HSBC, Citibank, Deutsche Bank, Standard Chartered and BNP Paribas, are among the many institutions active in this field. In Muslim countries, they cater for both the wholesale and the retail markets, but elsewhere they tend to restrict themselves to the wholesale market. HSBC and Lloyds TSB, however, also tap the retail market in the UK, along with specialized Islamic firms. Penetration is increasing in other parts of the world as well. In South Africa, for instance, one of the leading banks, ABSA, offers Islamic banking facilities to both business firms and consumers. Usually, a separate legal entity is set up for this purpose. However, this does not seem strictly necessary, as long as all money streams, including the funding of Islamic activities, are strictly separated from the bank's conventional business [YAQ 00].

3.3.14. *Tawarruq*

Islamic banks use the *tawarruq* structure to facilitate cash financing to their clients. In this structure, the bank directly or indirectly buys an asset and immediately sells it to a customer on a deferred-payment basis. The customer then sells the same asset to a third party for immediate delivery and payment. The result is that the customer receives an immediate cash payment with an obligation to make deferred payments to the bank for the marked-up price of the asset [SHA 09]. In modern Islamic banking, the bank usually performs all the transactions needed for *tawarruq* financing. *Tawarruq* financing is somewhat controversial and has been the subject of debate in Islamic financial circles because the customer has no real intention of buying or selling the underlying commodity that supports the financial transaction. Because of the absence of any exchange of actual goods, *tawarruq* financing is prohibited by the Islamic Fiqh Academy of Jeddah, Saudi Arabia. *Tawarruq* generates debts, adding to the gap between the real sector and the financial sector of the economy. It leads to a debt market, and a debt instrument does not represent any real asset. The customer's purpose when engaging in the transaction is merely to generate cash, which can be construed as inconsistent with *Shariah*. Mohammad Nejatullah Siddiqi, researcher in Islamic finance, has said: *The introduction of tawarruq into the body of Islamic economy is sure to act like a virus destroying the immune system that would protect it from increasing indebtedness leading to speculation, monetary fluctuations, instability and inequity* [SID 07].

3.3.15. *Deposits*

– *Current accounts*

It is permitted for legal and natural persons to deposit funds in current accounts, wadia (guard). These deposits, for the:

– customer;

- have no predetermined interest, as could be the case in conventional banks because there is a lack of risk,

- are capital guaranteed, as a free loan hassan card,

– Islamic financial institution;

- are used at will for halal operations,

- who must ensure that the balances are positive,

- and who receives income from investments;

– *Banking services*

Banking, Jawala (contract refers to an agreement wherein one party deposit undertakes to pay a predetermined commission to another to realize a specific service) are paying as is the case for conventional banks (services with VAT).

Islamic banking can apply for bank commissions, *Oujr*:

– rental coffers with Ijarah contract;

– Wakala agent contract, where the bank is Wakil such securities depository, holding a cash system service performs remittances, administered for the customer's account, etc.

These funds are guaranteed by the Islamic bank and the account holders receive free check books, services, money transfers, etc.

– *Savings accounts*

Hoarding is in principle prohibited. Savings accounts (safekeeping of goods with a discount on the original stated cost) based on the principle of current account Wadia, are provided to retain precautionary savings without charging interest, without control over the management of funds by the bank and without insurance that capital be returned (such as savings contracts in units of account offered actually in conventional finance).

Wadia in the current account, the bank is regarded as a simple administrator of deposits. Payment of principal is guaranteed and the applicant may be awarded a bonus, a gift, Ibah by the bank for the use of halal funds, customer loyalty, etc., at the discretion of the bank. The applicant may of course ask for a participatory management of their account by the bank, the *Taoufir*.

– *Participatory account*

The Tawfir is a participatory futures account where the applicant bank to load the fruiting-proud its assets approved by the Shariah operations. The bank then distributes the dream-naked in accordance with what had been expected. The Taoufir is a participatory savings account with a recommended capital management but not guaranteed.

– *Investment accounts*

They are based first on the principle of sharing profits and losses SPL on the association of factors, capital and labor. The amounts paid by investors for investment purposes are an essential source of funds of Islamic banks.

Example of Murabaha contract using an investment account:

Depositor funds invested	⇨Funds deposits ⇨	Financial Institution		⇨ Use of funds	Borrower
	⇦ Compensation ⇦	Manager *Mudarib*	Investor *Rab-el-mal*	⇦ Compensation ⇦	

Islamic finance must match the funding for investments and the underlying asset must be identifiable. Thus, for each project there are a multitude of variants. For example, in a project combining:

– Istinah Mudaraba and, in addition to the previous diagram, two parallel contracts Istina that link the bank with the contractor;

– with a lease is a contract will add Ijarah wa Ictina, etc.

– *Bank cards*

A credit card is a payment, often deferred debit. A *Fatwa* against these credit cards is often issued as they are used in conventional finance, withdrawals and payments. Bank cards contain interest and should not be used in Islamic finance. Only permitted is:

– withdrawal cards;

– payment cards when purchasing operations are backed by a tangible underlying asset (the purchase of the property paid by the card);

– prepaid cards which avoid interest.

So if the bank card does not generate any costs related to money, then it is allowed.

3.3.16. *Islamic investment funds*

– *The Murabaha funds*: they are collected and invested by the fund manager in Murabahas. They allow offering fixed income since the Murabaha contract allows to sell assets with a predetermined margin.

– *The Ijarah funds*: the principle is to buy shares in companies, as if they were assets and leasing them to customers. The shares remain the property of the financial institution and rents are payable by customers. Funds are raised and invested by the Manager, Mudarib funds in capital, which will then be in rentals and will provide fixed income.

– *Equities funds*: the profits when investing in shares or come from a share of annual dividends and other gains obtained by the sale of shares (difference between the price at the time of the sale and time of acquisition). If an entity has had to borrow money or make a marginal operation on his mended-interest, this does not discredit all its operations. It may well spend some of his illicit gains charitable investments (Zakat).

– *Hedge funds*: there are hedge funds which are guaranteed Sharia. Of course, all those which involve derivatives are prohibited in principle, but there are strategies to “bypass”. In Islamic finance you cannot sell anything that you do not own and in principle if it does not hold well on the day of the sale. To overcome this difficulty, the following operations have been used: the Salam, the Arboun, the Kiar and the Wad;

- the Salam allows to deliver assets at term (titles) the buyer pays entirely in cash;

- the Arboun, where a contract is made up of deposit (lost instead of recoverable payments) paid on signature of the contract and retained by the seller if the buyer fails. It is this difference between deposit and deposit that is not comparable to conventional options, regulation outstanding being at a future date agreed in advance between the seller and the buyer,

- the Kiar is a possibility of adding a condition in the contract,

- the Wad is a unilateral irrevocable contractual promise in principle. For example, the issuer of a contract will commit unilaterally to acquire or transfer an amount of one currency against another currency at a predetermined date and value. The buyer has the choice of whether to run the wad in exchange for a non-refundable commission, equivalent in conventional finance to a putt or a call.

In fact, the investor has invested in Sharia compatible securities while receiving non-compliant asset yields. This type of exchange yield is conventionally called Swap. One quibble is that:

> "Prohibition of Gharar and Jahala refers only to sales contracts and not the promises. Therefore, it is acceptable for a promise to purchase or sell exchangeable and binding, even without knowing the price at the time of the promise. The award will be known at the execution of the sale".
>
> "There is in Sharia no reason why an asset could not be sold at a price derived from the performance of separate assets, indices or other benchmark that would or would not Sharia compliant".

3.4. Overview of Islamic banking

3.4.1. *Classical Islamic banking*

During the Islamic Golden Age, early forms of proto-capitalism and free markets were present in the Caliphate, where an early market economy and early form of merchant capitalism was developed between the 8th and 12th Centuries, which some refer to as “Islamic capitalism”. A vigorous monetary economy was created on the basis of the expanding levels of circulation of a stable high-value currency (the dinar) and the integration of monetary areas that were previously independent [BEN 12].

A number of innovative concepts and techniques were introduced in early Islamic banking, including contracts, bills of exchange, long-distance international trade, the first forms of partnership (mufawada) such as limited partnerships (mudaraba), and the earliest forms of credit, debt, profit, loss, capital (al-mal), capital accumulation (nama al-mal), circulating capital, capital expenditure, revenue, checks, promissory notes, trusts, startup companies, savings accounts, transactional accounts, pawning, loaning, exchange rates, bankers, money changers, ledgers, deposits, assignments, the double-entry bookkeeping system and lawsuits.

Organizational enterprises similar to corporations independent from the state also existed in the medieval Islamic world, while the agency institution was also introduced. Many of these early capitalist concepts were adopted and further advanced in medieval Europe from the 13th Century onward. The common view of riba (usury) among classical jurists of Islamic law and economics during the Islamic Golden Age was that it is only riba and therefore unlawful to apply interest to money (exclusively gold and silver currencies) but that it is not riba and is therefore acceptable to apply interest to fiat money (currencies made up of other materials such as paper or base metals) to an extent. The definition of riba in classical Islamic jurisprudence was “surplus value without counterpart”. When “currencies of base metal were first introduced in the Islamic world, no jurist ever thought that paying a debt in a higher number of units of this fiat money was riba” as they were concerned with the real value of money (determined by weight only) rather than the numerical value.

3.4.2. *Modern Islamic banking*

The modern Islamic banking movement started in a humble way as a small community finance effort in Egypt (1963) and grew gradually to become a small emerging finance industry in the Middle East (1973). Today, with the increase in demand for oil and gas and the increase in energy prices, many of the Gulf’s oil-producing countries have accumulated large amounts of cash. Some of the owners of this cash have decided to use Islamic banks to manage it. This has helped the riba-free banking industry become well established and a high-growth industry. Islamic banking came to Europe in the early 1980s.

Islamic banking really got on the agenda after the Third Islamic Conference of Foreign Ministers, held in Jeddah in 1972. The finance ministers of 18 countries presented a plan to introduce Sharia principles in the financial and banking system and in the wake of the conference several countries took steps in this direction [LEW 01]. Then, in December 1973 the Conference of Finance Ministers of Muslim Countries, again held in Jeddah, issued a Declaration of Intent to establish an Islamic Development Bank (IDB), which duly started operations in 1975. The purpose of the bank is to foster economic development and social progress of member countries and Muslim communities in accordance with Sharia principles, through participation in equity capital and providing loans. More recently, the IDB launched a venture capital fund targeting high-tech ventures in Muslim countries [ALR 00].

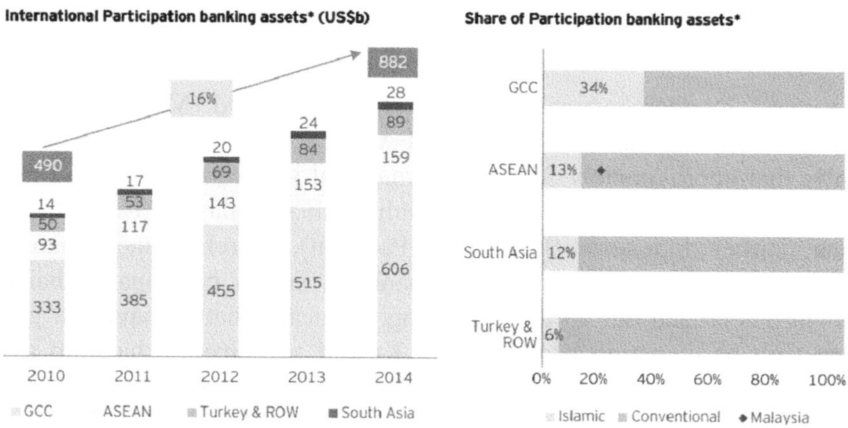

Figure 3.3. *International participation banking assets (source: Central banks, EY analysis [EY 16]). For a color version of this figure, see www.iste.co.uk/benbouheni/banking.zip*

Figure 3.3 shows that the participation banking assets grew strongly in 2014, with GCC gaining above average growth rate. Participation banking continues to show strong growth of approximately 16%, despite political and economic volatility in the major regions.

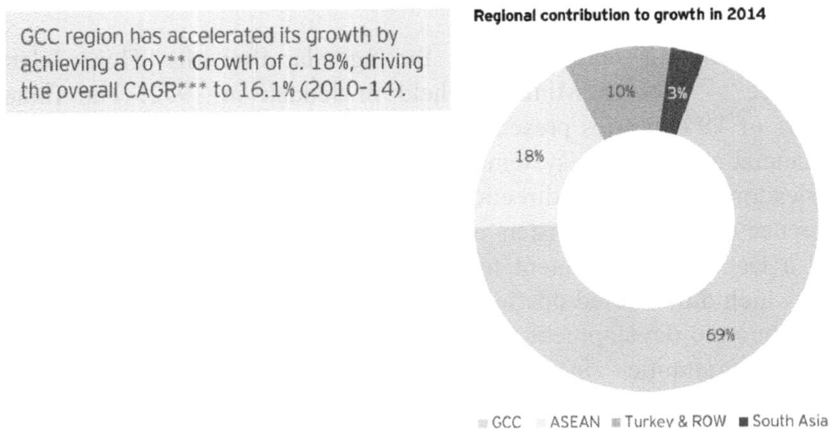

Figure 3.4. *Regional market contributions (source: Central banks, EY analysis [EY 16]). For a color version of this figure, see www.iste.co.uk/benbouheni/banking.zip*

Figure 3.4 demonstrates that Saudi Arabia and Malaysia are the respective leading markets in GCC and Asia Pacific. In addition, Figure 3.5 shows that approximately 93% of international participation banking assets is based out of nine core markets (Saudi Arabia, Malaysia, UAE, Kuwait, Qatar, Turkey, Indonesia, Bahrain and Pakistan). Therefore, more than 50% of Saudi assets are from participation banking. Turkey participation banking growth has eroded due to the prevailing political situation having a global impact on participation banking. And Kuwait participation banking assets now comprise 45% of the national banking system assets [EY 16].

Malaysia had the most developed market in the world for Islamic financial products, partly because of the presence of a significant number of players and partly because of strong government support [COO 08]. In 2008, Dubai and Saudi Arabia launched large government-backed Islamic banks. This move changed the traditional face of the Islamic banking industry, which has traditionally been populated by many small institutions (see [DUB 08]).

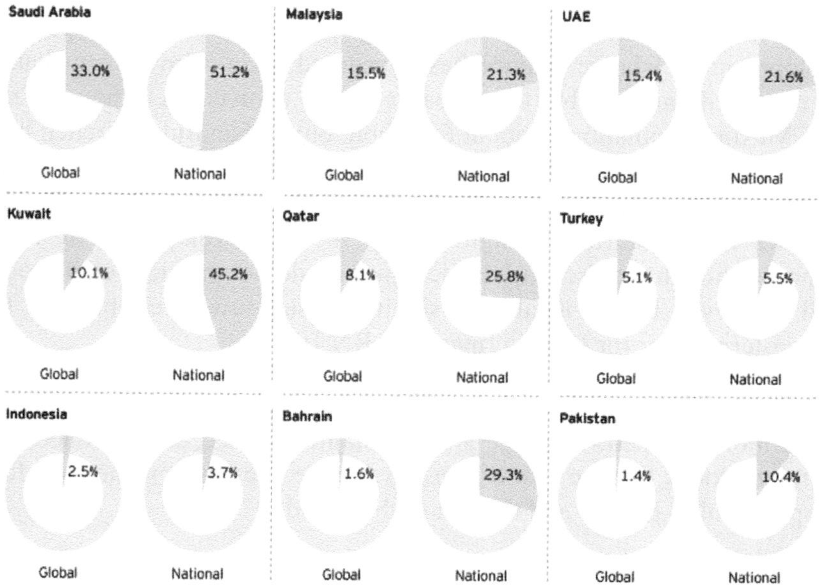

Figure 3.5. *Participation industry footprint (source: EY analysis [EY 16]). For a color version of this figure, see www.iste.co.uk/benbouheni/banking.zip*

Islamic banking assets worldwide have grown by more than 10% annually over the past 10 years, from about US $150 billion in the mid-1990s to a US $1 trillion in 2011 [BEN 15]. In addition, the value of assets managed by Islamic banks is expected to grow to US $4 trillion by 2020. Many European municipalities and governments are dealing in Islamic banking products, mainly bonds (Sukuk). In Asia, many countries have Islamic banks and/or finance companies. Malaysia has one of the pioneering and most sophisticated Islamic banking industries in the world.

The United Kingdom, where the Muslim population is three times less than in France, is home to five Islamic banks, the only licensed ones in the European Union, and lists £5.5 billion in Sukuk, or Islamic bonds, on its stock exchange. Since 2003 the United Kingdom has been reforming laws to ensure that Shariah-compliant investments are not prone to higher levies than their conventional equivalents [ARN 10].

Up to 2008 in France, and although some financial institutions seem to be willing now to enter into a licensing process for this purpose, the development of Islamic finance has concerned mainly investment banking and not retail banking, but this situation could evolve: even though France has a Muslim population of about 6 million, only a handful of French banks, such as BNP Paribas and Société Générale currently offer wholesale Islamic services. These types of structures are called “Islamic windows”. These windows have contributed significantly to the development of Islamic finance, although the French Islamic windows do not provide retail products at all. However, France is taking a significant step toward establishing Paris as a western center for Islamic finance [ARN 10].

France’s goals are to attract global funds, and, particularly, to make France more competitive in the area of Islamic finance, since France, being an international finance center, has to handle the phenomenon of forum shopping within Europe and the rest of the world.

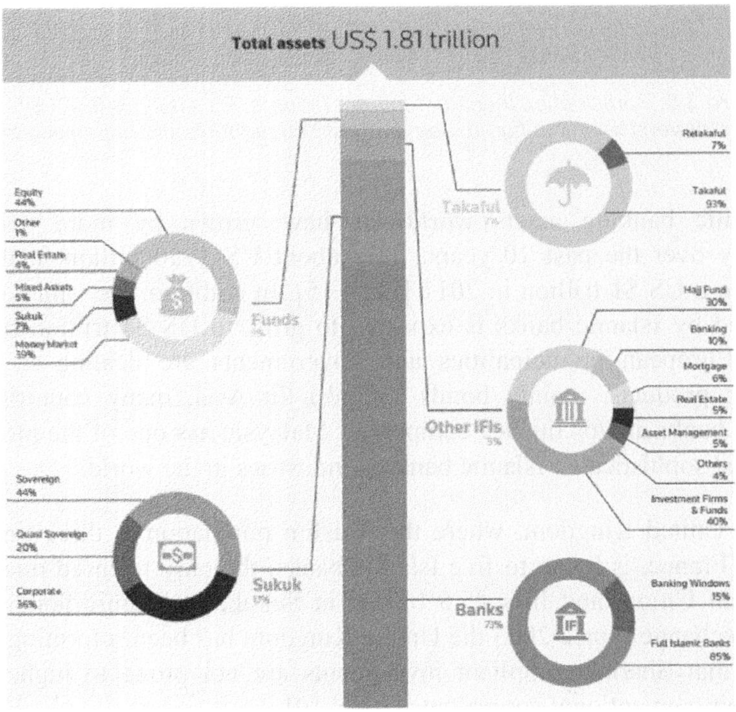

Figure 3.6. *Quantitative development landscape (source: Thomson Reuters, 2016). For a color version of this figure, see www.iste.co.uk/benbouheni/banking.zip*

Thomson Reuters [THO 16] estimated that Islamic finance assets globally reached US $1.81 trillion in 2014, up from US $1.66 billion a year earlier. Most of these Islamic finance assets (74%) are held by Islamic banks and most of the assets are located in Muslim-majority countries within the 57-member countries of the Organization of Islamic Cooperation (OIC).

By asset size alone, the five largest markets for Islamic banking are Iran (US $329 billion), Saudi Arabia (US $300 billion), Malaysia (US $174 billion), the United Arab Emirates (US $127 billion) and Kuwait (US $88 billion).

In the capital markets sector, which represents US $295 billion in total assets (16% of total Islamic finance assets), Sukuk issuance has fluctuated from US $70.4 billion in 2011 to a record high level of US $137 billion in 2012. Due to the slowdown in emerging markets and Malaysia's central bank curtailing its issuance, the Sukuk market may not reach the 2011 total before the year-end. However, despite the present headwinds as a result of a strong dollar and worries about Chinese growth prospects, the long-term picture for Sukuk is bright with 2014 seeing sovereign issuances from key non-Muslim sovereigns (United Kingdom, Luxembourg, South Africa and Hong Kong). The issuance trends in 2015 have been more muted, although Hong Kong returned with another Sukuk, Luxembourg announced its intention to return in 2016 and Indonesia issued a US $2 billion global Sukuk. The debut sovereign Sukuk issued by Luxembourg is a key part of their strategy to attract Islamic finance activity to the Grand Duchy.

3.5. The Islamic development bank

Established by the Articles of Agreement in October 1975, the IDB is a multilateral financial institution designed to foster economic development and social progress in the 53 member countries of the Organization of Islamic Countries (OIC) and in Muslim communities in non-member countries. IDB provides financial assistance by way of equity and lease financing (*Ijarah*), installment sale financing (*Murabahah*), and grant (interest-free) loans for projects and assistance in promoting foreign trade among member countries. Projects are financed from ordinary capital resources through interest-free loans, leasing, installment sale, and equity participation. More recently, the IDB has introduced the use of *istisnah* (construction and manufacturing) contracts [BEN 12].

By the year 2000, the IDB had financed inter-Islamic trade to the tune of over US $8 billion mostly using the mark-up technique. It also gives loans, taking only service charges according to actual administrative expenditures. But it does try to promote sharing-based modes of financing. It is also managing an investment portfolio in which individual Islamic banks place their surplus liquidity. Even though it cannot, and does not aspire to, serve as a lender of last resort for all Islamic banks, it is trying to help them solve their liquidity problems. It fosters technical cooperation between member countries and has established or sponsored a number of institutions for this purpose. The Islamic Chamber of Commerce and the Islamic Foundation for Science, Technology and Development are two of these. It is also distributing scholarships for higher learning and technical education to Muslim students in countries in which Muslims are in a minority.

In order to fulfill its mission, the IDB has established the Islamic Research and Training Institute (IRTI). It conducts in-house research, sponsors external research, publishes a research journal, conducts training courses, organizes seminars and conferences and maintains a database on Islamic countries' economies.

The IDB has also established the IRTI with the objectives of providing training facilities for professionals engaged in development activities in member countries and undertaking research in the areas of Islamic economics, finance and banking. IRTI serves as an information center, collecting and disseminating information in related fields. In addition to the publication of an academic journal on Islamic economics, IRTI arranges both professional and academic seminars and conferences to promote research on Islamic economics and banking. In 2005, the IDB Board of Governors approved the establishment of the International Islamic Trade Finance Corporation to finance trade activities of its member countries.

The IDB interacts with all regional and international financial institutions such as the International Monetary Fund, the World Bank and the Asian Development Bank.

According to Figures 3.7 and 3.8, Saudi Arabia continues to dominate the growth share of the market with a strong comeback by Kuwait and Qatar. Bahrain is also steadily gaining market share over traditional banks. Saudi Arabia, Qatar and Pakistan are enjoying double digit median banking growth (2010–2014).

3.6. Features of Islamic banking governance

Corporate governance relates to the manner in which the business of the bank is governed, including setting corporate objectives and the bank's risk profile, aligning corporate activities and behaviors with the expectation that the management will operate in a safe and sound manner, running day-to-day operations within an established risk profile, while protecting the interests of depositors and other stakeholders. It is defined by a set of relationships between the bank's management, its board, its shareholders and other stakeholders [VAN 08].

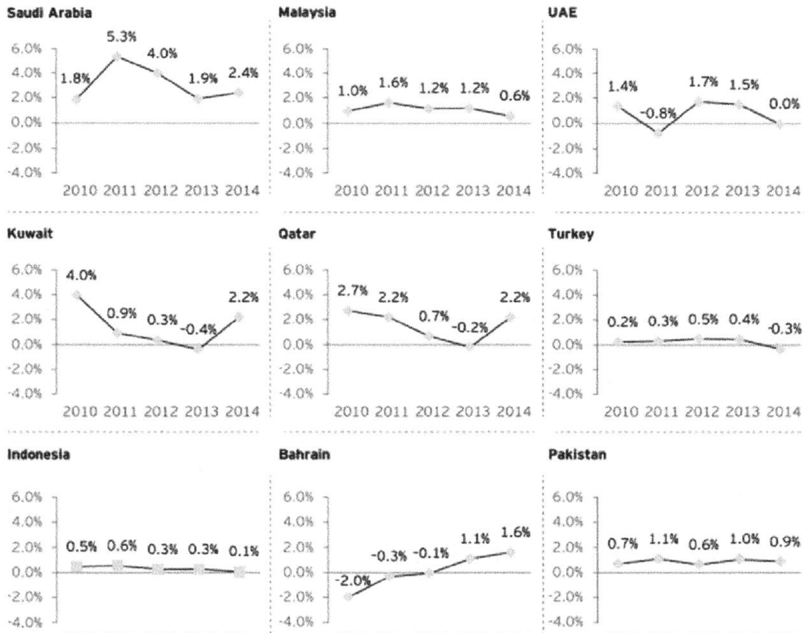

Figure 3.7. *Market share changes (source: EY analysis [EY 16])*

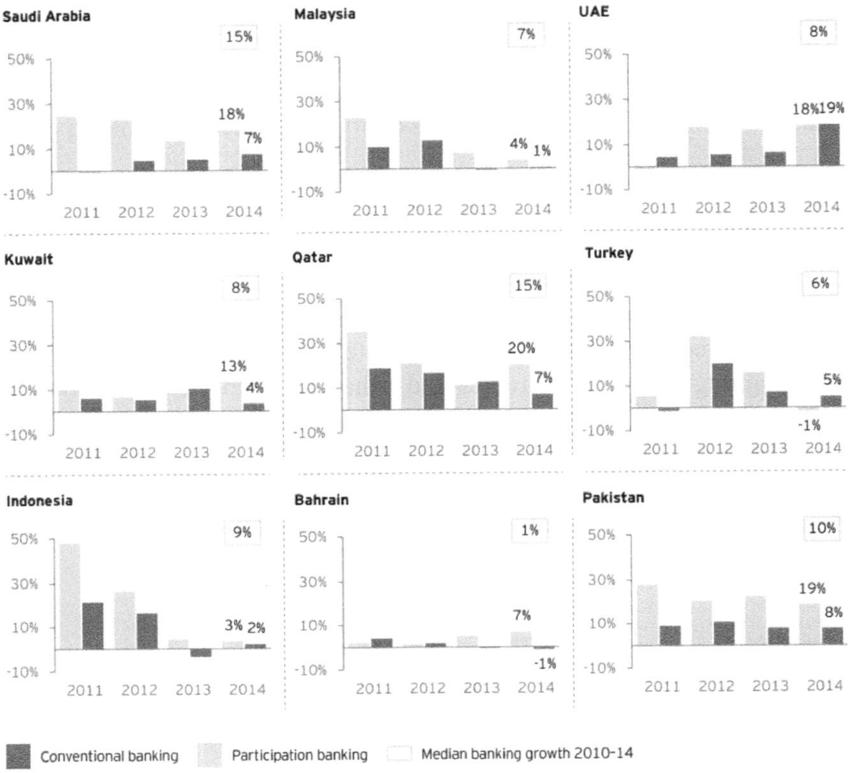

Figure 3.8. *Asset growth (source: EY analysis [EY 16]). For a color version of this figure, see www.iste.co.uk/benbouheni/banking.zip*

Corporate governance in banking has been analyzed extensively in the context of commercial banking. By contrast, little is written on corporate governance of Islamic banking, particularly the governance structures of Islamic finance sector, despite its rapid growth since the mid-1970s and increasing presence on world financial markets [YUN 07]. Hence, corporate governance is one of the vital elements of any corporation development and it is even bigger challenge to Islamic finance system due to its additional risk as compared to the commercial banking system.

The principles of Islamic banks are significantly different from those of conventional banks. Islamic banks are organized under and operate upon principles of Islamic law that requires risk sharing and prohibits the payment interest. In contrast, conventional banks are guided mainly by the profit-maximization principle. If the differences between the two types of banks are not just semantic, Islamic and conventional banks should be distinguishable from one another on the basis of financial information obtained from company balance sheets and income statements. However, since all banks operate in the same competitive environment and are regulated in the same way in most countries, it is possible that Islamic and conventional banks display similar financial characteristics [BEN 12].

Islamic banks generally have corporate governance structures and financial systems similar to those of conventional systems for handling agency problems between shareholders and management. In addition, a framework is needed to protect the financial interests of stakeholders, in this case, investment account holders. Generally, Islamic banks offer three broad categories of deposit–investment accounts: current accounts, unrestricted investment accounts and restricted investment accounts. Each category raises corporate governance issues, but those of unrestricted investment accounts are the most challenging. Islamic financial institutions carry assets based on partnership contracts, which converts them into stakeholders in the businesses to which they provide financing. This is similar to the "insider" system of governance in the German model of banking, where bankers may also be represented on the board of directors. Little attention is being paid to this aspect, but it does pose challenges for corporate governance.

First, Islamic bank assets are composed of profit and loss-sharing instruments (Mudarabah and Musharakah). Due to the high degree of asymmetry of information in equity and profit- and loss- sharing contracts, there is greater need for close monitoring by the Islamic bank. To minimize the costs, institutional arrangements that facilitate monitoring and governance are essential. Second, as the Islamic financial system places more emphasis on partnership-based instruments, Islamic bank participation in governance matters is critical, enhancing the responsibility and accountability of the management and the decision-makers. Weak corporate governance may impose a heavy cost. The extension of international standards and practices to Islamic banks may not be sufficient. Sound corporate governance requires the formulation of principles and enforcement (see [BER 04]). Many countries where Islamic finance is developing have weak contractual environments. Regulators often lack powers to enforce the rules, private actors are non-existent and courts are "underfinanced, unmotivated, unclear as to how the law applies, unfamiliar with economic issues, or even corrupt" [FRE 02].

Referring to El-Gamal [ELG 05], corporate governance of Islamic banking and regulatory recommendations are not so different from the Anglo–American system. Boards of directors and external market discipline will ensure that managers pursue the best interests of shareholders, while capital adequacy and other risk management regulatory requirements protect the interests of depositors. However, this solution is likely to appeal only to customers who are currently satisfied with conventional banking, and thus may undercut the very rationale for having Islamic banking.

Meanwhile, the solution to the fundamental corporate governance problems of Islamic banks can be easily found in the opening quote of Sheikh Saleh Kamel: The rhetoric of Islamic banking suggests that investment account holders are in fact shareholders, whose interests are aligned with the Islamic banks' owners. The solution is to align the corporate structure of Islamic banks with that rhetoric, through a process of metallization that puts those investment account holders on par with shareholders, and affords them the same corporate governance protections, through internal representation on the board of directors and external market discipline. In fact, it is interesting to note that early Islamic banking experiments in Pakistan, Malaysia and Egypt were inspired by European mutual forms of banking, and many utilized mutual forms to varying degrees.

The phenomenal growth of Islamic finance at the hands of large multinational banks, such as HSBC, Citi, etc., will no doubt continue in various areas of investment banking and fund management. Needless to say, those activities do not fall within the scope of banking proper, where primarily deposits finance assets. Those non-banking segments of Islamic finance can continue to grow – as they have to-date – within the same corporate governance and regulatory frameworks for conventional financial markets and institutions. In the meantime, metallization can help to bring Islamic banking proper (focusing on the depositary function of banks) within the familiar governance and regulatory framework of thrift institutions.

In mutually owned banks, shareholders and depositors are one and the same, which resolves the fundamental corporate governance problem in Islamic banking. However, since mutual bank shares are non-tradable, one of the main mechanisms of corporate governance through external market discipline (linking managers' compensation to stock prices) is missing. Of course, tying manager compensation to internal accounting entries (profits, volume of transactions, risk adjusted rates of return, etc.) is possible, but it lacks the external discipline and objectivity commonly associated with capital market pricing of stocks. This concern is somewhat ameliorated by the likely high concentration of shareholdings by current owners of Islamic banks, who will continue to have a strong incentive for internal monitoring of bank manager performance and risk-taking.

For Islamic banks, the basic concept is that both the mobilization and the use of funds are based on some form of profit sharing between the depositors, the bank and the users of funds. A typical Islamic bank performs the functions of financial intermediation by screening profitable projects and monitoring the performance of projects on behalf of the investors who deposit their funds with the bank. This process needs time, resources and skills and justifies the existence of information costs.

Tables 3.3 and 3.4 presents balance sheet of an Islamic bank, showing different activities and financial instruments.

Assets	Liabilities
Short-term trade finance (cash, murabahah, salaam)	Demand deposits (amanah)
Medium-term investments (ijarah, istisnah)	Investment accounts (mudarabah)
Long-term partnerships (musharakah)	Special investment accounts (mudarabah, musharakah)
Fee-based services (joalah, kifalah and so forth)	Reserves
Non-banking assets (property)	Equity capital

Table 3.3. *Theoretical Islamic bank balance sheet based on maturity profile*

Assets	*Liabilities*
Cash balances	Demand deposits (amanah)
Financing assets (Murabahah, salaam, ijarah, istisnah)	Investment accounts (mudarabah)
Investment assets (mudarabah, musharakah)	Special investment accounts (mudarabah, musharakah)
Fee-based services (joalah, kifalah and so forth)	Reserves
Non-banking assets (property)	Equity capital

Table 3.4. *Theoretical Islamic bank balance sheet based on functionality*

– *Liabilities*:

The liabilities side of the balance sheet is based on the "two-window" theoretical model of an Islamic bank. This model divides the "liability" or funding side of the bank balance sheet into two deposit windows, "two-window": one for demand deposits and the other for investment or special investment accounts. The investment accounts are not liabilities in a strict sense because investors–depositors in Islamic banks are like partners.

Conventional Banks	**Islamic Banks**
Assets	
Current assets	
Marketable securities	Cash
Standard loan	Investment: – Financing Musharka – Financing Mudaraba
Discovered	Interbank Murabaha
Other advances Murabaha Salam Istina	Credit sale: – Salam – Istisna – Murabaha
	Equity investments, real estate
Non-current assets	
Participation	Musharaka
Estate	Buildings
	Diminishing Musharka
Liabilities	
Current liabilities	
Deposits	Current account (Qard Hassan)
Loans and various financial debts	Investment Account (PSIA) – Restricted – Unrestricted Savings account Zakat and withholding tax Murabaha interbank non-current Provision (IRR)
Non-current liabilities	
	Islamic funds, Salam, Istina
Equities	Equities
Earnings	Earnings
Stocks, reserves	Profit to purify (Zakat)
	Reserves (PER)

Table 3.5. *Principles of balance sheet: conventional versus Islamic bank [KOP 08]*

– *Assets:*

Islamic banks have several choices of instruments with different maturities and risk-return profiles. For short-term maturities, trade financing or financial claims resulting from a sales contract – that is *Murabahah, salaam* and so forth – are available. For medium-term investments, leasing (*ijarah*), manufacturing contracts (*istisnah*) and various partnerships are possible. For long-term investments, partnerships in the form of *musharakah* can be undertaken. An Islamic financial intermediary may also engage an external entrepreneur on a *mudarabah* basis in which the bank acts as principal and the entrepreneur (user of the funds) acts as agent. In this capacity, an Islamic bank can form a syndicate with other financial or non-financial institutions to provide entrepreneurs with medium- to long-term capital [VAN 09].

4

Mechanisms of Corporate Governance, Banking Governance and Islamic Banking Governance

4.1. Mechanisms of corporate governance

According to Becht *et al.* [BEC 02], "corporate governance had been concerned with the resolution of collective action problems among dispersed investors and the reconciliation of conflicts of interest between various corporate claimholders".

They point out five mechanisms to solve the *collective action problem*: large shareholders, hostile takeovers and proxy voting contests, the board of directors, executive contracts linking compensation and company performance, and finally, well-defined CEO fiduciary duties combined with class-action suits. They reach the conclusion that the major problem now is balancing the trade-off between the regulation of large-shareholder supervisory power in order to protect the dispersed investors and the need to monitor managers to prevent them from self-dealing and abuse of shareholders.

In this section, we divide the mechanism into two kinds, external and internal, to facilitate comprehension, knowing that each country applies their specific mechanisms and there are no standard mechanisms.

4.1.1. *Internal mechanisms*

4.1.1.1. *Ownership structure*

Several studies have examined the ownership structure in corporate governance and considered it as a good mechanism to monitor and enhance the performance of corporations. Berle and Means [BER 32] argued that a firm's equity structure has a certain impact on the firm's value. They believed that when the firm had a widely dispersed ownership, the managers, who only had a limited shareholding, tended to misuse corporate resources, thus leading to an agency problem. Jensen and Meckling [JEN 76] further extended the concept and indicated that managers tended to pursue self-interest, leading to a lower firm value when there is a separation between ownership and control. Jensen and Meckling [JEN 76] also believed that the managers' interests tended to be more in line with those of the external shareholders when there was a larger insider shareholding. Related empirical studies also indicate that increases in the managers' and insiders' shareholdings have a positive influence on corporate performance and value. For example, Mueller and Spitz-Oener [MUL 06] found that corporate performance would be better for firms with higher insider shareholdings; Hanson and Song [HAN 03] showed that the firms' operating performances after asset sales would be better in firms with higher manager shareholding; Chen *et al.* [CHE 03] found that a firm's value would be higher when managers held more shares.

Pound [POU 88] pointed out that institutional shareholders are better equipped in terms of professional knowledge and monitoring skills than individual shareholders, and they can therefore monitor management more efficiently than relatively less knowledgeable or skilled individual investors. In this way, agency problems can be reduced. Current research also generally supports the monitoring mechanism on the part of institutional investors [BRI 88, AGR 90, MCC 90]. In addition, institutional monitoring also plays an important role in corporate performance. Cornett *et al.* [COR 07] indicated that more institutional investors or more institutional shareholdings would have a positive influence on a firm's performance. Sias and Starks [SIA 06] found that higher institutional shareholdings would have a positive impact on stock prices. The above findings support the concept that institutional shareholdings help enhance corporate governance.

An alternative approach to mitigating the collective action problem of shareholders is to have a semi-concentrated ownership structure with at least one large shareholder, who has an interest in monitoring management and the power to implement management changes. Although this solution is less common in the United States and the UK, because of regulatory restrictions on blockholder actions, some form of concentration of ownership or control is the dominant form of corporate governance arrangement in continental Europe and other countries. This literature emphasizes the idea that the ownership structure as a meaning mechanism directly effects the firm's value.

4.1.1.2. *Board structure*

The role of boards as a mechanism for corporate governance of banks takes on special relevance in a framework of limited competition, intense regulation and higher informational asymmetries due to the complexity of the banking business. Thus, the board becomes a key mechanism to monitor managers' behavior and to advise them on strategy identification and implementation. Bank directors' specific knowledge of the complexity of the banking business enables them to monitor and advise managers efficiently.

Jensen and Meckling [JEN 76] indicated that when the firm's ownership and management are separated, agency problems may occur, meaning that managers may seek to maximize their personal interests rather than the wealth of shareholders. However, the agency problem could be mitigated through appropriate monitoring. To resolve the potential conflicts of interest between managers and shareholders, it has become important for firms to think about how to improve corporate governance. Fama and Jensen [FAM 83] believed that the board of directors is an important factor that affects corporate governance. The main duty of the board of directors is to approve managers' decisions and monitor managers' performance, and it also has the authority to employ and lay off managers. Furthermore, Fama [FAM 80] and Williamson [WIL 83] thought that the board of directors was responsible for protecting the firm's benefit and monitoring management so as to reduce the agency problem.

Jensen [JEN 93] further pointed out that a board with more independent directors would be better able to monitor managers effectively. Fama [FAM 80], Connors [CON 89] and Baysinger and Hoskisson [BAY 90] also supported the idea that independent directors could objectively evaluate corporate development and could monitor management more effectively because they own more professional knowledge and adopt a more independent stance. Weisbach [WEI 88] also indicated that inside directors may play a less efficient role in monitoring since they are often less likely to challenge and monitor the CEO. Therefore, a higher ratio of independent directors is expected to have a positive effect on corporate performance [HUS 01, CHO 07]. Sharma [SHA 04] also found that a board with a higher ratio of independent directors would reduce the likelihood of fraud, and that independent directors once again would be confirmed to have a better monitoring function.

Jensen [JEN 93] and Rechner and Dalton [REC 89] indicated that having the chairman of the board concurrently serving as CEO would reduce the independence of the board, especially when the board was dominated by inside directors. Dayton [DAY 84] also agreed with this view and warned that when a CEO also serves as chairman, he or she is better able to manipulate a board meeting to achieve his or her own personal goals.

Sharma [SHA 04] provided evidence that there is a greater possibility of fraud in firms with the chairman of the board concurrently serving as CEO.

Muniandy [MUN 07] indicated that the auditors would ask for a higher audit fee from a firm of which the chairman of the board is also serving as the CEO due to the higher audit risks. Kesner and Dalton [KES 86] pointed out that the independence of the board would be harmed when the board was composed of relatives, who did not seem to be able to objectively evaluate the performance of their CEOs. Moreover, Lausten [LAU 02] found that CEOs were less likely to be replaced because of poor performance in family-controlled firms. Ali *et al.* [ALI 07] indicated that there exists a more serious agency problem between controlling and non-controlling shareholders in family-controlled firms. Santiago-Castro and Brown [SAN 07] also found that minority shareholders are more likely to be expropriated as a result of an increase in the size of the family-controlled shareholding. These findings suggest that family-controlled firms are characterized by worse corporate governance.

Recently, Berk and Demarzo [BER 14] noted that in most corporations, each share of stock gives a shareholder one vote in the election of the board of directors, so investors with the most shares have the most influence. When one or two shareholders own a very large proportion of the outstanding stock, these shareholders may either be on the board of directors themselves, or they may have the right to appoint a number of directors. The board of directors makes rules on how the corporation should be run, sets policy and monitors the performance of the company. The board of directors delegates most decisions that involve day-to-day running of the corporation to its management. The CEO is charged with running the corporation by instituting the rules and policies set by the board of directors. The size of the rest of the management team varies from corporation to corporation. The separation of powers within corporations between the board of directors and the CEO is not always distinct. In fact, it is not uncommon for the CEO to also be the chairman of the board of directors. The most senior financial manager is the chief financial officer, who often reports directly to the CEO. Figure 4.1 exhibits a typical organizational chart for a corporation.

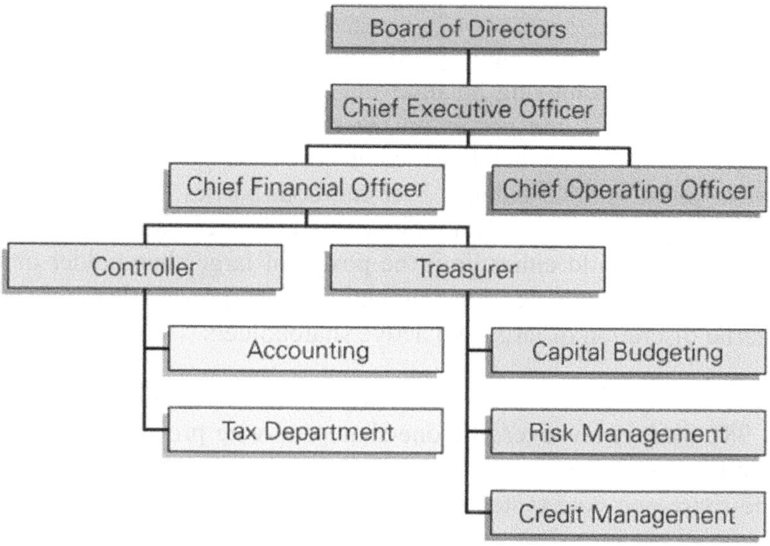

Figure 4.1. *Organizational chart of a typical corporation (source: [BER 14])*

4.1.1.3. *Executive compensation (incentive pay)*

Bank deregulation is associated with sharp increases in the share of equity-based CEO compensation in the banking industry [CHE 06, CUÑ 09, HUB 95]. Equity-based compensation may affect corporate investment choices by making the CEO wealth sensitive to both company risk and performance [GUA 99].

4.1.1.4. *Legal protection*

Corporate governance was defined as the "structure and the functioning of corporate policy" [ELL 60]. Therefore, the "corporate governance problem" was defined as the discrepancy between management and the shareholders in exercising "control". The first consideration is the difference between "large and active shareholders" and "small shareholders". Shareholders are the owners of the corporation. However, while a part of shareholders, "large and active shareholders", are actively involved in managerial functions, other shareholders, "small shareholders", are not active, in general, and they are expropriated and need protection.

The main issue concerning "good corporate governance practices" may be summarized as achieving balance and fairness between large and active shareholders' control and power on the one hand, and "small shareholder protection" on the other hand. Efficient corporate governance implies the attainment of an optimal balance between both parties. In a way, this is an issue of setting preferences without concrete reference values. So to get the right balance it should either limit the power of large shareholder or voting trusts, or should tolerate concentrated voting power that might limit managerial discretion of large and active shareholders.

In the United States, the system was "one shareholder has one vote" [DUN 98]. Today, however, the one-share-one-vote process is a worldwide universally accepted process. It is easy to see that one-shareholder-one-vote and one-share-one-vote systems are located at the extreme ends of a line. In today's system, one-share-one-vote means concentrated ownership and control. Therefore, researchers may choose to focus their investigation on small shareholder protection. Another important aspect of the corporate governance challenge is the requirement that the firm considers the interests of "other constituencies", or stakeholders of the firm, if it is to ultimately act in the best interests of the shareholders.

In Continental Europe (particularly Germany) and Japan, corporate governance relies more on large investors and banks to monitor managers; legal protection for investors is weaker and hostile takeovers very uncommon. In the rest of the world ownership is heavily concentrated in families, some outside investors and banks, and an extremely limited protection of investors. Legal protection of investors and concentration of ownership are considered complementary approaches to corporate governance. The successful governance models such as the Anglo-Saxon, German or Japanese models are characterized by protecting efficiently at least some kind of investors. However, in the French model there is no strong protection for the minorities and as a result there are many failures due to those practices and this neglect.

4.1.1.5. *Internal auditors*

Internal auditors have traditionally performed an independent appraisal of a bank's compliance with its internal control systems, accounting practices and information systems. Most modern internal auditors would, however, describe their task as providing assurance regarding the bank's corporate governance, control systems and risk management processes. Although audit committees play a valuable role in identifying and addressing areas of risk, the prime responsibility for risk management cannot be abdicated to them; rather it should be integrated into all levels of management.

The goals of an internal audit function are to accomplish the following: (1) enable management to identify and manage business risks; (b) provide an independent appraisal; (c) evaluate the effectiveness, efficiency and economy of operations; (d) evaluate compliance with laws, policies and operating instructions; (e) evaluate the reliability of information produced by accounting and computer systems; (f) provide investigative services to line management.

Contrary views exist regarding the value of audit committees. Such committees have been likened to a gleam of hope that boards cling to in an attempt to show that they are managing risk. It is logical that a board facing risk management problems will rush to the historical source of information about problems in the company, namely the auditors. The proponents of this view often point out that the auditors are simply checklist experts, while risk management has never been such a simple pursuit and should not be delegated to a committee, department or team.

The problems of internal auditors are exacerbated when they follow an inspection approach and they never become a partner in the risk management process, but remain an outsider not to be trusted to assist management in their operational risk management task through sound advice coming from the macroview that internal auditors should have of an organization.

The monitoring and directing of the internal audit functions are an integral part of the audit committee's overall responsibilities. Both the board and management must have a tool to ensure that policies are being followed and risks are being managed. Under a market-oriented approach, an audit extends beyond matters related directly to administrative controls and accounting.

The most important duties of internal auditors are to "provide assurance regarding corporate governance, control systems and risk management processes". Internal auditors should also review annual financial statements prior to their submission to the board of directors and ensure that appropriate accounting policies and practices are used in the development of financial statements. The review of financial statements must be detailed enough to allow internal auditors to be able to report on a range of aspects, including the accuracy of the balance sheet and income statement. The internal auditors also consider compliance with regulatory and legislative requirements, identify all significant discrepancies and disclosure problems, highlight differences between the annual report and management accounts, point to major fluctuations and check management's compliance with statutory and other requirements [VAN 08].

4.1.1.6. *Sharing control with employees*

Sharing control between creditors and shareholders may be an optimal mechanism to control, and in some cases it is between employees and providers of capital. The role of employee representatives on the board can be justified as a way of dampening shareholders' excessive urge to dismiss employees [BEC 02].

Sharing control with employees can be achieved by letting employees participate in share ownership of the company, by giving them board representation or by strengthening their bargaining power through, say, increased unionization. An important remark made by Holmstrom [HOL 99] and echoed by Roberts and Van den Steen [ROB 00] is that when employees cannot participate in corporate decision making, a likely response may be unionization and/or strikes. There are many examples in corporate history where this form of employee protection has proved to be highly inefficient, often resulting in extremely costly conflict resolutions.

Bolton [BOL 95] looks at yet another angle. He argues that state ownership is actually a form of governance with extreme dispersion of ownership. This structure tends to exacerbate problems of self-dealing. These problems, however, are not always best dealt with through privatization, which may also involve shareholder dispersion. Pointing to the example of Chinese Township and Village enterprises, Bolton argues instead that state ownership at the community level may be another way of mitigating the inefficiencies of state-owned firms.

An extreme result highlighted by Roberts and Van den Steen [ROB 00] is that it may even be efficient to have employee-dominated boards when only human capital investment matters. Examples of such governance structures are not uncommon in practice, especially in the professional services industry. Most accounting, consulting or law partnerships effectively have employee-dominated boards. Another example is universities, where academics not only have full job security but also substantial control rights.

Let us take the example of French law, which mandates that employees of large publicly listed companies allowed to elect directors for two reasons. First, privatized companies must reserve two or three (depending on board size) board seats for directors elected by employees by right of employment. Second, employee shareholders in any publicly listed firm have the legal right to elect one director whenever they hold at least 3% of outstanding shares. Additionally, French law allows but does not mandate that listed firms may adopt a two-tiered supervisory and management board structure, as per the German model. Taken together, these regulations and governance options have engendered employee representation on the boards of over one-fifth of the largest French companies, but have also created significant cross-sectional variation in the extent and type of employee board representation [GIN 11].

4.1.1.7. *Sharing control with creditors*

A number of studies have considered the question of dividing control between managers, shareholders and creditors and how different control allocations affect future liquidation or restructuring decisions. A critical factor in these studies is whether share ownership is concentrated or not [BEC 002].

Aghion and Bolton [AGH 92] consider a situation where ownership is concentrated and argue that family-owned firms want to limit control by outside investors because they value the option of being able to pursue actions in the future, which may not be profit maximizing. They may value family control so much that they may want to turn down acquisition bids even if they are worth more than the net present value of the current business. Or, they may prefer to keep the business small and under family control even if it is more profitable to expand the business. In some situations, however, they may have no choice but to relinquish some if not all control to the outside investor if they want to secure capital at reasonable cost.

Aghion and Bolton [AGH 92] show that under some conditions the efficient contractual arrangement is to have a state-contingent control allocation, as under debt financing or under standard venture capital arrangements. Although their model only considers a situation of bilateral contracting with incomplete contracts, it captures some basic elements of a multiconstituency situation and provides a rationale for extending control to other constituencies than shareholders.

Other studies that support the idea of dividing control with creditors have been carried out by Zender [ZEN 91], Diamond [DIA 91, DIA 93], Dewatripont and Tirole [DEW 94], Berglöf and von Thadden [BER 94], Aoki [AOK 90] and Aoki *et al.* [AOK 94]. All these studies propose that the threat of liquidation if performance is poor may be an effective incentive scheme for management. But in order to credibly commit to liquidate the firm if performance is poor, control must be transferred to fixed claimholders (creditors). As these investors get a disproportionate share of the liquidation value and only a fraction of the potential continuation value, they are more inclined to liquidate the firm than shareholders, who as the most junior claimholders often prefer to "gamble for resurrection". The commitment to liquidate is all the stronger the more dispersed debt is, as that makes debt restructuring in the event of financial distress more difficult (see [HAR 95], [DEW 95] and [BOL 96]).

Interestingly, Berkovitch and Israel [BER 96] have argued that when it comes to replacing managers, shareholders may be more inclined to be tough than creditors. The reason why a large shareholder is more likely to fire a poorly performing manager is that the shareholder effectively exercises a valuable option when replacing the manager, while the creditor does not. Sometimes the large shareholder may be too eager to replace management, in which case it may be desirable to let creditors have veto rights over management replacement decisions (or to have them sit on the board).

Another way of limiting shareholders' power to dismiss management is, of course, to have a diffuse ownership structure. This is the situation considered by Chang [CHA 92]. In his model, the firm can only rely on creditors to dismiss management, since share ownership is dispersed. Chang shows that creditors are more likely to dismiss a poorly performing manager the higher the firm's leverage. Since a large shareholder would tend to dismiss poorly performing managers too easily, Chang [CHA 92] shows that there is an efficient level of leverage, implementing a particular division of control rights.

4.1.2. *External mechanisms*

4.1.2.1. *The stock exchange*

The stock exchange is an important and a good mechanism of control; it encourages and forces listed corporations to be efficient and try to save and keep the value of their shares on the market.

4.1.2.2. *Hostile takeovers*

One of the most radical mechanisms for disciplining and replacing managers is a hostile takeover. This mechanism is highly disruptive and costly. Even in the United States and the UK, it is relatively rarely used. In most other countries, it is almost non-existent. Yet, hostile takeovers have received a great deal of attention from academic researchers. In a hostile takeover, the raider makes an offer to buy all or a fraction of outstanding shares at a stated tender price. The takeover is successful if the raider gains more than 50% of the voting shares and thereby obtains effective control of the company. With more than 50% of the voting shares, in due course he/she will be able to gain majority representation on the board and thus be able to appoint the CEO.

The formal analysis by Scharfstein [SCH 88] stands out. Building on the insights of Grossman and Hart [GRO 80], he considers the ex-ante financial contracting problem between a financier and a manager. This contract specifies a state contingent compensation scheme for the manager to induce optimal effort provision. In addition, the contract allows for ex-post takeovers, which can be efficiency enhancing if either the raider has information about the state of nature not available to the financier or if the raider is a better manager. In other words, takeovers are useful both because they reduce the informational monopoly of the incumbent manager about the state of the firm and because they allow for the replacement of inefficient managers. The important observation made by Scharfstein is that even if the firm can commit to an ex-ante optimal contract, this contract is generally inefficient. The reason for this is that the financier and manager partly design the contract to try and extract the efficiency rents of future raiders. Like a non-discriminating monopolist, they will design the contract so as to "price" the acquisition above the efficient competitive price. As a result, the contract will induce too few hostile takeovers on average.

Shleifer and Summers [SHL 88] have argued that some takeovers may be undesirable if they result in a "breach of trust" between management and employees. If employees anticipate that informal relations with current management may be broken by a new managerial team that has taken over the firm, they may be reluctant to invest in such relations and to acquire firm-specific human capital. They argue that some anti-takeover protections may be justified at least for firms where specific (human and physical) capital is important. A small formal literature has developed around this theme (e.g. [KNO 86, SCH 95, CHE 98]). One lesson emerging from this research is that efficiency depends critically on which type of anti-takeover protection is put in place. The main difficulty from a regulatory perspective, however, is that protection of specific human capital is just too easy an excuse to justify managerial entrenchment. Little or no work to date has been devoted to the question of identifying which actions or investments constitute "entrenchment behavior"[1] and which do not. It is therefore

---

1 The concept of entrenchment was developed by Shleifer and Vishny [SHL 89]. It is a strategy that focuses on the directors increasing their own utilities in their organization by increasing their private expenditure and/or the cost of their replacement. The management entrenchment or entrenchment behavior is a deliberated behavior realized by the manager considered as a more informed actor, which consists of serving his or her own interests at the expense of the shareholders as less informed actors.

impossible to say conclusively whether current regulations permitting anti-takeover amendments, which both facilitate managerial entrenchment and provide protections supporting informal agreements, are beneficial overall.

4.1.2.3. *External auditors*

The external audit report is normally addressed to shareholders, but it is used by many other parties, such as supervisors, financial professionals, depositors and creditors. The traditional approach to an external audit according to the requirements of generally accepted auditing standards (International Standards of Auditing) typically includes a review of internal control systems. External auditors traditionally look for fraud and mismanagement in the lending function. Audits rarely include a detailed credit analysis of borrowers, as this has traditionally been performed by bank supervisors.

External auditors, as an integral part of the risk management partnership, have a specific role to fulfill. If market discipline is to promote stability of the banking system, markets must first have information and the capacity to hold directors and management accountable for the sound operation of a bank. External auditors play a key role in improving the market's ability to determine which banks to do business with.

The approach of external auditing is crucial to the success or failure of a coordinated strategy of risk management. The work of the external auditor offers added protection for the consumer. It is therefore important for the profession to shift from a simple balance sheet audit to an evaluation of the risks inherent in the financial services industry. When such an approach has been adopted by all auditors of financial institutions, the risk management process will be significantly enhanced, which will benefit all users of financial services.

The role of the accounting and auditing profession has gained importance as part of the bank supervision process. Management letters and long form reports submitted by auditors can provide supervisors with valuable insights into various aspects of a bank's operations. This is especially important when auditors become aware of facts that may endanger the stability of a particular bank or of the banking system. In many countries, especially those where supervisory resources are scarce, supervisors should avoid repeating the work of external auditors. In such situations, auditors have a broader mandate prescribed by law, but at a minimum it is important to establish adequate liaison mechanisms [VAN 08].

4.2. Mechanisms of banking governance

Banks are themselves corporations, but they operate in a special way in comparison with corporations. Caprio and Levine [CAP 02], relying on Shleifer and Vishny's [SHL 97] comprehensive review on the banking governance, started by describing how small and large equity and debt holders exert corporate governance in a generic firm. They examined different mechanisms such as *diffuse shareholders, concentrated shareholders, diffuse debt holders* and *large creditors.* In addition regulation and supervision and Basel committee principles are considered as fundamental external mechanisms in banking.

4.2.1. *Internal mechanisms*

4.2.1.1. *Diffuse shareholders*

Diffuse shareholders exert corporate governance by directly voting on crucial issues, such as mergers, liquidation, and fundamental changes in business strategy, and indirectly by electing the boards of directors to represent the interests of the owners and oversee the myriad managerial decisions. Incentive contracts are a common mechanism for aligning the interests of managers with those of shareholders. The board of directors may negotiate managerial compensation contracts that link compensation with achieving particular results. Thus, diffuse shareholders may exert corporate governance directly through their voting rights and indirectly through the board of directors.

A variety of factors, however, keep diffuse shareholders from effectively exerting corporate control. There are large informational asymmetries between managers and small shareholders and managers have enormous discretion over the flow of information. Small shareholders frequently lack the expertise to monitor managers. Furthermore, the large costs associated with monitoring managers accompanied by each small investor's small stake in the firm may induce a "free-rider" problem: each investor relies on others to undertake the costly process of monitoring managers, so there is too little monitoring. Given the difficulties in acquiring information, the voting rights mechanism may not work effectively. Also, the board of directors will not represent the interests of the minority shareholders, if management captures the board. Finally, in many countries, legal codes do not adequately protect the rights of minority shareholders and legal systems frequently do not enforce the legal codes that are actually on the books concerning minority shareholder rights. These forces work to provide managers with significant discretion over the control of corporate assets.

4.2.1.2. *Concentrated shareholders*

The role of this banking governance mechanism is to avoid the conflict of interests between owners and managers. Large investors have the incentives to acquire information and monitor managers. Furthermore, large shareholders can elect their representatives to the board of directors and thwart managerial control of the board of directors. Large shareholders will also be more effective at exercising their voting rights than an ownership structure dominated by small, comparatively uninformed investors. Finally, well-informed, large shareholders can more effectively negotiate managerial incentive contracts that align owner and manager interests than poorly informed small shareholders whose representative, the board of directors, can be manipulated by management.

Concentrated ownership raises new corporate governance problems, however. Large investors may pay themselves special dividends and exploit business relationships with other firms they own that profit themselves at the expense of the corporation or bank. In general, large shareholders maximize the private benefits of control at the expense of small investors [DEA 85, ZIN 94]. Thus, while concentrated ownership is a common mechanism for confronting the corporate governance issue, it has its drawbacks. Again, the legal system's ability to thwart insider arrangements that exploit small stakeholders has important implications for the effectiveness of corporate governance.

4.2.1.3. *Diffuse debt holders*

Debt purchasers provide finance in return for a promised stream of payments and a variety of other covenants pertaining to corporate behavior, such as the value and risk of corporate assets. If the corporation violates these covenants or defaults on the payments, then debt holders typically obtain the rights to repossess collateral, throw the corporation into bankruptcy proceedings, vote in the decision to reorganize and vote on removing managers. Clearly, the effective exertion of corporate control with diffuse debt depends on the efficiency of the legal and bankruptcy systems.

There are barriers, however, to diffuse debt holders effectively exerting corporate governance. Small debt holders maybe unable to monitor complex organization and will face the same "free-rider" incentives as the small equity holders discussed above. Legal systems in many countries give companies the right of an automatic stay on assets and managers frequently remain in place pending a decision by the bankruptcy court. This makes repossession of assets difficult even for secured creditors and reduces the governance power of debt holders. Furthermore, inefficient bankruptcy proceedings frequently take years to complete, which further erode the corporate governance role of diffuse debt.

4.2.1.4. *Large creditors*

Because of their large investment, large debt holders are more likely to have the ability and the incentives to exert control over the firm by monitoring managers and influencing the composition of the board of directors. Large creditors obtain various control rights in the case of default or the violation of covenants. In terms of cash flow, concentrated debt holders can also renegotiate the terms of loans, which may avoid inefficient bankruptcies. Thus, large creditors frequently exercise substantial control rights and cash flow power over corporations.

Nevertheless, large creditors face obstacles. First, the effectiveness of large creditors relies importantly, though arguably to a lesser degree than with small debt holders, on legal and bankruptcy systems. If the legal system does not efficiently identify the violation of contracts and provide the means to bankrupt and reorganize firms, then creditors lose a crucial mechanism for exerting corporate governance. Second, large creditors, like large shareholders, may attempt to shift the activities of the corporation or bank to reflect their own preferences. For instance, large creditors may induce the company to forego good investments and take on too little risk because the creditor bears some of the cost but will not share the benefits [MYE 77].

More generally, large creditors may seek to manipulate the corporation's activities for personal gain.

4.2.1.5. *Delegated monitoring*

The issue of institutional investor incentives to monitor has been analyzed mainly in the context of bank monitoring. The first formal analysis of the issue of who monitors the monitor is due to Diamond [DIA 84]. He shows that, as a means of avoiding duplication of monitoring by small investors, delegated monitoring by a banker may be efficient. He resolves the issue of "who monitors the monitor" and the potential duplication of monitoring costs for depositors by showing that if the bank is sufficiently well diversified, then it can almost perfectly guarantee a fixed return to its depositors. As a result of this (almost safe) debt-like contract that the bank offers to its depositors, the latter do not need to monitor the bank's management continuously. They only need to inspect the bank's books when it is in financial distress, an event that is extremely unlikely when the bank is well diversified. As Calomiris and Kahn [CAL 91] and Diamond and Rajan [DIA 01] have emphasized more recently, however, preservation of the banker's incentives to monitor also requires a careful specification of deposit contracts. In particular, banks' incentives are preserved in their model only if there is no deposit insurance and the first-come first-served feature of bank deposit contracts is maintained. In other words, bankers' incentives to monitor are preserved only if banks are disciplined by the threat of a bank run by depositors.

In summary, the theoretical literature on bank monitoring shows that delegated monitoring by banks or other financial intermediaries can be an efficient form of corporate governance. It offers one way of resolving collective action problems among multiple investors. However, the effectiveness of bank monitoring depends on bank managers' incentives to monitor. These incentives, in turn, are driven by bank regulation. The existing evidence on bank regulation and banking crises suggests that bank regulation can at least be designed to work when the entire banking system is healthy, but it is often seen to fail when there is a system-wide crisis [GOR 98]. Thus, the effectiveness of bank monitoring can vary with the aggregate state of the banking industry. This can explain the perception that Japanese banks played a broadly positive role in the 1970s and 1980s, while in the 1990s they appear to have been more concerned with covering up loan losses than with effectively monitoring the corporations the lent to.

4.2.2. *External mechanisms*

There are many external forces that give an important contribution to solving the corporate governance problem, especially the banking governance.

4.2.2.1. *Market competition and takeovers*

With regard to the first, competition in the managerial labor market and the product market may also affect governance, as Fama [FAM 80], Jensen [JEN 93] and Hart [HAR 83] suggest. The banking industry is, arguably, competitive in both markets. Also, interstate banking deregulation most likely has resulted in more competition. Thus, the similarity in the production technology of banking firms as well as industry competition can impact the governance of banking firms. Specifically, according to contracting theory, contracts are easier to construct and are more likely to exist in industries where more precise (relative) performance measures are available and where it is not relatively costly to replace a CEO [PAR 97].

So in a competitive environment firms are forced to adopt corporate control mechanisms in order to minimize the cost of raising external finance. The second form of competition is takeovers: if a fluid takeover market exists, managers will have the incentives to maximize a firm's value in order not to be fired in a takeover.

Caprio and Levine [CAP 02] concluded that there is some scope to improve the corporate governance of firms. Government intervention should be aimed at forcing firms to be more transparent, at increasing competition, both in the product market and in takeovers, at protecting investors through a more efficient legal and bankruptcy system.

4.2.2.2. *National regulation and supervision*

We have to know that the consequences of a bank crisis can be damaging for an economy. Not only do the nature of their activities and the high debt ratios make banks very fragile institutions; but, because of the interconnectedness of banks, the failure of one institution can immediately affect other banks and firms they do business with. This is known as *contagion effect* and makes bank runs a very serious issue to deal with since they could potentially spread throughout the economy (which is called a banking panic) justifying the systemic interest to avoid bank failures and the associated high social cost [LLE 01].

For these reasons, many regulation and supervision instruments are implanted to assure the good function of banks, so regulation plays a special role for financial entities, since both the credit and payment systems and economic development depend on the bank's financial health. In the banking industry, regulators are one of the main stakeholders, yet their objectives may clash with those of the other stakeholders [DIA 84]. Although it is true that monitoring by regulators may represent an additional governance mechanism, their presence can also worsen governance problems. For example, regulators might discourage competition and discipline banks by imposing restrictions on ownership structures [PRO 97, MAC 03]. Or regulators might limit the power of markets to discipline the banks [CIA 01].

They may even pursue their own interests as a regulator [BOO 93, SAN 97]. Moreover, when regulators intervene directly in the shareholding of financial entities, this conflict of interest is compounded. Such a conflict casts doubts on the efficacy of supervision and modifies stakeholder incentive to control managers [LA 02].

Regulation might also be considered as an external governance force that acts macroeconomically, at the banking industry level as a whole, and microeconomically, at the level of the individual banks [CIA 01]. As part of their efforts to supervise banks, regulators monitor the functioning of bank boards. However, regulators are constrained by the laws of their countries, while large banks have diversified geographically, setting up branches around the world in countries with many different regulatory systems. In this changing scenario, we should expect bank boards to emphasize strategic decisions to cope with a highly competitive environment while ensuring that their bank complies with regulatory requirements in each of the countries in which the bank operates.

Regulation distinguishes the banking industry from other industries, although since the deregulation implemented in developed countries, the driving forces in corporate governance are private monitoring and competition. Caprio *et al.*'s [CAP 07] study shows the importance of the legal and institutional rather than the regulatory setting in banking governance. Moreover, empowering private monitoring of banks yields the greatest benefits in developed countries that have in place legal and institutional systems that work well [BEC 06a].

4.2.2.3. *International regulation (The Basel Committee on Banking Supervision)*

After the collapse of two large international banks in 1974 (Bankhaus Herstatt in Germany and Franklin National Bank in the United States), a standing committee of bank supervisory authorities was established under the Bank for International Settlements in Switzerland by the central bank governors from the G-10 countries (Belgium, Canada, France, Germany, Italy, Japan, Netherlands, Sweden, the UK and the United States) in cooperation with the monetary authorities of Luxembourg and Switzerland. It has a permanent secretariat based at the Bank for International Settlements in Basel, and meets there about once every 3 months. The Bank for International Settlements is owned by the central banks – it does not participate in Basel's policy making, provides a venue for the Committee's secretariat and for membership meetings. Traditionally, members came from western central banks but, since 1994, there have been 13 member central banks from emerging markets [HEF 05].

The main purpose of the Basel Committee is to consider regulatory issues related to activities of international banks in member countries. Their objective is to use concordats and agreements to prevent any international banking operation from escaping effective supervision.

The relevance of banks in the economic system and the nature of the banking business make the problems involved in their corporate governance highly specific, and banks have specific mechanisms available to deal with such problems. Hence, the Basel accords are considered as a significant mechanism specific for financial entities. The complexity of the banking business increases the asymmetry of information and diminishes stakeholders' capacity to monitor bank managers' decisions. Banks are a key element in the payment system and play a major role in the functioning of economic systems. They are also highly leveraged firms, due mainly to the deposits taken from customers. For all these reasons, banks are subject to more intense regulation than other firms, as they are responsible for safeguarding depositors' rights, guaranteeing the stability of the payment system, and reducing systemic risk.

4.3. Mechanisms of Islamic banking governance

Following Ben Bouheni and Ammi [BEN 15], the Islamic bank is using the same mechanisms as the conventional bank; in addition to the Shariah supervisory boards, the Shariah review unit and the Islamic Financial Services Board (IFSB) as the main mechanisms of monitoring in the Islamic Banking system.

In contrast to the conventional system, the Islamic financial system is based on the active participation of public policy institutions, regulatory and supervisory authorities and Shariah authorities. These institutions collectively monitor the performance of the firm and its faithfulness and commitment to explicit as well as implicit contracts.

4.3.1. *Shariah supervisory boards*

A distinctive feature of Islamic banks is the accordance of activities with the principles of Shariah. Islamic banks have created corporate governance structures and processes to reassure stakeholders that all transactions conform to Shariah principles and to ensure compliance. Shariah supervisory boards, operating either within the Islamic bank itself or through an external institution such as the central bank, ensure conformity with religious principles. Each board has the authority to design, develop and issue Shariah-compliant financial products and legal instruments. Shariah boards exist in all Islamic countries with the exception of the Islamic Republic of Iran, where the central bank guarantees and monitors compliance of the whole banking system with Shariah [VAN 08].

The internal tasks of Shariah supervisory boards vary according to the provisions stipulated in the particular Islamic bank's articles of association or by national regulators. However, a review of 13 Islamic banks for which sufficient information was available revealed that all Shariah supervisory boards are entrusted with ex-ante monitoring. Next to internal regulations, international and national regulators often implement guidelines for Shariah boards. These generally refer to the duty to ensure Shariah compliance of transactions and less frequently specify competencies, composition and decision-making authority.

The role and responsibilities of Shariah supervisory boards typically include advising the boards of directors, providing input to Islamic financial institutions on Shariah matters to enable firms to comply with Shariah principles, setting Shariah-related rules and principles and overseeing compliance to ensure that policies and procedures prepared by Islamic financial institutions are in conformity with Shariah and issuing verdicts (fatwa) to create confidence with respect to Shariah compliance [SAF 09, MOL 15].

The key differentiation between conventional banks and Islamic banks in terms of governance is the ethical underpinning and the existence of Shariah supervisory boards in Islamic banking. Working under the guidance of Shariah supervisory boards, the management of Islamic banks have the opportunity to raise operational issues with Shariah scholars who can examine them in the light of Islamic rules and principles and give specific rulings [USM 98]. Contrasting Islamic banks with conventional banks, Zaher and Hassan [ZAH 01, 159) observe that "Under the Islamic financing system, investment or financing is targeted to the specific needs of the entity. Financiers or investors will need to satisfy themselves as to the reliability of the project, their lease rentals or the return promised in any financing deal. The investors and financiers have to exercise due diligence and careful monitoring of their investment. There is not much room for raising a variety of unsecured debts that are not targeted to the specific needs of borrowers".

4.3.2. *The Shariah review units*

In addition to Shariah boards, most Islamic banks, particularly those complying with standards of the Accounting and Auditing Organization for Islamic Financial Institutions (AAOIFI), have established another internal Shariah review structure: the Shariah review unit. These units are independent of other departments or are an integral part of the institution's audit and control department. They perform an array of tasks similar to that of the audit department: reviewers generally use all powers necessary to ascertain that all financial transactions implemented by management comply with Shariah board rulings. In this respect, the role of the internal review unit is limited to complementary monitoring. This makes its task secondary, if more focused and defined, to that of the Shariah boards, which are the ultimate arbiters in matters of Shariah compliance. In some instances, Shariah review units have been given exclusive responsibility for monitoring. These units face many of the same challenges as Shariah boards, in particular, regarding independence and competence.

Structure of an Islamic bank balance sheet according to the standards of the	
FAS (AAOIFI)	IAS-IFRS (IASB)
Assets classified by kind	*Assets classified by liquidity order*
Cash, Central bank Debts from *Mourabahas*, net of deferred profits - *Moudaraba* - *Musharaka* - *Sukuk* Ijara *assets* Ijara *wa ictina* assets Real-estate investments	Cash, Central bank Financial assets - at fair value in the results - held for trading - available for sale Loans and debts Financial-leasing operations Financial assets held to maturity
Liabilities	*Liabilities*
Liabilities *classified by kind* Central banks Current deposits (*wadia*) *Wakala*[2] *Sukuks* issued	Liabilities *by order of payability* Central banks Current deposits Medium- and long-term deposits Securities issued
Unrestricted profit sharing investment Accounts (PSIAs) (open)	
- PSIA - on credit institutions - on the clientele - PER (profit equalization reserve) - IRR (investment risk reserve)	
Stockholders' equity	Stockholders' equity
Social capital Reserves Profit/loss Profit/loss pending allocation to charity	Social capital Reserves Profit/loss

Table 4.1. *Structure of an Islamic bank's balance sheet under the FAS and IFRS standards*

2 A *Wakala* is an agency contract in which the bank, *Wakil* for example, is a depositary of securities, has a department for cash inflows and outflows, carries out transfers of funds, acts as the client's administrator, etc. It may be included among the unrestricted joint investment pools. It all depends on the terms of the deposit contract.

Beyond internal arrangements, the broader Shariah governance framework may include features put in place by regulators, such as the provision of financial information to persons outside the institution. Among regulatory arrangements, centralized Shariah boards are the most noteworthy in relation to Shariah governance. While there are significant differences across countries, centralized Shariah boards are usually concerned with ex-ante monitoring, mostly understood as standardization of Shariah interpretation, and with ex-post monitoring of Shariah compliance. They are also concerned with issues related to upholding Shariah compliance and offer arbitration and recourse to settlement of Shariah disputes among members of the same Shariah board. Private mechanisms for external monitoring of Shariah compliance are limited. In particular, private rating agencies have not yet developed the necessary skills or have enough incentives to monitor Islamic banks' Shariah compliance. "Islamic rating" has so far been the exclusive domain of government-sponsored organizations such as the International Islamic Rating Agency and the Malaysian Rating Corporation [VAN 08].

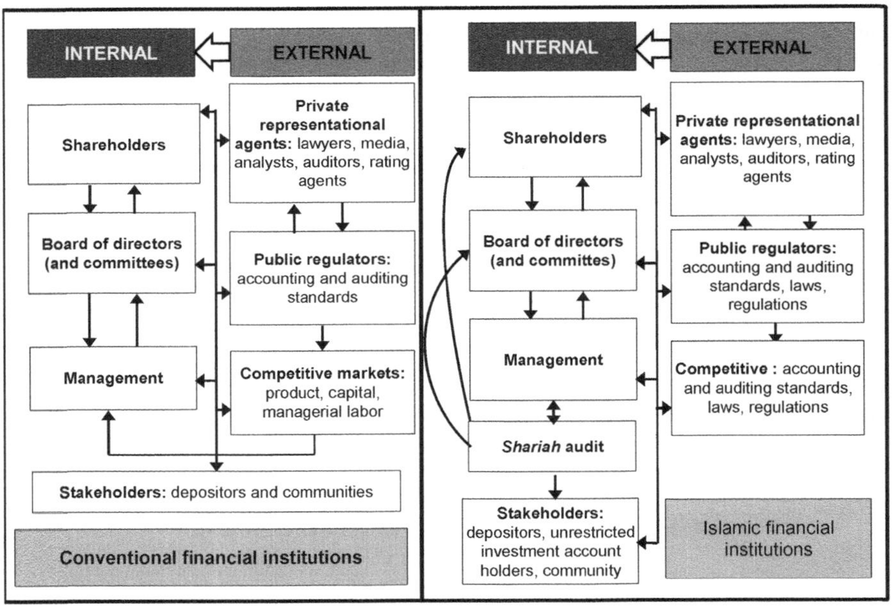

Figure 4.2. *Corporate governance structure: conventional banks versus Islamic banks (source [GRA 06])*

4.3.3. *The Islamic Financial Services Board*

The IFSB, which is based in Kuala Lumpur, was officially inaugurated on November 3, 2002 and started operations on March 10, 2003. It serves as an international standard-setting body of regulatory and supervisory agencies that have a vested interest in ensuring the soundness and stability of the Islamic financial services industry, which is defined broadly to include banking, capital market and insurance. In advancing this mission, the IFSB promotes the development of a prudent and transparent Islamic financial services industry through introducing new, or adapting existing, international standards consistent with *Shari'ah* principles, and recommending them for adoption.

4.3.4. *The Islamic International Rating Agency*

The Islamic International Rating Agency in Bahrain started operations in July 2005. It rates creditworthiness, Shariah compliance and corporate governance of financial institutions, and also insurers' financial strength. It has to compete with the large international rating agencies [HAL 06].

PART 2

Banking Performance

5

Performance Measurement

5.1. Performance measurement: definitions

Though the term performance measurement has been used since the late 1970s, there has not yet been a universal definition for it. The Government Accountability Office defines performance measurement as an assessment of an organization's performance, including the measures of:

– productivity, which quantifies the outputs and inputs of an organization;

– effectiveness, which determines the relationship of an organization's, outputs to what an organization is intended to accomplish;

– quality, which examines an output or the process by which an output is produced;

– timeliness, which evaluates the time involved producing an appropriate output.

The most quoted definition of performance measurement is that of Neely *et al.* [NEE 02c]: "the process of quantifying the efficiency and effectiveness of past actions". While this definition does emphasize effectiveness as well as efficiency, it is unlikely to make managers stop and challenge their performance measurement systems. In particular, it focuses exclusively on the past and does not give an indication of what they should quantify or why.

This is why Moullin [MOU 02] recommended another definition: "the performance measurement evaluating how well organizations are managed and the value they deliver for customers and other stakeholders". His definition gives much more guidance to people involved in performance measurement. In particular, it will encourage them to consider the extent to which their organization measures the value they deliver to their customers and whether it covers the main aspects of how it is managed. There has been an interesting discussion in the performance measurement. When Bocci [BOC 04] criticized the definition given by Neel *et al.* [NEE 02c], he said that performance measurement does not mean only quantifying but also comparing to a reference. For him, performance measurement can be considered a sort of primary process and can be part of larger and different processes: we measure performance to evaluate the performance of the organization on the inside or from the outside, and to manage this performance. So the aims of performance measurement could be quite different.

Moreover, Bocci commented on Moullin's definition, saying that there should be a difference between performance measurement and performance evaluation definitions. Especially in the public sector considering performance measurement in such a way is one of the main barriers that people need to overcome if the organization wants to move from measurement set to judge to measurement consciously adopted to support decision making process.

Moullin [MOU 05] replied saying that evaluating was a better term as this included interpretation and analysis: "someone somewhere is going to ask how well an organization is doing or what is responsible for the drop in sales. We can't hide behind the numbers forever". Pratt [PRA 05] agreed pointing out that evaluating was much better than quantifying as it encompasses qualitative as well as quantitative measures. Neely also commented that in essence he agreed with Moullin and Pratt – delivering value to stakeholders is clearly essential to an organization's success [NEE 05], although later in the article he says that the concept of stakeholder adds no clarity to the definition, because the question of which stakeholder matters is so context dependent.

According to Kelvin [KEL 02], "when you can measure what you are speaking about and express it in numbers, you know something about it". Likewise, Anon said, "you cannot manage what you cannot measure".

5.2. Performance measurement tools

The measure of performance might be dependent on the industry that we wish to study. Venkatram and Ramanujam [VEN 86] classify the different approaches to the measurement of business performance, which they consider to be a subset of the broader domain of organizational effectiveness. In this scheme, business performance would consist of financial plus operational performance. *Financial performance* uses financial indicators to represent the economic achievements of the firm, assuming this way the superiority of financial goals. Among these indicators, we would find growth sales, profitability (return on assets (ROA) and return on equity (ROE)), earnings per share (EPS) and market measurements (market-to-book value, stock returns and Tobin's *Q*[1]). On the other hand, *operational performance* broadens the concept of business performance by including the key operational success factors that might lead to financial performance, such as market share, product quality, marketing effectiveness, reputation of the company, new product introduction and manufacturing value-added.

Recently, Biazzo and Garengo [BIA 12] compare performance measurement models using both the eight dimensions of performance measurement strategies (strategy alignment, strategy development, focus on stakeholders, balance, process orientation, depth, breadth, dynamic adaptability, causal relationships, and clarity and simplicity), and the three typologies defined by De Toni and Tonchia [DE 01] (vertical, balanced and horizontal):

– *Vertical architectures* are defined as models that are strictly hierarchical (or strictly vertical) and are characterized by cost and non-cost performances on different levels of aggregation, until they ultimately become economic-financial ones [BER 88, LOC 94, PAR 94, RAN 96]; the first hierarchical model was that of Gold [GOL 55], which connected productivity with ROI;

– *Balanced architectures* are models that are balanced scorecards or dashboard, where several separate performances are considered

1 Brainard and Tobin [BRA 68] and Tobin [TOB 69] define the ratio between the firm's market value and the replacement cost of its capital stock as "Q" and propose that this ratio be used to measure the firm's incentive to invest in capital. This ratio has become known as Tobin's average *Q*.

independently; these performances correspond to different perspectives of analyses (financial, internal business processes, customers, learning/growth), which substantially remain separate and whose links are defined only in a general way [MAS 91, KAP 92, KAP 96];

– *Horizontal architectures* (by process) are models that focus on the value chain and take the internal customer-supplier relationship into consideration [SIN 89, MOS 93].

They conclude that the use of the type of models designed by De Toni and Tonchia [DE 01] shows a clear difference between the structure of most generic models (performance measurement matrix, performance pyramid system, results and determinants framework and balanced scorecard), which are mainly vertical, and those of the two specific models for SMEs (organizational performance measurement by Chennell and integrated performance measurement for small firms), which feature an horizontal type of structure. On the one hand, there is emphasis on the difference between the models for large enterprises and those for small and medium enterprises and, on the other hand, there is evidence of a time-related evolution of the considered models. However, in our study the techniques will be divided into two categories with reference to the study of Gupta [GUP 11].

5.2.1. *Classical methods*

The classical methods are based on earnings (profit). Managers have been using these traditional methods to measure the financial performance. Some of the main traditional measures used in performance measurement are given in the following.

5.2.1.1. *Ratio analysis*

Financial ratio analysis is the calculation and comparison of ratios which are derived from the information in a company's financial statements. The level and historical trends of these ratios can be used to make inferences about a company's financial condition, its operations and attractiveness as an investment. Financial ratio analysis groups the ratios into categories which tell us about different facets of a company's finances and operations [GUP 11].

The different categories of ratios are given below:

1) *Leverage ratios*: They show the extent to which debt is used in a company's capital structure. According to Berk and Demarzo [BER 14], an important piece of information that we can learn from a firm's balance sheet is the firm's leverage, or the extent to which it relies on debt as a source of financing. The *debt– equity ratio* is a common ratio used to assess a firm's leverage. This ratio is calculated by dividing the total amount of short- and long-term debt (including current maturities) by the total stockholders' equity:

$$\text{Debt-Equity Ratio} = \frac{\text{Total Debt}}{\text{Total Equity}} \quad [5.1]$$

– *Debt-to-capital ratio*:

$$\text{Debt-to-Capital Ratio} = \frac{\text{Total Debt}}{\text{Total Equity} + \text{Total Debt}} \quad [5.2]$$

2) *Liquidity ratios*: They give a picture of a company's short-term financial situation or solvency. We distinguish three main ratios:

– *Current ratio*:

Current assets/current liabilities

– *Quick ratio*:

(Cash + short-term investments + A/R)/ current liabilities

– *Cash ratio*:

- Cash/current liabilities.

3) *Profitability ratios*: According to Berk and Demarzo [BER 14], the income statement provides very useful information regarding the profitability of a firm's business and how it relates to the value of the firm's shares. The gross margin of a firm is the ratio of gross profit to revenues (sales):

– *Gross margin*:

$$\text{Gross Margin} = \frac{\text{Gross Profit}}{\text{Sales}} \quad [5.3]$$

A firm's gross margin reflects its ability to sell a product for more than the cost of producing it. Because there are additional expenses of operating a business beyond the direct costs of goods sold, another important profitability ratio is the operating margin, the ratio of operating income to revenues:

– *Operating margin*:

$$\text{Operating Margin} = \frac{\text{Operating Profit}}{\text{Sales}} \quad [5.4]$$

The operating margin reveals how much a company earns before interest and taxes from each dollar of sales. We can similarly compute a firm's earnings before interest and tax (EBIT) margin = (EBIT/sales). By comparing operating or EBIT margins across firms within an industry, we can assess the relative efficiency of the firms' operations.

– *EBIT margin*:

$$\text{EBIT} = \frac{\text{EBIT}}{\text{Sales}} \quad [5.5]$$

In addition to the efficiency of operations, differences in operating margins can result from corporate strategy. Finally, a firm's net profit margin is the ratio of net income to revenues:

– *Net profit margin*:

$$\text{Net Profit Margin} = \frac{\text{Net Profit}}{\text{Sales}} \quad [5.6]$$

The net profit margin shows the fraction of each dollar in revenues that is available to equity holders after the firm pays interest and taxes.

4) *Operational ratios*: They use turnover measures to show how efficient a company is in its operations and use of assets. Although financial ratio analysis is well developed and the actual ratios are well known, practicing financial analysts often develop their own measures for particular industries and even individual companies. The following ratios are the most common and used:

– *Return on equity*:

Return on equity (ROE) is the most significant indicator for profit, which measures the banking management in all its dimensions, and offers an image over the way to use the capitals brought by shareholders, the effect of their retainer in bank's activity. Following, Berk and Demarzo [BER 14], a high ROE may indicate the firm is able to find investment opportunities that are very profitable. This indicator is determined as followed:

$$\text{Return on Equity} = \frac{\text{Net Income}}{\text{Book Value of Equity}} \quad [5.7]$$

It is considered as the report between the net profit after deduction of all expenses and taxes and book value of equity. The specialty literature allots important studies to this indicator, considered one of the most characteristic barometers of some commercial enterprise performances. In the banks situation, a normal margin of this indicator is appreciated to be situated between the significant thresholds of 10% and 30%.

Figure 5.1 exhibits combined profitability of the top 20 participation banks, which has increased during the year by 1 billion USD to surpass 7 billion USD in 2014, growing with an asset growth rate of 14% (2010–2014). This resulted in healthy growth of ROE, which has positively contributed toward increasing shareholders' equity (22 banks have crossed the equity landmark of 1 billion USD). Figure 5.2 shows that Iran's Islamic banks dominated the regional rankings in term of ROE.

– *Return on assets*:

This indicator is an expression of profitability for the entire activity of a banking society. This indicator, known also as profit to assets or the assets profitability, measures the effect of management capacity to use the financial and real resources of an institution in order to generate profit. It is believed that the return of assets indicator is the most exact measure of banking activity due the fact that it directly expresses the result, according to the specific management of banking intermediates, of active operations optimization, related to a volume of resources considered. The formula of this indicator is:

$$\text{Return on Assets} = \frac{\text{Net Income}}{\text{Total Assets}} \qquad [5.8]$$

	Average ROE* (2014)	Average assets	Average growth 2010-14
Leading Participation banks by assets	12.6%	US\$23b	14.0%
Comparable conventional average	14.5%	US\$87b	11.0%

Figure 5.1. *Profitability and shareholders' equity in focus: top 20 participation banks [EY 16]*

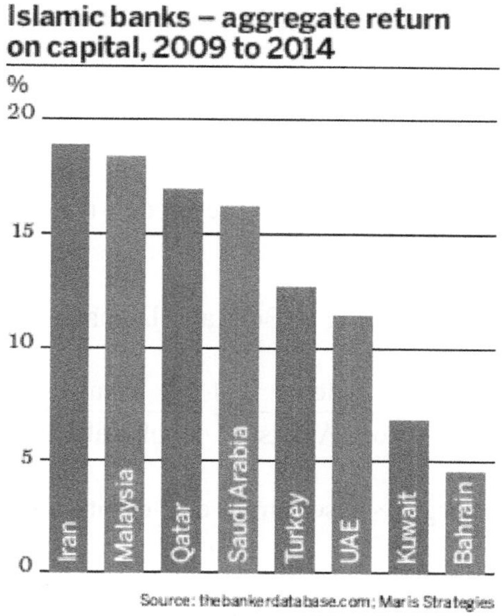

Figure 5.2. *ROE of Islamic banks from 2009 to 2014 [BAN 15]*

ROA is an indicator of how profitable a company is before leverage and is compared with companies in the same industry. Since the figure for total assets of the company depends on the carrying value of the assets, some caution is required for companies whose carrying value may not correspond to the actual market value. ROA is a common figure used for comparing performance of financial institutions (such as banks), because the majority of their assets will have a carrying value that is close to their actual market value. The limits of indicator's variations are generally between 0.5% and 1.6%. The small value (< 1%) is specific to big banks, while an extra unit dimension of indicator is a characteristic of small and medium banks. As a performance measure, return on assets (ROA) has the benefit that it is less sensitive to leverage than ROE. However, it is sensitive to working capital – for example an equal increase in the firm's receivables and payables will increase total assets and thus lower ROA [BER 14].

For further insight into a firm's ROE, the DuPont Identity (named for the company that popularized its use) is used. This tool expresses the ROE in terms of the firm's profitability, asset efficiency and leverage. Harrison *et al.*

[HAR 13] mention that the ultimate goal of the DuPont analysis is to explain the rate of return on common stockholders' equity (ROE) in a detailed fashion by breaking it down into its component elements: rate of return on sales, asset turnover and leverage. The first two components of the model combine to give rate of return on total assets (ROA). When the last component (leverage) is combined into the model, it produces rate of return on common stockholders' equity (ROE).

The DuPont identity according to Berk and Demarzo [BER 14] is:

$$ROE = \left(\frac{\text{Net Income}}{\text{Sales}}\right) \times \left(\frac{\text{Sales}}{\text{Total Assets}}\right) \times \left(\frac{\text{Total Assets}}{\text{Book Value of Equity}}\right) \qquad [5.9]$$

ROE = Net profit margin × asset turnover × equity multiplier

ROE = ROA × leverage

Developing ROE:

$$ROE = {}^{Ni}/E = \left({}^{Oi}/_{S}\right) \times \left({}^{S}/_{A}\right) \times \left({}^{Ni}/_{Oi}\right) \times \left({}^{L}/_{E}\right)$$

[Operational margin] × [Asset turnover] × [cost of debt] × [arm of leverage]

[Economic profitability] × [debt structure]

where:

Oi = operational income

E = equities

Ni = net income

S = sales

A = total assets

L = total liabilities

Arouri *et al.* [ARO 10] showed that if we analyze the financial statements of non-financial companies in stock exchange, for the same year presented in the IFRS and national accounting standards, these ratios are significantly altered.

Figure 5.3 shows that the growth of Islamic finance in the Gulf region was underpinned by the gains of fully Shariah-compliant Qatari banks. Between 2009 and 2014, these lenders posted an AAGR of 21.09%. Qatar's Islamic banks have also been putting these assets to good use. Over the same period, they achieved an aggregate ROA of 2.28% (see Figure 5.4). However, aggregate ROE is 16.93% (see Figure 5.2), which indicates the high capitalization levels of Qatari lenders.

– *Return on invested capital*:

The return on investment or return on invested capital (ROIC) is used as an indicator of the company's efficiency; in other words, how much profit the company is able to generate given the resources provided by its investors. Investors usually look for companies with ROI that are high and growing.

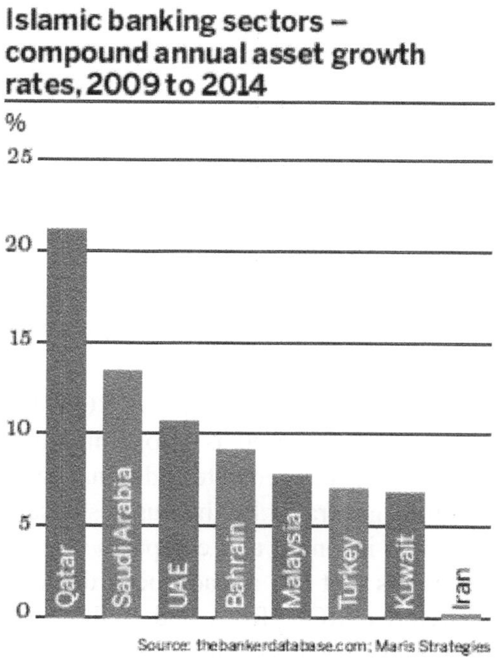

Figure 5.3. *Annual asset growth rates (AAGR) from 2009 to 2014 (source: [BAN 15])*

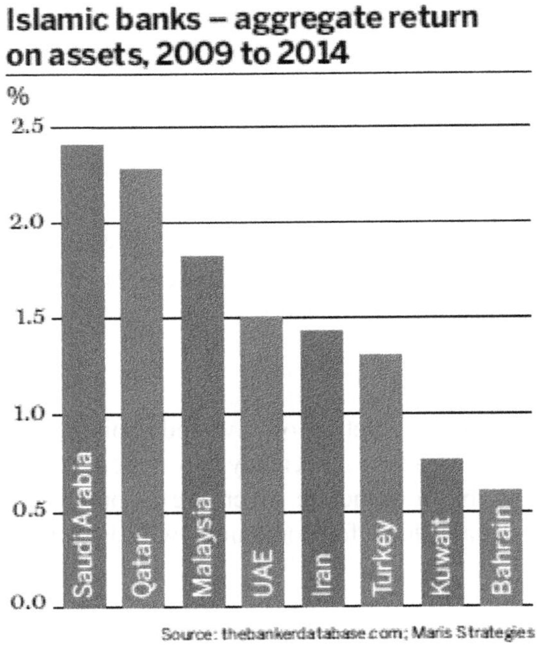

Figure 5.4. *ROA of Islamic banks from 2009 to 2014 (source: [BAN 15])*

The formula of this indicator is:

$$\text{Return on Invested Captial} = \frac{\text{EBIT(1-Tax Rate}}{\text{Book Values of Equity + Net Debt}} \qquad [5.10]$$

Decision makers often look for ways to improve ROIC by reducing costs, increasing gains or accelerating gains. It is also a measure of how well a company uses reinvested earnings to generate additional earnings. The ROIC measures the after-tax profit generated by the business itself, excluding any interest expenses (or interest income), and compares it to the capital raised from equity and debt holders that has already been deployed. Of the three measures of operating returns (ROE, ROA and ROIC), ROIC is the most useful in assessing the performance of the underlying business.

5) *Solvency ratios*: Give a picture of a company's ability to generate cash flow and pay it financial obligations. We classify two categories of ratios in the following [BER 14]:

– *Working capital ratios*: It is possible to use the combined information in the firm's income statement and balance sheet to gauge how efficiently the firm is utilizing its net working capital. To evaluate the speed at which a company turns sales into cash, firms often compute the number of accounts receivable days, that is the number of days' worth of sales accounts receivable represents:

- *Accounts receivable turnover*

$$\text{Accounts Receivable Days} = \frac{\text{Accounts Receivable}}{\text{Average Daily Sales}} \qquad [5.11]$$

An increase in average days to collect payment from its customers could be a cause for concern (perhaps indicating the firm is doing a poor job of collecting from its customers or is trying to boost sales by offering generous credit terms).

There are similar ratios for accounts payable and inventory. For these items, it is natural to compare them to the firm's cost of sales, which should reflect the total amount paid to suppliers and inventory sold. Therefore, accounts payable days is defined as:

- *Accounts payable turnover*

$$\text{Accounts Payable Days} = \frac{\text{Accounts Payable}}{\text{Average Daily Cost of Sales}} \qquad [5.12]$$

Similarly, inventory days = (inventory/average daily cost of sales). Turnover ratios are an alternative way to measure working capital. We compute turnover ratios by expressing annual revenues or costs as a multiple of the corresponding working capital account.

- *Inventory turnover*

$$\text{Inventory Days} = \frac{\text{Inventory}}{\text{Average Daily Cost of Sales}} \qquad [5.13]$$

Suppose an inventory turnover is 400/20 = 20, indicating that company sold roughly 20 times its current stock of inventory during the year. Similarly, accounts receivable turnover = (annual sales/accounts receivable) and accounts payable turnover = (annual cost of sales/accounts payable). Note that higher turnover corresponds to shorter days, and thus a more efficient use of working capital.

– *Accounts receivable turnover*

$$\text{Accounts Receivable Turnover} = \frac{\text{Annual Sales}}{\text{Accounts Receivable}} \quad [5.14]$$

– *Accounts payable turnover*

$$\text{Accounts Payable Turnover} = \frac{\text{Annual Cost of Sales}}{\text{Accounts Payable}} \quad [5.15]$$

– *Inventory turnover*

$$\text{Inventory Turnover} = \frac{\text{Annual Cost of Sales}}{\text{Inventory}} \quad [5.16]$$

While working capital ratios can be meaningfully compared over time or within an industry, there are wide differences across industries.

– *Interest coverage ratios*: Lenders often assess a firm's ability to meet its interest obligations by comparing its earnings with its interest expenses using an interest coverage ratio. One common ratio to consider is the firm's EBIT as a multiple of its interest expenses. A high ratio indicates that the firm is earning much more than is necessary to meet its required interest payments.

Berk and Demarzo [BER 14] consider that as a benchmark, creditors often look for an EBIT/interest coverage ratio in excess of 5× for high-quality borrowers. When EBIT/interest falls below 1.5, lenders may begin to question a company's ability to repay its debts. Depreciation and amortization expenses are deducted when computing EBIT, but they are not actually cash expenses for the firm. Consequently, financial analysts often compute a firm's earnings before interest, taxes, depreciation and amortization, or EBITDA, as a measure of the cash a firm generates from its operations and has available to make interest payments[2].

- *EBITDA/interest*:

$$EBITDA = EBIT + depreciation\ and\ amortization$$

Declining in interest coverage could be a source of concern for a company.

6) *Valuation ratios*: To gauge the market value of the firm, analysts use a number of ratios. The most common is the firm's price–earnings ratio or EPS:

– *Earnings per share*:

Earnings (profit) are the central performance indicator for shareholders. Thus, the very common measure of performance is the EPS that divides total annual earnings by the number of shares in issue. EPS are the earnings returned on the initial investment amount. The EPS formula does not include preferred dividends for categories outside of continued operations and net income. EPS for continuing operations and net income are more complicated in that any preferred dividends are removed from net income before calculating EPS.

$$EPS = \frac{\text{Market Capitalization}}{\text{Net Income}} = \frac{\text{Share Price}}{\text{Earnings per Share}} \qquad [5.17]$$

The EPS ratio is a simple measure that is used to assess whether a stock is over- or undervalued based on the idea that the value of a stock should be proportional to the level of earnings it can generate for its shareholders. EPS ratios can vary widely across industries and tend to be highest for industries with high expected growth rates [BER 14].

2 EBITDA is generally calculated by combining EBIT from the income statement and depreciation and amortization, because firms often do not separately list depreciation and amortization expenses on the income statement from the statement of cash flows. Note also that because the firm may ultimately need to invest to replace depreciating assets, EBITDA is best viewed as a measure of the firm's short-run ability to meet interest payments.

– *Market value versus book value*:

Successful firms are often able to borrow in excess of the book value of their assets because creditors recognize that the market value of the assets is far higher than the book value. Thus, it is not surprising that the book value of equity will often differ substantially from the amount investors are willing to pay for the equity. The total market value of a firm's equity equals the number of shares outstanding times the firm's market price per share:

$$\textit{Market value of equity} = \textit{Shares outstanding} \times \textit{market price per share}$$

The market value of equity is often referred to as the company's market capitalization (or "market cap"). The market value of a stock does not depend on the historical cost of the firm's assets; instead, it depends on what investors expect those assets to produce in the future.

$$\text{Market-to-Book Ratio} = \frac{\text{Market Value of Equity}}{\text{Book Value of Equity}} \qquad [5.18]$$

The market-to-book ratio for most successful firms substantially exceeds 1, indicating that the value of the firm's assets when put to use exceeds their historical cost. Variations in this ratio reflect differences in fundamental firm characteristics as well as the value added by management. Analysts often classify firms with low market-to-book ratios as value stocks, and those with high market-to-book ratios as growth stocks [BER 14].

– *Enterprise value*:

A firm's market capitalization measures the market value of the firm's equity, or the value that remains after the firm has paid its debts. The enterprise value of a firm (also called the total enterprise value) assesses the value of the underlying business assets, unencumbered by debt and separate from any cash and marketable securities. It is computed as follows:

$$\text{Enterprise value (EV)} = \text{Market value of equity} + \text{net debt (or debt} - \text{cash)} \qquad [5.19]$$

The enterprise value can be interpreted as the cost to take over the business [BER 14].

5.2.1.2. *Income statement (P&L)*

The income statement, or statement of financial performance, lists the firm's revenues and expenses over a period of time. The last or "bottom" line of the income statement shows the firm's net income, which is a measure of its profitability during the period. The income statement is sometimes called a profit and loss, or "P&L" statement, and the net income is also referred to as the firm's earnings.

The net income is equal to the profit that a firm has after subtracting costs and expenses from the total revenue. Revenues and expenses are the key inflows and outflows of assets that occur during a business's operating cycle. Therefore, *revenues* are the amount of assets received in exchange for the delivery of goods or services to customers. However, *expenses* are measures of the assets that a company gives up or consumes in order to deliver goods or services to a customer. The net income can be distributed among holders of common stock as a dividend or held by the firm as retained earnings. The net income is an accounting term. In some countries – such as the UK – profit is the usual term. Often, the term income is substituted for net income, yet this is not preferred due to the possible ambiguity. The items deducted will typically include tax expense, financing expense (interest expense) and minority interest. Likewise, preferred stock dividends will be subtracted too, though they are not an expense. For a merchandizing company, subtracted costs may be the cost of goods sold, sales discounts, and sales returns and allowances. For a product company advertising, manufacturing and design and development costs are included:

Net revenue – cost of goods sold = gross margin

Gross margin – operating expenses = earnings before interest and tax (EBIT)

Earning before interest and tax – interest expense + interest income income before taxes
Income before taxes – income taxes = income after taxes (and before extraordinary items)

Income before extraordinary items + extraordinary items = net income

Net income – preferred dividends = net income available to common

The income statement, or statement of operations, reports revenues and expenses for the period. The bottom line is net income or net loss for the period. In accounting, the word "net" refers to an amount after a subtraction. Net income is the profit left over after subtracting expenses and losses from revenues and gains. Net income is the single most important item in the financial statements [HAR 13].

5.2.1.3. *Market value added*

Market value added (MVA) is the difference between the current market value of a firm and the capital contributed by investors. If MVA is positive, the firm has added value. If it is negative, the firm has lost value. The amount of value added needs to be greater than the firm's investors could have achieved investing in the market portfolio, adjusted for the leverage (beta coefficient) of the firm relative to the market [GUP 11].

MVA is calculated as:

$$\text{Market value added (MVA)} = \text{Market value} - \text{invested capital} \quad [5.20]$$

The higher the MVA is, the better it is. A high MVA indicates the company has created substantial wealth for the shareholders. MVA is equivalent to the present value of all future expected economic value added (EVA). Negative MVA means that the value of the actions and investments of management is less than the value of the capital contributed to the company by the capital markets. This means that wealth or value has been destroyed. The aim of a firm should be to maximize MVA. The aim should not be to maximize the value of the firm, since this can be easily accomplished by investing ever-increasing amounts of capital.

5.2.1.4. *Cash flow statements*

Cash flow statements show how much cash comes in and goes out of a company over the quarter or the year, that is how much actual cash a company has generated, and is critical to understanding a company's growth. It shows how the company is able to pay for its operations and future growth.

Berk and Demarzo [BER 14] mention the income statement provides a measure of the firm's profit over a given time period. However, it does not indicate the amount of cash the firm has generated. There are two reasons that net income does not correspond to cash earned. First, there are non-cash entries on the income statement, such as depreciation and amortization. Second, certain uses of cash, such as the purchase of a building or expenditures on inventory, are not reported on the income statement. The firm's statement of cash flows utilizes the information from the income statement and balance sheet to determine how much cash the firm has generated, and how that cash has been allocated, during a set period.

The statement of cash flows is divided into three sections: operating activities, investment activities and financing activities. The first section, operating activity, starts with net income from the income statement. It then adjusts this number by adding back all non-cash entries related to the firm's operating activities. The next section, investment activity, lists the cash used for investment. The third section, financing activity, shows the flow of cash between the firm and its investors. Cash flow categories are explained by Harrison *et al.* [HAR 13] as follows:

– *Operating activities*: Companies operate by selling goods and services to customers. Operating activities result in net income or net loss, and they either increase or decrease cash. The income statement shows whether the company is profitable. The statement of cash flows reports whether operations increased the company's cash balances. Operating activities are most important, and they should be the company's main source of cash. Continuing negative cash flow from operations can lead to bankruptcy.

– *Investing activities*: Companies invest in long-term assets. A company buys fixtures and equipment, and when these assets wear out, the company sells them. Both purchases and sales of long-term assets are investing cash flows. Investing cash flows are the next most important after operations.

– *Financing activities*: Companies need money for financing. Financing includes issuing stock, paying dividends, borrowing and repayments of borrowed funds. The company may also pay loans and repurchase its own stock.

– Liquid funds end of the period (as presented by [PLE 12]):

+ Cash flows from operations

+ Cash flows from investments

+ *Cash flows from financing*

= Increase/decrease in liquidity

+ *Liquid funds beginning of period*

= Liquid funds end of the period

Companies produce and consume cash in different ways, which is why the cash flow statement is divided into three sections: cash flows from operations, financing and investing. Therefore, investors are attracted to companies that produce plenty of free cash flow or liquid funds end of the period.

Operating income (EBIT)
+/− Adjustment for items with no cash flow effects (depreciation, provision, etc.)
+/− Change in net working capital (inventories, receivables and operating liabilities)
+/− Corporate tax
= Cash flow from operating activities
+/− Investments in non-current assets, net
= Cash flow after investments (free cash flow, FCF)
+/− Financing items
= Net cash flow for the period (change in cash)

Table 5.1. *The relationship between cash flow based performance measures (source: [PLE 12])*

The fund flow statement, referred to as statement of "source and application of funds", provides insight into the movement of funds and helps to understand the changes in the structure of assets, liabilities and equity capital. The information required for the preparation of funds flow statement is drawn from the basic financial statements such as the balance sheet and profit and loss account. "Funds flow statement" can be prepared on total resource basis, working capital basis and cash basis. The most commonly accepted form of fund flow is the one prepared on working capital basis.

Plenborg and Petersen [PLE 12] explain the weaknesses in cash flow-based performance measures. They mention that no attention is made to uncompleted transactions in moving from one period to the next – this is a problem for growth firms and firms with transactions that span a considerable period of time (e.g. shipyards, software implementation). Cash flows can be manipulated through, for instance, investments postponed, suppliers not being paid, etc. They note that the association between the information content of performance measures and the length of the transaction. A correlation coefficient close to zero indicates that a performance measure's ability to measure value creation (stock returns) is the same across transactions of different lengths. A negative correlation coefficient indicates that the longer a time span for a transaction, the worse the profit measure is at measuring the true underlying performance.

5.2.1.5. *Variance analysis*

Variance analysis is usually associated with explaining the difference (or variance) between actual costs and the standard costs allowed for the good output. Variance analysis helps management to understand the present costs and then to control future costs. Variance analysis is also used to explain the difference between the actual sales and the budgeted sales.

5.2.1.6. *Standard costing*

Standard costing is a method that helps to control costs and business operations. It aims to eliminate waste and increase efficiency in performance by setting up standards or formulating cost plans. The word standard means a benchmark or yardstick. The standard cost is a predetermined cost that determines in advance what each product or service should cost under given circumstances. It is a system of cost accounting that is designed to find out how much the cost of a product should be under the existing conditions. The actual cost can be ascertained only when production is undertaken. The predetermined cost is compared to the actual cost and a variance between the two enables the management to take necessary corrective measures.

The traditional models, which Bourne *et al.* [BOU 00] defined as models based on accounting systems and financial information, were not included the adequacy with the current managerial needs.

They suffer from some serious limitations, which are the main reason that these traditional methods based on earnings cannot be used as a reliable measure of performance measurement today. Hence, there is the need of new approaches for the performance measurement, which takes stakeholder's perspective into consideration and shareholders wealth into consideration too.

5.2.2. *Modern methods*

For many years, it has been recognized that performance measurement can influence a company's behavior and consequently affect the successful implementation of company strategy [SKI 71]. Performance measurement must be designed and implemented in accordance with a company's business strategy in order to link the strategy to the objectives of functions, groups of people and individuals [BIE 97, KAP 96, NAN 92, SCH 99], as well as to operational aspects [GRE 98, LYN 91, MEE 95, NEE 02b].

The lack of alignment between performance measurement and business strategy in traditional models has been found to be one of the main obstacles to achieving the expected results from a performance measurement [ATK 97, BOU 00, DIX 90, GOO 91, KAP 92, KAP 96, KEE 9, LYN 91, MCA 02, NEE 94, SIN 86].

In fact, the models proposed after the mid-1980s, such as the balanced scorecard [KAP 96] and the performance pyramid system [LYN 91], stress the alignment between strategy and performance measurement.

In a successful total quality organization, performance will be measured by the improvements seen by the customer as well as by the results delivered to other stakeholders, such as the shareholders. Viewing the performance of an organization is also an important step when formulating the direction of the strategic activities. Modern approaches take into consideration the wealth maximization concept and other non-financial aspects such as innovation, customer satisfaction and employees' motivation. Some of the modern techniques include: The Performance Prism [NEE 02a], the cambridge performance measurement process [NEE 96], TPM process [JON 00], step TPM process [ZIG 99], total measurement development method (TMDM) [TAR 00], activity-based costing and management, quality management, customer value analysis, performance pyramid system [LYN 91], the balanced scorecard [KAP 93, KAP 96, KAP 01].

In this section, the focus will be on the EVA, the most commonly used tool for measurement of banks performance.

5.2.2.1. *Economic value added*

EVA framework developed by the Stern Stewart & Company is gradually replacing the traditional measures of financial performance due to its robustness and its immunity from "creative accounting" [GUP 11].

EVA is an estimate of true economic profit after making corrective adjustments to GAAP accounting, including deducting the opportunity cost of equity capital. By taking all capital costs into account, including the cost of equity, EVA shows the financial amount of wealth a business has created or destroyed in a reporting period. EVA can be calculated as follows:

$$\text{EVA} = \text{NOPAT} - \text{WACC} \times \text{capital employed} \qquad [5.21]$$

where NOPAT refers to net operating profits after taxes. NOPAT is equal to earnings before interest and tax (EBIT) minus adjusted taxes (AT), EBIT refers to the earnings before interest and tax, and WACC refers to weighted average cost of capital. It comprises following two components:

$$\text{Cost of debt} = \text{Borrowing rate} \times (1 - \text{marginal tax rate}).$$

$$\text{Cost of equity} = \text{Risk-free rate} + \text{risk premium} \times \text{Beta}$$
(capital asset pricing model)

$$\text{WACC} = \text{D/V} \times \text{Cost of Debt} + \text{E/V} \times \text{Cost of Equity}$$

where:

D = average debt

E = average equity (market capitalization)

V = D + E (total value of firm).

The risk free rate is equivalent to a government's long-term bond yield. Beta measures the volatility of share price relative to the market. Market risk premium is the extra return investors expect from equity market over and above risk-free rate.

Capital employed: is taken to be total assets subtracted with non-interest bearing liability in the beginning of the period. This definition does not consider the capital infused into the business at different times during the year and hence has a favorable impact on the resulting values. However, use of average capital employed shall correct this bias.

5.2.2.2. *Principles of EVA*

EVA was developed to help managers to incorporate two basic principles of finance into their decision making:

– the primary financial objective of any company should be to maximize the wealth of its shareholders;

– the value of a company depends on the extent to which investors expect that future profits will differ from the cost of capital. By definition, a sustained increase in EVA will result in an increase in the market value of a company. This approach has proved valid and effective for many types of organizations. This is because the level of EVA is not what really matters. Current performance already is reflected in share prices. It is the continuous improvement in EVA that brings continuous increases in shareholder wealth.

5.2.2.3. *Objectives of EVA*

EVA is one among various frameworks within a value-based management framework. EVA is based on the common accounting based items like interest bearing debt, equity capital, net operating profit, etc. The idea behind EVA is that shareholder must earn a return that compensates the risks taken by him. The main objectives of EVA are given below:

– the foremost objective of the EVA is the true performance measurement of an organization after taking into consideration the stakeholders' perspective;

– the main objective of EVA is to determine which business units' best utilize their assets to generate returns and maximize shareholder value; it can be used to assess a company, a business unit, a single plant, office or even an assembly line;

– EVA aims at determining a company's true profit, once taxes and the cost of supporting capital have been taken into account. It helps to identify whether a business or project is earning more or less than the capital originally invested in it;

– EVA aims to ascertain the financial health of the organization and its capacity to generate shareholder "value";

– EVA aims at the financial assessment of an organization, which is important for the company's long-range success and planning;

– EVA is a financial tool, which signifies the gain, or loss that remains after assessing a charge for the cost for all types of capital employed in an organization. EVA helps in ascertaining the "value" of the organization in a given time period;

– the other objective of EVA is to help the managers in setting organizational goals on the basis of financial assessment and keeping into consideration the main motive of shareholders wealth maximization;

– EVA gives the true economic profit and helps the managers in determining the bonuses, corporation valuation and analyzing equities. It aims at acting as a motivator of the managers and presenter of the true and fair picture of the organization to the investors and the shareholders.

The traditional performance measures, based on cost accounting information, provide little to support organizations on their quality journey, because they do not map process performance and improvements seen by the customer. In a successful total quality organization, performance will be measured by the improvements seen by the customer as well as by the results delivered to other stakeholders, such as the shareholders.

6

Corporate Governance and Performance

Corporate performance is a very ambiguous concept that has different dimensions and there are many methods to measure it depending on the context chosen. We should always keep in mind that the adequate definition and measure of performance might be dependent on the nature of corporations and the business objectives.

Let us follow Venkatram and Ramanujam [VEN 86] who classify the different approaches to the measurement of business performance, which they consider to be a subset of the broader domain of organizational effectiveness. In this scheme, business performance would consist of financial plus operational performance. Financial performance uses financial indicators to represent the economic achievements of the firm, assuming in this way the superiority of financial goals. Among these indicators, we would find growth sales, profitability (e.g. ROA and ROE), EPS and market measurements (market-to-book value, stock returns and Tobin's Q). On the other hand, operational performance broadens the concept of business performance by including the key operational success factors that might lead to financial performance, such as, market share, product quality, marketing effectiveness, new product introduction and manufacturing added-value.

Van Den Berghe [VAN 01] states that performance is finally the outcome of many interlinking factors where corporate governance is the only one possible element within the whole set of performance drivers. Good corporate governance has long been considered a crucial role for stakeholders in the business environment. Though the goal of corporate governance differs from one firm to another, or from one country to another, the main important concern is to provide an impetus for a good code of mechanisms to uplift and govern the organization. But with the current business pressures, corporate governance structure changes very quickly. Financial innovation and globalization force executives to adopt a rigorous re-evaluation of corporate governance principles.

Many studies exist linking good corporate governance with better performance. There is empirical evidence suggesting that countries that have implemented good corporate governance measures have generally experienced a more robust growth of corporate sectors and higher ability to attract capital than those that have not [SEC 05]. Fianna and Grant [FIA 05] explain that good corporate governance helps to bridge the gap between the interests of themselves and of a company, by increasing investor confidence and lowering the cost of capital for the company. Furthermore, they also add that it also helps in ensuring company honors, its legal commitments and forms value-creating relations with stakeholders. Coles *et al.* [COL 01] and Durnev and Han [DUR 02] also found that companies with better corporate governance enjoy higher valuation. However, there is a growing argument that corporate governance still needs to be renovated and revised.

6.1. Ownership structure and performance

Ownership structure is considered to be an important mechanism in corporate governance. The earliest research dates back to Berle and Means [BER 32] when they presented the theory of the separation of ownership and control right.

Hence, Berle and Means [BER 32] suggested a positive correlation between ownership concentration and firm profitability. Since more concentrated structures would suffer less the governance problem arising from the separation between ownership and control, the opportunities for managerial self-dealing would be reduced, and consequently, that would have a positive influence on the company's profit rates.

Later, Jensen and Meckling [JEN 76] further group shareholders into internal and external shareholders. They argue the rising of internal shareholders with control rights can effectively stimulate management, reduce agency costs and improve corporate performance. Nowadays, the conclusion still seems imperfect, but as pioneers, the research of Jensen and Meckling along with Berle and Means provides important theoretical guidance and empirical evidence for recent research.

In the case of family control, greater alignment of interests is assumed to result in greater firm performance. Anderson and Reeb [AND 03] support this notion by showing that U.S. family firms achieve higher operating performance and valuation relative to non-family firms. Saito [SAI 08] reports a similar result for Japanese firms. In contrast, bank control is generally considered to inhibit performance due to the conflicting objectives assigned to the firm.

More recently, Kang and Kim [KAN 12a] used data on listed firms from 1994 to 2002 to explore the different effects of three types of ownership structure; government shareholding, marketized corporate shareholding and private shareholding. They found that marketized state-owned enterprises outperform firms controlled by the government, indicating that partial privatization of state-owned Chinese firms improved corporate governance. Non-controlling large shareholders of marketized state-owned enterprises and private enterprises played active roles in corporate governance. In addition, the ownership concentration of a controlling shareholder decreased the incentives to expropriate minority shareholders.

However, Demsetz and Lehn [DEM 85] after examining the impact of ownership structure on firm value in a single regression model claim that the loss of control by the owners could be offset by a lower cost of capital or other benefits of diffuse ownership, causing the optimal degree of ownership concentration to vary across firms according to differences in firm size, the instability of the environment, the presence of regulation in the industry or the amenity potential of the firm's product for the owners.

Mayer [MAY 98] relies on the existing literature to make a theoretical overview of the interrelation between corporate governance, competition and performance. According to this author, corporate governance can bear on performance through five different channels: incentives, disciplining, restructuring, finance/investment and shareholders commitment/trust.

He argues that incentives, disciplining and corporate finance are not the main features that differentiate financial systems. Instead, they are the diverse types of ownership and control across countries that seems to mostly influence the formulation and implementation of corporate strategy. This way, while insider systems (characterized by concentrated ownership and large shareholder monitoring, and common in Continental Europe and Japan) might be better at implementing policies that involve relations with stakeholders; outsider systems (dispersed ownership, management-controlled firms frequent in the United States and the UK) are more flexible and can better adapt to changes. Eventually, product market competition will determine the effectiveness of the different governance systems and, consequently, their impact on performance, through the shaping of the required ownership and control structure.

In their paper, Nickell *et al.* [NIC 97] also look for an interaction between competition, ownership and performance. They use a productivity growth model on a panel of 580 UK manufacturing companies from 1982 to 1994 to show us, confirming previous studies, that product market competition, financial market pressure and shareholder control are all associated with some degree of productivity growth. Furthermore, they find some significant evidence that financial market pressure and shareholder control can substitute for competition as a disciplinary mechanism of management. Thomsen and Pedersen [THO 00] argue that this relationship between ownership and performance may be influenced by the governance system and, thus, they analyze the relation between ownership structure and economic performance in the largest European companies.

Demsetz and Villalonga [DEM 01] use simultaneous equations to examine 223 U.S. firms over the period 1976–1980, a sub-sample of the Demsetz and Lehn [DEM 85] data. They consider two dimensions of ownership structure, managerial ownership and ownership concentration among outside shareholders; and after controlling for capital structure, advertising and research intensity, firm size, profit volatility, stock market risk and industry dummies for the financial, media and utilities sectors, they find no significant impact of ownership structure on firm value, as measured by Tobin's Q.

Continuing in this line of arguments, Thomsen *et al.* [THO 06] use Granger tests for causality on data on ownership and firm value over a 10-year period (1988–1998) for 876 of the largest EU and U.S. companies. Their results confirm the existence of a *system effect* in the relationship between block holder ownership and firm value (using Tobin's Q). While in the United States and UK they find no evidence of causality either way, corroborating previous research by Demsetz and Lehn [DEM 85] and Demsetz and Villalonga [DEM 01], in Continental Europe a strong negative effect of block holder ownership on firm value is observed, though only significant for firms with high initial level of block holder ownership. According to the authors, the high levels of block holder ownership in continental Europe would have reduced the value of the firm, at least from the point of view of minority investors. In addition, some recent research also shows that the relationship between ownership and performance is both static and dynamic [FAH 09]. Arosa *et al.* [ARO 10] provide new evidence regarding the way in which ownership concentration influences non-listed firm performance focusing on the conflict between majority and minority shareholders, using data from 586 non-listed Spanish firms. Their results show that for family firms, the relationship between ownership concentration and firm performance differs depending on which generation of the family manages the firms.

Yixiang [YIX 11], by using China's 509 listed companies from Shanghai and Shenzhen during 1999–2008, concludes that there is a two-way interaction effect between the proportion of largest shareholding and corporate performance, then whether in a static or dynamic model, the proportion of management ownership is uncorrelated with performance; and finally some weak evidence shows there exists an intertemporal effect between ownership structure and corporate performance.

6.1.1. *CEO ownership*

Many studies show a positive relationship between CEO ownership and firm performance (e.g. [BET 93, GIB 93, JEN 76, JEN 90]) and some show mixed results [DAL 03]. Acquisitions can materially influence acquiring firms' share prices, and CEOs with a consequential stake in the firm are expected to approach acquisitions with appropriate diligence. Westphal [WES 99] finds that CEOs with consequential ownership solicit and act upon board member advice and counsel.

CEOs are expected to increase their own diligence, and avoid the temptation to grow the firm for reasons other than shareholder wealth maximization. However, if a CEO's ownership in the firm is either excessive or negligible, CEO interests will be less aligned with those of shareholders.

In the case of excessive ownership, the CEO is often inclined to pursue risk-reducing acquisitions as his or her wealth portfolio becomes less diversified [FAM 73, LIN 65, MEU 01, WRI 96], reducing shareholder returns.

When CEO ownership is negligible, CEOs' and shareholders' interests will again be misaligned. In this situation, however, executives are often risk averse because managers' employment income is tied to the enterprise; and they are confronted with risks associated with their income as the maintenance of that income is dependent on achieving predetermined performance targets. In the event of corporate underperformance or failure due to risk-taking, CEOs may not only lose their current employment income, but also suffer in the managerial labor market [FAM 80]. In effect, the present value of the income annuity for the number of years left to the retirement of senior managers is reduced [WRI 05].

6.2. Board structure and performance

Empirical research on boards greatly increased in the wake of the seminal work by Baysinger and Butler during the 1980s. The original work investigated whether specific board structures and composition could affect companies' market value. In Chile, controlling shareholders run companies acting as the prototypical owner-manager [JEN 76]. Consequently, the controlling shareholders tend to choose the majority of board members among those to whom they have close family and/or business relationships.

Hence, the structure of this key internal mechanism of governance of companies is suboptimal to deal with potential horizontal agency conflicts between controlling and minority shareholders. In such contexts, the presence of a few truly independent directors may greatly improve the monitoring capacities of Chilean boards, reducing agency costs and increasing company value.

Therefore, it is necessary to carefully distinguish board members that are independent of the controlling shareholder. That, however, requires establishing a proper definition of independence in the concentrated ownership case. Chile's Corporations Law defines an independent director as one that could gain a seat in the board without the controlling shareholder's votes. However, controlling shareholders also have incentives to improve the corporate governance of the companies they control by electing professional board members [MAK 94]. Hence, there are two types of independent directors. Outside directors are those board members elected without the controlling shareholder votes. Conversely, professional directors are those board members elected with the controlling shareholder votes, but are independent because of their profile and the lack of formal family or other ties to the controlling shareholder. In general, the professional directors have previously worked on government, universities, or business associations. In order to ensure independence, the professional directors considered are only those that fitted the above profile and that are a board member of only one company controlled by the same controlling shareholder. Of course, a non-independent board member is any director working as an officer in any company of the controlling shareholder.

Therefore, "outsiders" are independent board members elected by minority shareholders, while "professionals" are independent board members elected by the controlling shareholders.

In his study, Bennedsen [BEN 02] finds two motives behind the establishment of boards when law does not impose this. In his model, besides the governance motive (boards exist because they create firm value by monitoring the management and governing the firm), there is a second reason (distributive motive): boards help in solving conflicts between controlling and non-controlling owners. The strong presence of this distributive motive leads him to argue that increased investor protection could reduce its relative importance, permitting boards to be more focused on governance, thus boosting the value of the firm.

While the formal theory on the board of directors has been quite limited, the number of empirical studies is considerable. Hermalin and Weisbach [HER 03] in their empirical study on the issue reached the following conclusions: there is no relation between board composition and corporate performance and there is a negative relationship between board size and corporate performance.

Many studies across countries generally fail to report any significant association between board composition and firm performance and potential reasons for this contrast are considered.

The work of Andres *et al.* [AND 05] also does not establish a statistically significant association between firm performance and board composition across a sample of OECD countries. Brennan [BRE 06] points out the impact of corporate governance characteristics on firm performance is likely to vary across jurisdictions and from this perspective, cross-country research can provide valuable incremental insights.

However, O'Connell and Cramer [OCO 11] explore the relationship between firm performance and both board size and board composition for companies quoted on the Irish Stock Market. They found that: board size exhibits a significant negative association with firm performance and the relationship between board size and firm performance is significantly less negative for smaller firms.

6.2.1. *Board size*

Prior studies found a negative association between board size and corporate performance (e.g. [YER 96, EIS 98]). This association is consistent with the view that both coordination/communication problems and agency problems become more severe as a board grows larger.

The agency problems arise from dysfunctional norms of behavior in boardrooms. Lipton and Lorsch [LIP 92] argue that directors normally do not criticize the policies of top managers or hold candid discussions about corporate performance. These problems are more pronounced with larger boards, because the cost to any individual director of not exercising diligence in monitoring management falls in proportion to the total number of board directors. Similarly, Jensen [JEN 93] contends that when a board has more than seven or eight directors, the directors are less likely to function effectively and are easier for the CEO to control. The coordination/communication problems are more straightforward. When a board becomes larger, it is more difficult for the firm to arrange board meetings and for the board to reach a consensus. As a result, larger boards are less efficient and slower in decision-making. According to Jensen [JEN 93], as a board increases in size, the costs of the agency problems and the coordination/communication problems overwhelm the potential advantages from having more directors to draw on, leading to a lower level of corporate performance.

The effects of agency problems within larger boards on the variability of corporate performance are less clear. As a board becomes larger, it is easier for the CEO to influence and control the board's decisions [JEN 93]. In other words, larger boards are more captive to the CEO, making the CEO more powerful in decision-making. The evidence on the relation between CEO power and the variability of corporate performance is mixed. On the one hand, Adams, Almeida and Ferreira [ADA 05] find that firms with more powerful CEOs have a more variable performance. Built up on the studies of group decision-making, their idea is that when the CEO is less powerful relative to the other top executives, he/she has to gain agreement or approval from a larger number of executives, similar to the situation where a larger group makes the decision. Although Adams *et al.* [ADA 10] focus on the relative power between the CEO and the other top executives, their arguments apply to the relative power between the CEO and the board. On the other hand, several prior studies suggest that firms with more powerful CEOs may have less variable performance. For instance, Amihud and Lev [AMI 81] show that powerful managers have an incentive to engage in risk-reduction activities such as diversifying conglomerate mergers. Similarly, Bertrand and Mullainathan [BER 03] document that managers protected by anti-takeover laws engage in less destruction of old plants and less creation of new plants. It is therefore an empirical issue as to whether a larger board's effect on CEO power is associated with more or less variable firm performance.

On the other hand, the study of Coles *et al.* [COL 06] find that firms that require more advice derive greater value from having larger boards. Linck *et al.* [LIN 06] find evidence that smaller boards are not necessarily better than larger boards, Aggarwal *et al.* [AGG 06] show that larger boards are more desirable for not-for-profit organizations that pursue more objectives, and Raheja [RAH 05] suggests that because optimal board size is a function of the directors' and the firm's characteristics, a large board may be optimal under certain circumstances.

Moreover, Harris and Raviv [HAR 06] show that movements in factors that exogenously affect both board size and firm performance, such as profit potential and the opportunity cost of outside directors, induce a negative association between board size and firm performance. While most prior studies of corporate boards are agency theory-based, this study presents a non-agency explanation for the effect of board size on the variability of corporate performance [HER 03]. The research on firm-level volatility is limited, and this study suggests that the size of a firm's board is associated with the variability of the firm's performance [CAM 01, ADA 05].

However, the question about the board size is still necessary, so what is the best; small board size or large board size? And in which case can you rely on the small board and in which case is the large board size more efficient?

6.2.2. *CEO duality*

There is a duality when the CEO is both the chairman and the CEO of the firm; the chairman of the board is responsible for monitoring and evaluating the performance of the executive directors, including the CEO. The CEO has responsibility for the day-to-day running of the company as well as setting, and implementing, corporate strategy [WEI 01]. Fama and Jensen [FAM 83] posit that when CEO duality exists there is an "absence of separation of decision management and decision control". In the absence of clear separation of decision-making and monitoring functions, the board is ineffective because of the lack of independence created when CEO dominance exists. The CEO needs to monitor his or her own decisions and activities [VAN 83]. The impact of board independence on the firm's internal monitoring mechanisms has been extensively covered in the literature on corporate governance [FAM 83, LOR 89, PI 93, BAL 96].

Different theoretical arguments have been used either to support or to challenge CEO duality. Davis *et al.* [DAV 97] assert that corporate performance can be enhanced when the executive manager has the full authority over his corporation by serving also as the chairman, as less conflict is likely to occur. Other authors such as Brickley *et al.* [BRI 97] argue that there is no one optimal leadership structure as both duality and separation perspectives have related costs and benefits. Hence, duality will benefit some firms while separation is likely to be advantageous for others.

Empirical evidence is somewhat inconclusive. While some studies (e.g. [DON 91, LIN 05]) support the positive impact of CEO duality on corporate performance, others (e.g. [REC 91, PI 93]) find that duality leads to inferior shareholder value. Yet other studies (e.g. [BER 78, CHA 85, REC 89, BAL 96, ABD 04]) find that CEO duality and corporate performance are not correlated.

6.3. Incentive pay and performance

Considering now incentive pay as a governance mechanism, Murphy [MUR 99] makes a comprehensive review of the empirical and theoretical research on executive compensation. His findings suggest that pay-performance sensitivity is positive and small, but with a tendency to increase over time. Nonetheless, the causality is debatable; since, on the one hand, managers may be more likely to accept performance-related pay when they expect good performance (it is not uncommon that managers influence their own pay), and on the other, there is typically more room for extra compensation packages, including performance-related pay, when the company is doing well.

Even if it has been a stronger alignment between executives and shareholders during the last decades as a result of the increased reliance on equity-based forms of compensation, especially on stock options plans, [DAI 03a, DAI 03b], when reviewing the research on governance through ownership and regarding the relationship between CEO compensation (shareholdings versus salary) and firm performance, find little agreement on any strong relationship. Even when such a relationship has been consistently demonstrated, the causality is not clear. Likewise, there is no firm evidence on the efficacy of the recent trend consisting of compensating members of the board of directors with stock [DAI 03b].

6.4. Legal protection and performance

La Porta *et al.* [LA 00] examine 371 large firms from 27 wealthy economies and conclude that better investor protection is associated with higher corporate valuation. This would be explained, according to the authors, by the fact that outside investors would be willing to pay a higher price for financial assets when a better legal protection makes sure that they will receive their rents.

6.5. Audit committee and performance

The major contribution of this study is that it provides further empirical evidence lending support for the adoption of good corporate governance practices such as was prescribed by the Cadbury Committee [CAD 92]. A further contribution made by this study is that it provides fresh evidence from an emerging market – Malaysia. This country was one of the Asian countries affected by the Asian economic crisis and subsequently revamped its corporate governance structures, including the mandatory requirement for all listed companies to have an audit committee since January 2001 [MIC 01]. Audit committees in Malaysian listed companies are required to have at least three directors, a majority of whom are independent and the chairman of the audit committee should be an independent non-executive director [MIC 01]. There has been no prior study in Malaysia examining whether having more independent directors on audit committee moderates the auditor's perceived inherent risk when CEO duality is present. Prior research papers have investigated the association of audit committee and audit fees mainly outside of Asian countries, predominantly in the United States, the UK and Australia.

PART 3

Banking Risk-Taking

7

Banking Governance and Performance

In a survey of empirical literature on corporate governance, Börsch-Supan and Köke [BÖR 00] suggest that firms should ideally utilize the firm's equity value or total factor productivity to measure performance. In particular, they argue that Tobin's Q, the main measure for firm performance in most of the studies, might be the best measure available, though its use implies the assumption that the current market value of shares coincides with the real value.

7.1 Board composition in banking

The board structure is an important mechanism for banks, so it is inevitable to study the board composition, the board size and the board's degree of independence, to understand the impact of this mechanism on the bank performance. Simpson and Gleason [SIM 99] find no effect of the size of directors on the probability of financial distress. However, a study by Adams and Mehran [ADA 05] identifies a significant positive correlation between board size and bank performance, as measured by Tobin's Q. This positive effect of larger boards would be in opposition to most previous findings for other industries [HER 03].

Regarding the presence of independent directors, these same authors find no significant relation between the degree of board independence and performance [ADA 05], agreeing with previous studies by Pi and Timme [PI 93], Griffith *et al.* [GRI 02] and Simpson and Gleason [SIM 99], the latter studying the effect of board independence on the probability of financial distress.

In more recent study, Adams and Mehran [ADA 11], by examining the relationship between bank performance and two features of board structure (board composition and size) and using 34 years of data, found that board composition has a weak relationship with performance and board size and performance are positively related. Hence, they suggested one possible explanation for this result is that larger boards have more directors with subsidiary directorships. These directors may be particularly suited to dealing with organizational complexity.

Another important characteristic of the board is the so-called *CEO duality*. In the cases where the CEO is also the chairman of the board, it may increase governance difficulties. This is at least what Pi and Timme [PI 93] presume in their study of a sample of large publicly traded US commercial banks for the years 1988–1990. The results they get appear to confirm the expectations: banks with a dual CEO underperform banks where the CEO and the chairman of the board are different people. Looking at it from a different perspective, Simpson and Gleason [SIM 99] find that CEO duality is related to a significant lower probability of financial distress. Their interpretation lies on the idea that a powerful dual CEO–chairman of the board would take less risky decisions in order to protect his or her position, and therefore, they suggest, CEO duality could be encouraged by regulators wanting to avoid financial distress in banks. Finally, Griffith *et al.* [GRI 02] provide evidence on the insignificance of the relationship.

7.2. Ownership structure

The two studies that find conflicting results, the impact of ownership concentration on bank performance, are Pi and Timme [PI 93] and Prowse [PRO 95]. With the first study, bank performance is shown to be unrelated to the level of blockholdings, however, the second postulates the benignity of ownership concentration, claiming that large shareholders are more motivated to monitor the bank's management, and prowse shows that banks that present lower levels of ownership concentration are more likely to go through an intervention by regulators.

In this same way, Caprio *et al.* [CAP 03] provide international evidence of higher levels of concentration of cash flow rights having a beneficial effect on bank valuations around the world, this relationship being stronger in countries where the legal protection of investors is poorer.

Most of the studies about the role of managerial equity ownership in corporate governance debate the existence of an inverse relationship between managerial ownership and bank performance (the *management entrenchment* hypothesis), both measured in accounting and market terms [GRI02], and the possibility that managerial shareholdings would motivate managers to work harder, thus increasing the firm's financial performance (the *convergence-of-interests* hypothesis [PI 93]).

Following Demsetz and Lehn [DEM 85], Hirschey [HIR 99] tests whether bank performance might be influenced by size, growth, leverage and, possibly, managerial equity ownership. For a sample of US commercial BHCs during the 1992–1996 periods, he finds that after controlling for firm size, there is no evidence of poorer performance among closely held banks. Since high managerial equity ownership is only typical for small banks, he suggests that the inferior performance of closely held banks could be due to scale inefficiencies. This explanation would be in line with Demsetz and Lehn [DEM 85], who found ownership concentration to be dependent on firm size, but not significantly related to performance. Providing further support to this idea, Simpson and Gleason [SIM 99] show that the shareholding owned by the CEO and other officers and directors had no significant effect on the bank's performance.

The findings of Pi and Timme [PI 93], however, suggest the existence of different implications of managerial shareholdings for dual and non-dual CEOs. This way, they find that when the CEO is the chairman of the board, CEO ownership is insignificant or significantly negative related to performance; while for banks with a nonchairman–CEO, they obtain a significantly positive link between the two variables.

Making use of very different methodologies, De Young *et al.* [DE 01] and Griffith *et al.* [GRI 02] both reach the conclusion of a nonlinear relationship between managerial shareholdings and bank performance. De Young *et al.* [DE 01] examine this relationship at small, closely held U.S. commercial banks that are mostly not publicly traded, presenting a broad range of ownership and management arrangements, and they find that hiring a professional manager can potentially increase small closely held bank performance. Furthermore, the likelihood of this better performance increases when managers own shares in the company, but only up to a certain level when management would become "entrenched", showing that there is an inverted U-shaped relationship between hired managers' shareholdings.

Using data from the largest U.S. BHCs for the years 1995–1999, Griffith *et al.* [GRI 02] find that performance of commercial banks is related to CEO ownership, but again, this relationship is not always positive. Bank performance increases until CEO ownership reaches the 12% level and decreases until 67% is achieved. This way, for a small share of CEO ownership, we would observe the effects predicted by the alignment ofinterests hypothesis (managers' interests converge with shareholders), while when CEO ownership exceeds a certain level, its positive effects on performance are offset due to the management entrenchment hypothesis (the powerful manager focuses now on protecting his job and maximizing his utility, neglecting shareholders' interests). The rise in value experienced at levels of ownership above percentage is interpreted by the authors as the marginal impact of convergence of interests being greater than that of entrenchment once majority ownership is obtained. In their study, they use economic measures of performance, such as EVA, MVA and Tobin's Q.

7.3. Incentive pay

The study of Barro and Barro [BAR 90] is one of the first to study the relation between pay, performance and turnover of CEOs in the banking industry. They use data from large commercial US banks over the period 1982–1987 and employ a logit regression model. Their findings suggest that changes in CEO pay are positively related to performance (both measured in accounting and market terms), though the sensitivity of this relationship declines over the CEO tenure. CEO compensation is not affected by regional average performance, only by relative performance. For newly hired CEOs, the pay is positively influenced by bank size. In addition, they observe a positive link between CEO turnover and age (from the early 1950s on). Finally, they obtain a negative relationship between CEO turnover and stock returns, but not with accounting earnings; this might be explained by the possible manipulation of accounting returns, they argue.

Corroborating the positive sign of pay-performance sensitivities in the banking industry, Bosworth *et al.* [BOS 03] make use of three different measures of efficiency, in addition to profitability, in order to measure the performance of a sample of US BHCs. Furthermore, their results seem to suggest that executive compensation packages cause large BHCs to expand beyond their optimal size.

Despite the positive sign, the observed pay-performance sensitivities are lower in regulated industries, and among them, banking, when compared to corporations belonging to other economic sectors [MUR 99]. As a consequence, several studies investigate these pay-performance sensitivities in banks taking into account the presence of regulation [CRA 95, SIG 01, JOH 03].

Since major deregulation took place in the US banking industry during 1981–1982, Crawford *et al.* [CRA 95] divide their sample into the regulated subsample (1976–1981) and the deregulated subsample (1982–1988) and find that pay-performance sensitivities (for all CEO compensation components) increase substantially in the second period as compared to the previous one. The reason behind these higher sensitivities, they argue, would be the increased need of CEO monitoring by the bank shareholders after deregulation. In addition, they provide evidence showing that CEO pay-performance sensitivities are greater for riskier banks, giving further support to their initial hypothesis saying that deregulation increases CEO discretion. Consequently, CEOs with their compensation tied to performance would after deregulation engage in riskier activities that will report higher returns.

The impact of deregulation in pay-performance sensitivities is also investigated by Sigler and Porterfield [SIG 01]. These authors decided to focus on a sample of publicly traded commercial US banks over a period after the deregulation of the banking industry (1988–1997), so that regulatory requirements did not perturb the sensitivity of the relationship, and they found, confirming previous results by Barro and Barro [BAR 90] and Crawford *et al.* [CRA 95], a strong positive link between changes in CEO total compensation and bank performance.

Furthermore, John and Qian [JOH 03] compare CEO compensation and pay-performance sensitivity for two samples of US commercial banks and manufacturing firms, confirming the existence of lower sensitivities for banks, which they attribute to the presence of regulation and the higher leverage. Furthermore, they observe that sensitivity declines with bank size.

7.4. Regulation and supervision

While relatively little evidence exists on the relationship between regulations and supervision and various aspects of bank performance and efficiency, the literature on bank regulations and supervisory practices is plentiful. Barth *et al.* [BAR 04] provide empirical evidence on the impact of specific regulatory and supervisory practices on bank development, performance and stability using survey data for a sample of 107 countries. The results suggest that there is no statistically significant relationship between capital stringency, official supervisory power, bank performance and stability. In contrast, the evidence produced indicates that encouraging and facilitating private monitoring can boost bank performance. Balancing their results indicates that restrictions on bank activities cannot only be detrimental for banking performance, but also increase the probability of banking crises. Similarly, Demirguc-Kunt *et al.* [DEM 04] investigate the impact of bank regulations, market structure and national institutions on the cost of financial intermediation as measured by accounting ratios (net interest margin and overhead costs). They use the databases by Barth *et al.* [BAR 01, BAR 04] for 1,400 banks operating in 72 countries over 1995–1999. The results show that tighter regulations on banking services and activities increase the costs of financial intermediation.

Beck *et al.* [BEC 06] use data on 2,500 firms across 37 countries to examine the relationship between supervisory strategies and corporate financing obstacles. Their results show that strengthening the power of supervisory agencies may actually reduce the integrity of bank lending with adverse implications on the efficiency of credit allocation. Thus, private monitoring may have a positive impact on the banking industry in terms of efficient operations and sounder banks.

Then, Pasiouras [PAS 08] investigate the impact of several types of regulations on bank efficiency for a sample of 715 commercial banks operating in 95 countries in 2003. Their results suggest that market discipline is significant in facilitating banks' technical efficiency. In a more recent study, Pasiouras *et al.* [PAS 09] investigate the link between bank regulations and parametric cost and profit efficiency levels for 615 publicly listed commercial banks operating in 74 countries over 2000–2004. Their findings substantiate the role of market discipline and of supervisory power in increasing both profit and cost efficiency, while the results on capital requirements and restrictions on bank activities are mixed.

Similarly, the empirical evidence by Barth *et al.* [BAR 10] indicates that tighter restrictions on bank activities exert a negative impact on bank efficiency, while greater capital restrictions are marginally and positively associated with bank efficiency. Barth *et al.* [BAR 10] also find that, although there is no significant relation between official supervisory power and bank efficiency, there is a significant and positive relationship between the latter and supervisory authority independence. The analysis is based on an international sample of 4,050 bank observations operating in 72 countries during 1999–2007. The evidence broadly supports the role of market discipline. It also shows that the impact of different aspects of regulations on bank performance and efficiency is mixed.

Chortareas *et al.* [CHO 11], by using a sample of 22 EU countries over 2000–2008 to study the relationship between bank regulations, supervisory practices and bank performance, find that strengthening capital restrictions and official supervisory powers can improve the efficient operations of banks. They indicate also that interventionist supervisory and regulatory policies such as private sector monitoring and restricting bank activities can result in higher bank inefficiency levels.

In a related line of research, some recent studies take all bank governance reforms together in the same model to investigate their impact on performance. Developed by Berger *et al.* [BER 04], this approach was illustrated by Berger *et al.* [BER 05] and Williams and Nguyen [WIL 05] in a case study and cross-country settings, respectively. For example, Berger *et al.* [BER 05] study the effects of corporate governance on bank performance using data from Argentina in the 1990s; their results suggest that corporate governance changes' effects on state-ownership are the most robust. While they find dramatic improvement in the performance of state-owned banks after their privatization, they do not find similar improvement for banks involved in M&A. Williams and Nguyen [WIL 05] study the impact of bank governance changes on performance of banks across a sample of South East Asian countries during the Asian crisis. Their results favor a policy of bank privatization, but consistent with the findings of

Berger *et al.* [BER 05] they do not find conclusive evidence on the impact of foreign acquisitions.

7.5. BCBS

The Basel Committee on Banking Supervision (BCBS) has called attention to the need to study, understand and improve the corporate governance of financial entities. The BCBS especially advocates a governance structure composed of a board of directors and senior management (Enhancing Corporate Governance for Banking Organizations, September 1999 and February 2006). The core of the BCBS message is the conviction that good corporate governance increases monitoring efficiency. Furthermore, the Committee believes that corporate governance is necessary to guarantee a performance, a sound financial system and, consequently, a country's economic development.

In other words, the Committee acts as an advisory body the purpose of which is to produce recommendations of concordats and accords, rather than laws *sensu stricto*, encouraging the harmonization of member countries' regulatory standards. This is meant not only to ensure efficient supervision of the international banking sector, but also to promote competition by ensuring that banks worldwide comply with the same bylaws, and thus face similar costs. Jackson *et al.* [JAC 99] note, for example, that "when banks are required to maintain equity cushions exceeding what they would otherwise choose it is natural for banks to view capital standards as a form of regulatory taxation". Thus, to the extent that international regulation imposes the same standards on banks, it may be perceived as a roller leveling the global financial playing field.

8

Banking Risk Analysis

8.1. Risk exposure for conventional banks

8.1.1. *Definition of risk*

Banking risk is defined as the probability that an actual return on an investment will be lower than the expected return. Financial risk is divided into many categories: capital risk, country risk, default risk, delivery risk, economic risk, exchange rate risk, interest rate risk, liquidity risk, operational risk, payment system risk, political risk, market risk, credit risk, refinancing risk, reinvestment risk, settlement risk, sovereign risk, underwriting risk, etc. In a profit-maximizing bank, a unit could be the whole bank. The risk may also be measured in terms of different financial products. But the objective of the bank as a whole will be to add value to the bank's equity by maximizing the risk-adjusted return to shareholders. In this sense, a bank is like any other business, but for banks, profitability is going to depend on the management of risks. Large universal banks will focus on the risk analysis on the banking book (the traditional asset–liability management), the trading book (where banks are buying and selling bonds, equity, etc.), and in the risk management advice they give to corporate customers.

Corporate treasurers of non-financial firms can incur large losses as a result of poor financial risk management. But it rarely leads to insolvency, if the core business operations are sound. By contrast, for banks, risk management is their core business. In the extreme, inadequate risk management may threaten the solvency of a bank, where insolvency is defined as a negative net worth, that is, liabilities in excess of assets [HEF 05].

8.1.1.1. *Categories of banking risks*

Referring to Heffernan [HEF 05], banking risks are classified as following:

– *Market risk* is defined as the risk to a financial portfolio from movements in market prices such as equity prices, foreign exchange rates, interest rates, and commodity prices, or due to some events on the market.

Thus, market risk includes a very large subset of other risks, which are currency and interest rate risk. If exchange rates are flexible, any net short or long open position in a given currency will expose the bank to foreign exchange or currency risk, a form of market risk. In this case, it is the market for foreign exchange, and the relative price of currencies given by the exchange rate. A bank with global operations will have multiple currency exposures. The currency risk arises from adverse exchange rate fluctuations that affect the bank's foreign exchange positions taken on its own account, or on behalf of its customers. However, the interest rate (price of money) risk arises due to interest rate mismatches. Banks engage in asset transformation, and their assets and liabilities differ in maturity and volume. The traditional focus of an asset–liability management group within a bank is the management of interest rate risk, but this has expanded to include off-balance sheet items.

– *Liquidity risk* is defined as the particular risk from conducting transactions in markets with low liquidity as evidenced in low trading volume and large bid-ask spreads. Under such conditions, the attempt to sell assets may push prices lower, and assets may have to be sold at prices below their fundamental values or within a time frame longer than expected.

Following Heffernan [HEF 05], the liquidity of an asset is the ease with which it can be converted to cash. A bank can reduce its liquidity risk by keeping its assets liquid (i.e. investing in short-term assets), but if it is excessively liquid, its returns will be lower. All banks make money by having a gap between their maturities, that is, more short-term deposits and more long-term loans: "funding short and lending long". They can do this because of fractional reserve lending – only a fraction of deposits are held in reserve, and the rest are loaned out. Liquidity can be costly in terms of higher interest that might have been earned on funds that have been locked away for a specified time.

Liquidity is necessary for banks to compensate for expected and unexpected balance sheet fluctuations and to provide funds for growth [IQB 07]. It represents a bank's ability to accommodate the redemption of deposits and other liabilities and to cover the demand for funding in the loan and investment portfolio. A bank is said to have adequate liquidity potential when it can obtain needed funds (by increasing liabilities, securitizing or selling assets) promptly and at a reasonable cost. The price of liquidity is a function of market conditions and the market's perception of the inherent riskiness of the borrowing institution [VAN 08].

– *Credit risk* is the risk that an asset or a loan becomes irrecoverable in the case of outright default, or the risk of an unexpected delay in the servicing of a loan. Since bank and borrower usually sign a loan contract, credit risk can be considered a form of counterparty risk. However, the term counterparty risk is traditionally used in the context of traded financial instruments (e.g. the counterparty in a futures agreement or a swap), whereas credit risk refers to the probability of default on a loan agreement.

The bank would avoid credit risk by choosing assets with very low default risk but low return, but the bank profits from taking risk. Credit risk rises if a bank has many mediums to low quality loans on its books, but the return will be higher. So banks will opt for a portfolio of assets with varying degrees of risk always that taking into account that a higher default risk is accompanied by higher expected return. Since much of the default risk arises from moral hazard and information problems, banks must monitor their borrowers to increase their return from the loan portfolio [HEF 05].

– *Operational risk* is defined as the risk of loss due to physical catastrophe, technical failure and human error in the operation of a firm, including fraud, failure of management and process errors.

The Bank for International Settlements defines operational risk as: "The risk of direct or indirect loss resulting from inadequate or failed internal processes, people, and systems, or from external events" [BIS 01].

The Basel Committee of the Bank for International Settlements (BIS) and the Solvency Committee of the International Association of Insurance Supervisors (IAIS) define operational risk as the risk of losses resulting from inadequate or failed internal processes, people and systems or from external events. Although designed for financial institutions, this definition should be applicable for any industry, institution or individual.

The Basel and Solvency approach to operational risk divides it into seven major categories, 18 secondary categories, and 64 subcategories. The great majority is not unique to financial services and can provide a good framework for addressing operational risk in any industry.

Pareto developed an 80–20 rule that works with few exceptions. In this case, about 10–15 of the 64 categories will probably represent at least 80% of an organization's risk exposure.

Based on Base II (2004), the key types of operational risk are identified as follows:

– *Physical capital*: it can be expressed in the form of: damage to physical assets, business disruption, and system failure, problems with execution and delivery, and/or process management. Technological failure dominates this category and here, the principal concern is with a bank's computer systems. A crash in the computing system can destroy a bank. Most banks have a duplicate system that is backed up in real time, in a secret location, should anything go wrong with the main computer system. More generally, the loss of physical assets, such as buildings owned, is a form of operational risk. However, banks take out insurance against the risk of fire or other catastrophes, and to this extent, they have already hedged themselves against the risk, hence they are fully hedge.

– *Human capital*: this type of risk arises from human error, problems with employment practices or employees' health and safety, and internal fraud. The bank might find itself being fined for breach of health and safety rules, or brought before an employment tribunal accused of unfair dismissal.

– *Legal:* the main legal risk is when a bank is sued. It can arise as a result of the treatment of clients, the sale of products, or business practices. There are many examples of banks being taken to court by disgruntled corporate customers, who claim they were misled by advice given to them or business products sold, even contracts with customers may be disputed.

– *Fraud*: fraud may be internal or external to the bank:

- *internal fraud* such as (1) unauthorized activities (transactions not reported (informational), transaction type unauthorized (with monetary loss), mismarking of position (international), etc.) and (2) theft and fraud (fraud/credit, fraud/worthless deposits, theft/ extortion/embezzlement/ robbery, misappropriation of assets, forgery, check kiting, smuggling, account takeover/impersonation, etc.

- *external fraud* such as (1) theft and fraud (theft/robbery, forgery, check kiting) and (2) system security (hacking damage, theft of information (with monetary loss), etc.).

However, Van Greuning and Bratanovic [VAN 09] concluded that banks are exposed to three categories of risks: financial, operational and environmental risks:

– *Financial risks* comprise two types of risk. Traditional banking risks, including balance sheet and income statement structure, credit and solvency risks; and treasury risks, based on financial arbitrage. The main categories of treasury risk are liquidity interest rate, currency and market risks.

– *Operational risks* are related to a bank's overall business processes and the potential impact thereon of compliance with bank policies and procedures, internal systems and technology, information security, measures against mismanagement and fraud, and business continuity concerns. Another aspect of operational risk encompasses the bank's strategic planning, governance and organizational structure, management of staff careers and internal resources, product and knowledge development and customer acquisition approach.

– *Environmental risks* are associated with a bank's business environment, including macroeconomic and policy concerns, legal and regulatory factors and the overall financial sector infrastructure and payment systems of the jurisdictions in which it operates. Environmental risks include all types of exogenous risks that, if they were to materialize, could jeopardize a bank's operations or undermine its ability to continue in business.

8.2. Risk exposure for Islamic banks

Van Greuning and Iqbal [VAN 08] note that Islamic banks are exposed to many types of risks: *financial risks* (currency risk, liquidity, credit, market, etc.), *operational risks* related to a bank's organization and functioning, including computer-related and other technologies, *business risks* associated with a bank's business environment, including macroeconomic and policy concerns, legal and regulatory factors and the financial sector's infrastructure, such as payment systems and auditing professions, and *event risks* which include all types of exogenous risks, political, contagion, banking crisis, etc.

In the case of Islamic banks, added attention must be paid to the contractual role of the bank concerned, when analyzing the risks inherent in the bank's assets and liabilities:

– In *murabahah* transactions, Islamic banks are exposed to credit risks when the bank delivers the asset to the client but does not receive payment from the client in time. In case of a non-binding murabahah, where the client has the right to refuse delivery of the product purchased by the bank, the bank is further exposed to price and market risks.

– In *bay'al-salaam* or *istisnah* contracts, the bank is exposed to the risk of failure to supply on time, to supply at all, or to supply the quality of goods as contractually specified. Such failure could result in a delay or default in payment, or in delivery of the product, and can expose Islamic banks to financial losses of income as well as capital.

– In the case of *mudarabah* investments, the Islamic bank is exposed to an enhanced credit risk on the amounts advanced to the mudarib (agent). The nature of the mudarabah contract is such that it does not give the bank appropriate rights to monitor the mudarib or to participate in management of the project, which makes it difficult to assess and manage credit risk. The bank is not in a position to know or decide how the activities of the mudarib can be monitored accurately, especially if losses are claimed.

In addition, they believe that Islamic banks are also exposed to *Shariah risk* that is related to the structure and functioning of Shariah boards at the institutional and systemic level. This risk could be of two types: the first is due to nonstandard practices in respect of different contracts in different jurisdictions, and the second is due to the failure to comply with Shariah rules.

The relationship between the bank and the investors–depositors is not only that of an agent and principal, it is also based on an implicit trust between the two that the agent will respect the desires of the principal to comply fully with the Shariah. This relationship distinguishes Islamic banking from conventional banking and is the sole justification for the existence of Islamic banks. If the bank is unable to maintain this trust and the bank's actions lead to non-compliance with the Shariah, the bank risks breaking the confidence of the investors–depositors. Therefore, the bank should give high priority to ensuring transparency in compliance with the Shariah and take actions to avoid lack of compliance [VAN 08].

Recently, in its World Islamic banking Competitiveness Report, Ey [EY 16] noted that GCC[1] banks consider cyber-security risk the most serious threat to achieving their digital aspirations. Its assessment shows customers are also equally nervous about the prospects of data breaches. They expect intuitive security processes and much more clarity on terms of use. The emerging challenge for banks is to balance the need for security, cost of execution and customer expectation.

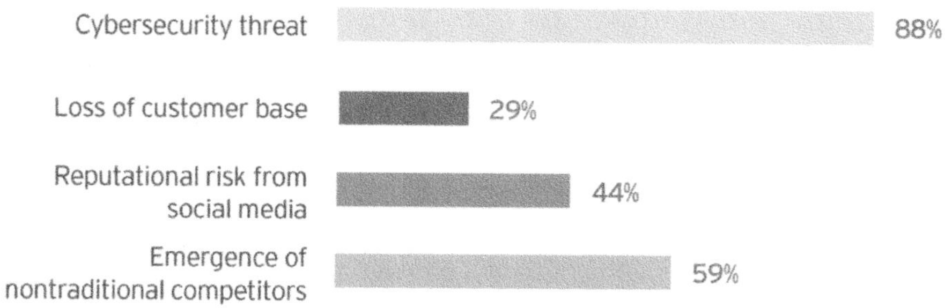

Figure 8.1. *Risks are identified and often mitigated (source: [EY 16])*

1 The Cooperation Council for the Arab States of the Gulf, known as the Gulf Cooperation Council (GCC) is a regional intergovernmental political and economic union consisting of all Arab states of the Persian Gulf, except for Iraq. Its member states are Bahrain, Kuwait, Oman, Qatar, Saudi Arabia, and the United Arab Emirates.

9

Banking Risk Management

9.1. Traditional risk management techniques

9.1.1. *Asset–liability management*

Asset–liability management (ALM) is the proactive management of both sides of the balance sheet, with a special emphasis on the management of interest rate and liquidity risks [HEF 05].

9.1.1.1. *Interest rate risk*

For some banks, it may be more important to manage interest rate risk arising from off-balance sheet business. ALM measures their performance in terms of net interest income (loan income less cost of deposit), the market value of equity (the market price of bank stock) or the economic equity ratio (new equity value/new loan value) for an unexpected change in interest rates. To the extent that changes in net interest income affect bank stock market valuations, the three measures will be very closely linked. There are many techniques to manage interest rate risk such as GAP analysis, duration analysis and duration GAP analysis.

GAP analysis is the most well-known ALM technique, used to manage interest rate risk, though it can also be used in liquidity risk management. The "gap" is the difference between interest sensitive assets and liabilities for a given time interval. In gap analysis, each of the bank's asset and liability categories is classified according to the date the asset or liability is repriced, or "time buckets": groupings of assets or liabilities. Analysts compute incremental and cumulative gap results. An incremental gap is defined as earning assets minus any funding sources in each time bucket;

cumulative gaps are the cumulative subtotals of the incremental gaps. If total earning assets must equal total funding sources, then by definition, the incremental gaps must always total zero, and therefore the last cumulative gap must be zero. Analysts focus on the cumulative gaps for the different time frames.

The assets and liabilities on the banking book can be summarized with a formula for a maturity gap:

$$\text{Maturity gap} = W_A\text{RSA} - W_L\text{RSL} \quad [9.1]$$

where:

W_A: weighted average of rate sensitive assets;

W_L: weighted average of rate sensitive liabilities.

The bigger the maturity gap, the more a bank's net worth will be affected by a change in interest rates.

Duration analysis expands on the gap analysis presented above by taking duration into account. The objective is to consider the impact on shareholders' equity if a risk-free rate, for all maturities, rises or falls, but takes the procedure one step further. Duration analysis allows for the possibility that the average life (duration) of an asset or liability differs from their respective maturities.

Duration is the present value weighted average term to reprising, and was originally applied to bonds with coupons, correcting for the impurity of a bond: true duration is less than the bond's term to maturity. The duration of an "impure" bond (that is one with a coupon) is expressed as follows:

$$\text{Duration} = T\,\{1 - [\text{coupon size}/(\text{MV} \times r)]\} + [(1 + r)/r]\,[1 - (\text{DPVR}/\text{MV})] \quad [9.2]$$

where:

T: time to redemption;

r : market (nominal) interest rate;

MV: market value;

DPVR: discounted present value of redemption.

Duration analysis is most well known for its use in bond portfolio management where billions in fixed income funds are managed using duration as a measure of interest rate sensitivity. Risk managers in banks, insurance companies and other financial institutions have utilized duration analysis to control or measure their institution's exposure to interest rate risk. Many investment banks and other financial institutions have used duration measurements in value – at-risk analyses, as in Risk Metrics – to estimate the possible losses that may result from adverse interest movements. Traders in fixed income securities use duration notions in their everyday evaluations of bond price movements.

Duration gap analysis estimates a bank's overall interest rate exposure on the balance sheet, taking into account that duration gaps are present. The duration of the assets and liabilities are matched as in standard gap analysis. The off-balance sheet interest sensitive positions of the bank are placed in time bands, based on the maturity of the instrument. The position in each time band is netted, and the net position is weighted by an estimate of its duration, where duration measures the price sensitivity of fixed rate instruments with different maturities to changes in interest rates. If the duration of designated deposits and liabilities are matched, then the duration gap on that part of the balance sheet is zero. This part of the balance sheet is immunized against unexpected changes in the interest rate. In this way, immunization can be used to obtain a fixed yield for a certain period of time because both sides of the balance sheet are protected from interest rate risk. Hence, the use of duration to measure interest rate sensitivity should be limited to small changes in the interest rate.

Saunders [SAU 02] shows how a duration model can be used to measure the overall gap of the bank's exposure to interest rate risk, i.e. the duration gap. Begin by summing up the bank's duration of, respectively, its assets and liabilities portfolio:

– D_A: the market value weighted average of the individual durations of each asset in the portfolio.

– D_L: the market value weighted average of the individual durations of each liability":

$$\Delta E = \Delta A - \Delta L \qquad [9.3]$$

where:

ΔE: the change in net worth of the bank;

ΔA: the change in market value of assets for a given change in interest rates;

ΔL: the change in market value of liabilities for a given change in interest rates.

Saunders [SAU 02] shows that the net worth of the bank can be expressed as:

$$\Delta E = -(\text{Adjusted duration gap}) \times \text{asset size} \times \text{interest rate shock} \qquad [9.4]$$

where:

$$\text{Interest rate shock} = \Delta R/(1 + R)$$

where R is the yield to maturity, and will change, for example, as a result of a change in the interest rate set by the central bank:

$$\text{Adjusted duration gap} = \text{duration gap } D_A - GD_L$$

where D_L is adjusted for the proportion of assets funded by liabilities (e.g. deposits or other borrowed funds) rather than equity. That is, D_L is adjusted for gearing or leverage: $G = L/A$, where A is total assets and L is the bank's liabilities excluding equity.

9.1.1.1.1. Liquidity risk

Short-term liquidity risk is defined as a firm's ability to pay all short-term obligations. And long-term liquidity risk is defined as a firm's ability to pay all long-term obligations [PLE12]. The liquidity risk is the risk that a bank is unable to meet its liabilities. It is associated with the liabilities side of the balance sheet when depositors unexpectedly withdraw their financial claims. Assuming the liquidity preferences of a bank's customers are roughly constant, the problem usually arises if there is a run on the bank as depositors try to withdraw their cash. A bank liquidity crisis is normally triggered either by a loss of confidence in the bank or because of poor management practices, or if the bank is a victim of a loss of confidence in the financial system caused, possibly, by the failure of another bank. However, if the bank experiences an unusually high deposit withdrawal rate, and lacks the cash or is unable to borrow the money quickly, it is faced with liquidating its longer term investments, possibly in a market where other banks and investment houses are also selling, pushing down prices.

A bank can also experience liquidity problems on the asset side of the balance sheet, caused by large numbers of unexpected loan defaults. Banks have also been caught out granting credit lines, which they do not expect to be drawn down, but which are subsequently used by the borrowers. If an economy goes into recession relatively quickly, these banks may see firms drawing down their credit lines all at once, which will put pressure on their liquidity. There is also liquidity risk linked to off-balance sheet transactions and to a slow-down or collapse in the payments system.

If a bank does experience liquidity problems, the central bank is usually willing to lend to them at some penal rate, which is costly for the bank. Also, the central bank will have to be reasonably certain that the problem is one of illiquidity and not insolvency. Banks will borrow funds on the interbank markets or from other sources before they approach the central bank, but again this is costly for the bank, and undermines its profitability.

The goal of liquidity risk management should be to avoid a situation where the net liquid assets are negative. Gap analysis can be used to manage this type of risk. The gap is defined in terms of net liquid assets: the difference between net liquid assets and volatile liabilities. Liquidity gap analysis is similar to the maturity ladder for interest rate risk, but items from the balance sheet are placed on a ladder according to the expected time the cash flow (which may be an outflow or an inflow) is generated. Net mismatched positions are accumulated through time to produce a cumulative net mismatch position. The bank can monitor the amount of cash which will become available over time, without having to liquidate assets early, at penal rates [HEF 05].

According to Plenborg and Petersen [PLE 12], liquidity cycle could be measured as following:

$$\text{Liquidity cycle} = \frac{365}{\text{Turnover rate of net working capital}} \qquad [9.5]$$

$$\text{Liquidity cycle} = \frac{365}{\left(\frac{\text{Cost of gold sold}}{\text{Inventory}}\right)} + \frac{365}{\left(\frac{\text{Revenue}}{\text{Accounts receivable}}\right)} + \frac{365}{\left(\frac{\text{Purchase, material}}{\text{Accounts payable}}\right)} \qquad [9.6]$$

Therefore, knowledge of a company's liquidity is important, as lack of liquidity may lead to loss of business opportunities and, in the worst cases, to suspension of payments.

9.1.2. Financial derivatives

Financial derivatives can be defined as financial instruments that derive their value from the prices of one or more other assets such as equity securities, fixed-income securities, foreign currencies, or commodities. According to Bodie and Merton [BOD 98], the most commonly used financial derivatives by financial institutions to manage risk exposure are forward contracts, futures, options and swaps.

9.1.2.1. *Forward contracts*

A forward contract obligates one party to buy an underlying asset at a fixed price (forward price) at a certain future date (maturity date) from a counterparty, who is obligated to sell the assest at that fixed price [STU 05]. All transactions are negotiated over the counter (OTC), which means that they are not traded via an exchange.

A forward contract is an agreement to buy (or sell) an asset (for example currencies, equities, bonds and commodities such as wheat and oil) at a future date for a price determined at the time of the agreement. For example, an agreement may involve one side buying an equity forward, that is purchasing the equity at a specified date in the future, for a price agreed at the time the forward contract is entered into. Forward contracts are not standardized and are traded OTC. If the forward agreement involves interest rates, the seller has the opportunity to hedge against a future fall in interest rates, whereas the buyer gets protection from a future rise in rates. Currency forward contracts allow both agents to hedge against the risk of future fluctuations in currencies, depending on whether they are buying or selling [HEF 05].

9.1.2.2. *Future contracts*

A future contract is a standardized contract traded on an exchange and delivered at some future, specified date. The contract can involve commodities or financial instruments, such as currencies. Unlike forward contracts, future contracts are homogeneous, specifying quantity and quality, time and place of delivery, and method of payment [HEF 05].

9.1.2.3. *Swap contracts*

Swap contracts serve to exchange a cash flow related to the debt obligation of two counterparties. The main instruments are interest rate, currency, commodity and equity swaps. Like forward, swap contracts are bilateral agreements, designed to achieve specified risk management objectives. Negotiated privately between two parties, they are invariably OTC and expose both parties to credit risk. The swap market has grown rapidly since the late 1980s [HEF 05]. Referring to Stulz [STU 04], a swap contract exchanges cash flows over a specific period. The principal used to compute the flows is the "notional amount".

9.1.2.4. *Option contracts*

According to Heffernan [HEF 05], with option contracts, the agent pays for more flexibility because he is not obliged to exercise it. The price of the option gives the agent the flexibility. The first type of option traded on an exchange [CHI 73] was a *call option*. The holder of a European call option has the right, but not the obligation, to buy an asset at an agreed (strike) price, on some specified date in the future. If the option is not exercised, the buyer loses no more than the premium he pays plus any brokerage or commission fees. The holder of a call option will exercise the option if the price of the asset rises and exceeds the strike price on the date specified.

The call option is said to be *in the money* because the strike price is below the stock price. If the strike price exceeds the market price – the call option is *out of the money* because money is lost if the option was exercised. Though there is no point in exercising the option, the holder does not necessarily lose out because the whole point of buying the call option is to gain some flexibility, which in turn can be used as a hedge during the life of the option. Exchange traded *put options* first appeared in 1977, and give the holder the right (but not the obligation) to sell an underlying asset at an agreed price at some specified date in the future. This time, if, on the specified date, the price of the asset is less than the strike price, the holder will profit by exercising the option and pocketing the difference between the strike price and the share price (if an equity).

However, Stulz [STU 05] states that a call option on a stock gives its holder the right to buy a fixed number of shares at a given price by some future date, while a put option gives its holder the right to sell a fixed number of shares on the same terms. The specified price is called the exercise price. When the holder of an option takes advantage of this right, they are said to exercise the option.

The purchase price of an option – the money that changes hands on the first day – is called the option premium. Options enable their holders to lever their resources, while at the same time limiting their risk.

9.1.2.5. *Hybrid derivatives*

These are hybrids of the financial instruments discussed above. Variable coupon facilities, including floating rate notes (FRNs), note issuance facilities and swaptions, fall into this category. A swaption is an option on a swap: the holder has the right, but not the obligation, to enter into a swap contract at some specified future date. Variable coupon securities are bonds where the coupon is revalued on specified dates. At each of these dates, the coupon rate is adjusted to reflect the current market rates. As long as the reprising reflects the current interest rate level, this type of security will be less volatile than one with a fixed rate coupon. FRNs have an intermediate term, whereas other instruments in this category will have different maturities. All the periodic payments are linked to an interest rate index, such as Libor. A FRN will have the coupon (therefore the interest rate payments) adjusted regularly, with the rates set using Libor as a benchmark. Note that issuance facilities are a type of financial guarantee made by the bank on behalf of the client, and have features similar to other financial guarantees such as letters of credit, credit lines and revolving loan commitments [HEF 05].

9.2. International risk management tools

9.2.1. *Basel I*

The 1988 Basel committee focused on the effective supervision of international banking operations through greater coordination among international bank supervisors and regulators. A document was written to recommend some standards and regulations for banks; the main recommendation of this document is that in order to lower credit risk, banks should hold enough capital at least 8% of its weighted risk assets.

The 1988 Basel Accord established a single set of capital adequacy standards for international banks of participating countries from January 1993. With the arrival of a new revised accord, the 1988 Accord will be known as Basel I henceforth. Basel I require all international banks to set aside capital based on the (Basel) risk assets ratio:

$$\text{Basel capital ratio} = \frac{\text{capital}}{\text{risk} - \text{weight assets}} = \frac{\text{capital (tier 1 and 2)}}{\text{assets (weighted by credit type)} + \text{credit risk equivalents}} \quad [9.7]$$

Under the Accord, banks were required to hold a backing for weighted assets of no less than 8% total capital and at least 4% of tier 1, or core, capital. Core capital was defined as issued and fully paid ordinary shares/common stock plus non-cumulative perpetual preferred stock and disclosed reserves. Supplementary capital (tier 2) consisted simply of all other capital (i.e. undisclosed reserves, property where the value changes, bonds).

Assets were to be weighted according to their risk with:

– no risk (0% weight) being assigned to cash, gold and bonds issued by OECD government;

– 20% weight characterizing claims on agencies of OECD governments and local public sector entities;

– 50% weight attributed to mortgage loans;

– 100% weight assigned to all claims on the private sector, non-OECD governments, real estate, investments and all other assets.

Even though weights, as proposed under Basel I, were hardly unambiguous, the standards were immediately adopted by the G-10 governments and by the late 1990s the Accord had spread to over 100 countries worldwide [JAC 99].

Clearly, the main purpose of the implemented regulations was to put a check on banks' activities as originators of credit by encouraging them to boost their capital positions. However, as the risk asset ratio might be increased by altering either the numerator or the denominator in the ratio, banks could improve their position not only by securing larger amounts of capital, but also by restructuring their balance sheets and resorting to arbitrage, in particular securitization. This would certainly be a viable option if banks were to perceive the new Basel framework as a form of undue taxation. Nevertheless, certain conditions with regard to the financial market ought to be satisfied for securitization to flourish. Hence, the popularity of this particular form of capital arbitrage seems, at least *a priori*, to be somewhat dependent on the institutional framework of a given country [JAB 10].

The Basel Committee began to address the treatment of market risks in a 1993 consultative document, and the outcome was the 1996 Amendment of Basel I to be implemented by international banks by 1998. It introduced a more direct treatment of off-balance sheet items rather than converting them into credit risk equivalents, as was done in the original Basel I.

The different forms of market risk recognized in the amendment include: equity price risk (market and specific), interest rate risk associated with fixed income instruments, currency risk and commodities price risk. Debt securities (fixed and floating rate instruments, such as bonds, or debt derivatives), forward rate agreements, futures and options, swaps (interest rate, currency or commodity) and equity derivatives will expose a bank to market risk.

In the numerator of the Basel ratio, a third type of capital, tier 3 capital, can be used by banks but only when computing the capital charge related to market risk, and subject to the approval of the national regulator. Tier 3 capital is defined as short-term subordinated debt (with a maturity of less than 2 years), which meets a number of conditions stipulated in the agreement, including a requirement that neither the interest nor principal can be repaid if it results in the bank falling below its minimum capital requirement.

Whether the amendment raises or lowers the capital charge of a bank depends on the profile of its trading book. However, as will be shown in the following, banks using the "standardized" approach are likely to incur higher capital charges, unless positions are well hedged or debt securities are of a high investment grade [HEF 05].

9.2.2. *Basel II*

A "revised framework" known as Basel II was released in June 2004 [BCB 04] after many issues with Basel I, most notably that regulatory arbitrage was rampant [JAC 99]. Basel I gave banks the ability to control the amount of capital they required by shifting between on-balance sheet assets with different weights, and by securitizing assets and shifting them off balance sheet – a form of disintermediation. Banks quickly accumulated capital well in excess of the regulatory minimum and capital requirements, which, in effect, had no constraining impact on bank risk taking:

> "New Capital Regulation Rules, known as Basel II, will more closely align regulatory requirements with economic risk, and will have a profound effect on banking industry structures and practices" [BAR 02].

$$\underset{\text{Basel 1 (with 1996 Amendment)}}{\frac{\text{Capital (tier 1 \& 2)}}{\text{Credit risk + market risk}}} \qquad \underset{\text{Basel 2 (2006/7)}}{\frac{\text{Capital (tier 1 \& 2)}}{\text{Amended credit risk + market risk + operational risk}}} \qquad [9.8]$$

Thus, the proposal consists of three interactive and mutually reinforcing pillars (Figure 9.1).

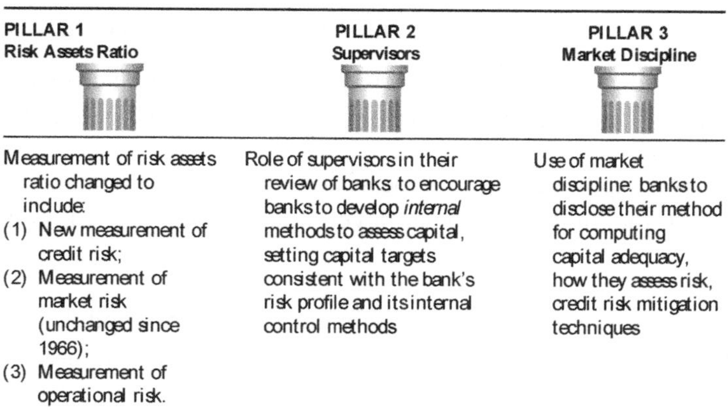

Figure 9.1. *The "three-pillar" approach (source: [HEF 05])*

The definition of tier 1 and 2 capital used in Basel I is retained. However, over the longer term, the Basel Committee plans to review what constitutes eligible tier 1 capital. The minimum requirements to set aside, 4% of capital (for tier 1) or 8% (for tier 2), remains unchanged. The market risk measure introduced in the 1996 amendment is part of the new risk assets ratio and was discussed at length earlier in the chapter. The only change proposed is to have one system for determining the trigger charge. There are important changes in the measurement of credit risk and, for the first time, an attempt to measure and impose a capital requirement for operational risk [HEF 05].

9.2.3. *Basel III*

In 2012, the Bank of International Settlements decided to implement Basel III, a comprehensive set of reform measures developed by the Basel Committee on Banking Supervision, to strengthen the regulation, supervision and risk management of the banking sector. These measures aim to:

– improve the banking sector's ability to absorb shocks arising from financial and economic stress, whatever the source;

– improve risk management and governance;

– strengthen banks' transparency and disclosures.

The reforms target:

– bank-level, or microprudential, regulation, which will help raise the resilience of individual banking institutions to periods of stress;

– macroprudential, system wide risks that can build up across the banking sector as well as the pro-cyclical amplification of these risks over time.

These two approaches to supervision are complementary as greater resilience at the individual bank level reduces the risk of system wide shocks.

Banks are required to have a minimum amount of capital to be able to absorb losses and still operate as going concerns. However, during the recent crisis, the losses that banks suffered in their trading books have far exceeded minimum capital requirements [BCB 09c]. As a result, the Basel committee has undertaken an extensive revision of bank regulation, which has resulted in several new measures [BCB 09c, BCB 10b]. To increase the loss-absorbing capacity of bank capital, the Basel Committee has introduced two additional capital requirements for the trading book, the "incremental risk capital" charge and the stressed value-at-risk [VAR 11].

9.3. Market risk management

By the mid-1980s, the majority of investment and commercial banks expanded into trading assets, hence new management techniques were created, especially the market risk management. For this reason, it is important to introduce them.

The central components of a market risk management system are risk adjusted return on capital (RAROC) and value at risk (VAR). RAROC is used to manage risk related to different business units within a bank, but is also employed to evaluate performance. VAR focuses solely on giving banks a number, which, in principle, they use to ensure they have sufficient capital to cover their market risk exposure. In practice, the limitations of VAR make it necessary to apply other techniques, such as scenario analysis and stress tests [HEF 05].

9.3.1. *Risk-adjusted return on capital*

Following Heffernan [HEF 05], the RAROC approach consists of assessing the amount of credit risk embedded in all areas of the bank. By measuring the risk of the credit portfolio, the bank could decide on how much capital should be set aside to ensure that the exposure of its depositors was limited for a given probability of loss. The difference between RAROC and the more traditional measures such as ROA or ROE is that the latter two measures do not adjust for the differences in degree of risk for related activities within the bank.

RAROC is defined as:

$$\frac{\text{Position's return adjusted for risk}}{\text{total capital}}$$

where:

– position's return: measured as (revenue – cost – expected losses), adjusted for risk (volatility);

– capital: the total capital (equity plus other sources of external finance).

RAROC measures the risk inherent in each activity, product or portfolio. The risk factor is assigned by looking at the volatility of the assets' price, usually based on historical data. After each asset is assigned a risk factor, capital is allocated to it.

9.3.2. *Market VAR*

VAR is a modeling technique that typically measures a bank's aggregate market risk exposure and, given a probability level, estimates the amount a bank would lose if it were to hold specific assets for a certain period of time. Inputs to a VAR-based model include data on the bank's positions and on prices, volatility, and risk factors [VAN 08].

The simplistic approach to market risk assessment is the VAR concept. VAR measures a bank's aggregate market risk exposure, given a probability level, by estimating the amount a bank would lose if it were to hold specific assets for a certain period of time.

The risks covered by the model include all markup risk, currency, equity and commodity positions inherent in the bank's portfolio for both on- and off-balance sheet positions.

VAR-based models typically combine the potential change in the value of each position that would result from specific movements in underlying risk factors. The distinguishing feature of VAR is the emphasis on losses arising as a result of the volatility of assets, as opposed to the volatility of earnings. The first comprehensive model developed was by Morgan [MOR 94].

VAR is defined as:

$$VAR_x = V_x \times dV/dP \times \Delta P_t$$

where:

V_x: the market value of portfolio x;

dV/dP: the sensitivity to price movement per dollar market value;

ΔP_t: the adverse price movement (in interest rates, exchange rates, equity prices or commodity prices) over time *t*.

Time *t* may be a day (daily earnings at risk), a month, etc. Under the Basel market risk agreement, the time interval is 10 days.

VAR estimates the likely or expected maximum amount that could be lost on a bank's portfolio as a result of changes in risk factors, i.e. the prices of underlying assets over a specific time horizon, within a statistical confidence interval. VAR models of market risk focus on four underlying instruments, and their corresponding prices: bonds (interest rates at different maturities), currencies (exchange rates), equity (stock market prices) and commodities (prices of commodities such as oil or wheat).

9.3.3. *Monte Carlo methods*

Monte Carlo methods provide approximate solutions to a variety of mathematical problems by performing statistical sampling experiments. They can be loosely defined as statistical simulation methods, where statistical simulation is defined in quite general terms to be any method that utilizes sequences of random numbers to perform the simulation. Thus, Monte Carlo methods are a collection of different methods that all basically perform the same process. This process involves performing many simulations using random numbers and probability to obtain an approximation of the answer to the problem. The defining characteristic of Monte Carlo methods is its use of random numbers in its simulations. In fact, these methods derive their collective name from the fact that Monte Carlo, the capital of Monaco, has many casinos and casino roulette wheels are a good example of a random number generator [PEN 02].

With a given a set of estimates of the volatilities, and correlations for financial instruments, the future distribution of a portfolio's return can be estimated through Monte Carlo simulation. Monte Carlo simulation provides a statistical estimate. This takes the form of a sample frequency distribution. Given this estimate of the distribution of future value changes, calculation of VAR proceeds in the same manner as described for the historical simulation, that is the percentile corresponding to the desired confidence level, will be selected [HAS 04].

9.3.4. *The beta method*

In lieu of forecasting market risk by using historical prices for the actual securities in the equity portfolio, a simplifying technique is often applied that maps the different stocks to an equity index, using the stock's beta (correlation) to the same index. It is possible, therefore, to describe the equity portfolio's exposure to market risk in terms of index positions rather than as positions in the actual securities [HAS 04].

9.4. Credit risk management

Techniques for credit risk management are well known because the banking sector has had a long history of experience in this area. Nonetheless, loan quality problems are an important cause of bank failure [HEF 05].

9.4.1. *Minimizing credit risk*

As Heffernan [HEF 05] concludes, there are five key ways a bank can minimize credit risk: through accurate loan pricing, credit rationing, use of collateral, loan diversification and more recently through asset securitization and/or the use of credit derivatives. The weights applied to each of the methods will vary, depending on whether the loan is commercial or retail:

– *Pricing the loan*: Any bank will wish to ensure the "price" of a loan (loan rate) exceeds a risk adjusted rate, and includes any loan administration costs, that is:

$$RL = i + ip + fees$$

where:

R_L: interest rate charged on the loan.

i: market interest rate, such as LIBOR or an equivalent term.

ip: risk premium, negatively related to the probability of the loan being repaid (ip = 0 if repayment is certain).

In the above equation, *ip* and *i* are positively related, for one of two reasons. In the case of a variable rate loan, if the market rate rises, so will the interest rate charged on the loan, and the borrower will find it more difficult to repay the loan, so the probability of default increases. Or, at very high market rates, the loan rate will rise, attracting riskier borrowers (due to adverse selection), so the chances of the loan being repaid fall.

– *Credit limits*: This method gives the potential for adverse selection, since most banks do not rely solely on loan rates when taking a lending decision. Instead, the availability of a certain type of loan may be restricted to a selected class of borrowers, especially in retail markets. Branch managers are given well-defined credit constraints and borrowers usually discover they may not borrow above some ceiling. In retail markets, banks normally quote one loan rate and then restrict the amount individuals or small firms can borrow according to criteria such as wealth or collateral. By contrast, in the wholesale markets, credit limits are of secondary importance; loan rates (and the risk premium) normally vary from business to business because banks have more information on the value of a firm, such as independent auditor reports on a company's financial performance.

– *Collateral or security*: Banks also use collateral to reduce credit risk exposure. However, if the price of the collateral (for example, houses, stock market prices) becomes more volatile, then for an unchanged loan rate, banks have to demand more collateral to offset the increased probability of loss on the credit. Another problem that can arise is if the price of collateral is negatively correlated with the ability of the borrower to repay, that is as the probability of default among a borrower class increases, the price of the collateral declines.

– *Diversification*: Additional volatility created from an increase in the number of risky loans can be offset either by new injections of capital into the bank or by diversification. New loan markets should allow the bank to diversify and so reduce the overall riskiness of the loan portfolio, provided it seeks out assets, which yield returns that are negatively correlated. So banks are able to diversify away all non-systematic risk. Banks should use correlation analysis to decide how a portfolio should be diversified.

– *Credit derivatives and asset securitization*: A method of reducing credit risk exposure, provided a third party assumes responsibility for the credit risk of the securitized assets. Hence, credit risk derivatives can be used to insure against a loan default.

9.4.2. *Assessing the default risk*

Most banks have a separate credit risk analysis department; their goal is to maximize shareholder value-added through credit risk management. Managerial judgment always plays a critical role, but a good credit risk team will use qualitative and quantitative methods to assess credit risk:

– *Qualitative method*:

It is used to evaluate credit risk, which involves using a checklist to take into account factors specific to each borrower. Sinkey [SIN 02] distinguished what he calls the "fives C" to be used in a qualitative assessment of credit risk:

- Character: Is the borrower willing to repay the loan?

- Cash flow: Is the borrower reasonably liquid?

- Capital: What assets or capital does the borrower have?

- Collateral or security: Can the borrower put up security (e.g. deeds to a house, share certificates which will be owned by the bank in the event of default)?

- Conditions: What is the state of the economy? How robust will the borrower be in the event of a down turn?

However, Heffernan [HEF 05] checked nine elements:

- past credit history (usually kept by credit rating agencies);

- the borrower's gearing (or leverage) ratio (how much the loan applicant has already borrowed relative to his/her assets);

- the wealth of the borrower;

- whether borrower earnings are volatile;

- employment history;

- length of time as a customer at a bank;

- length of time at a certain address;

- whether or not collateral or security is part of the loan agreement;

- whether a future macroeconomic climate will affect the applicant's ability to repay.

– *Quantitative method*:

A quantitative approach to credit risk analysis requires the use of financial data to measure and predict the probability of default by the borrower. Different models include the following:

– *Credit scoring*: The data from observed borrower behavior are used to estimate the probability of default, and to sort borrowers into different risk classes. The type of information gathered is listed above but here, a weight is applied to each answer, and a score obtained. The weights are obtained from econometric techniques such as discriminate or logic analysis. Here a large amount of historical data from two populations is obtained, from the population that defaults and a group, which does not default.

Discriminate analysis assumes that a borrower will come from one of two populations: those that defaults are in population 1 (P1) and population 2 (P2) consists of firms that do not default. Data from past economic performance are used to derive a function that will discriminate between types of firms by placing them in one of two populations. Thus, if Z is a linear discriminate function of a number of independent explanatory variables, then:

$$Z = \sum a_i X_i, \qquad i = 1,2,\ldots,n$$

where X_i are the independent explanatory variables, such as credit history, wealth, etc.

– *The Altman (1968) Z-score*: Model derived from discriminate analysis and used for larger corporations. Based on financial/accounting ratios, each firm is assigned a Z score and, depending on that score, the loan either is granted or refused. The higher the Z score, the lower the probability of defaults; if Z is lower than 1.81 (In the Altman model, the $Z = 1.81$ is the average of Z scores of the defaulting and non-defaulting firms), the default risk is considered too high and no loan is made.

Relationship banking also plays its part, especially in countries such as Germany and Japan. If a corporation has done business with a bank for a long period of time, then an application for a new loan will involve a combination of banker judgment and credit scoring. This may also apply to personal customers with a long-standing credit history at a bank.

Small businesses are more difficult. They vary considerably in their activities, and failure rates among small and medium-sized enterprises can be as high as 95%. This makes it difficult to apply credit-scoring models to this group [HEF 05].

9.4.3. *Credit VAR*

It is a marked-to-market approach, focusing on a loan loss value and/or a risk–return trade-off for a portfolio of debt. In the VAR approach, there is more than one single credit migration. Instead of an asset either being a good asset or in default, in credit VAR, there is the possibility of multiple migrations, that is a range of upgrades or downgrades.

Credit VAR has been the target of criticisms raised with respect to market VAR. Indeed, some of the underlying assumptions, such as a normal distribution, become even more problematic. For detailed accounts of VAR, Saunders [SAU 03] explains a range of credit portfolio models, including credit metrics and credit risk plus. Many banks use a version of the default mode model, which is most useful when applied to portfolios of untraded personal or commercial loans. The credit VAR models are more appropriate for bond portfolios, which are traded on the market, receive a debt rating and are reasonably liquid.

9.5. Management of operational risk

According to the revised Basel Committee revised report, "operational risk is defined as the risk of loss resulting from the inadequate or failed internal processes, people and systems or from external events. This definition includes legal risk". Furthermore, "legal risk includes, but is not limited to, exposure to fines, penalties, or punitive damages resulting from supervisory actions, as well as private settlements". However, operational risk management is the process of identifying, measuring or assessing operational risk and then developing strategies to manage/mitigate the risk. There are qualitative and quantitative methods to manage operational risk.

9.5.1. *Qualitative methods*

9.5.1.1. *The advanced measurement approach*

The advanced measurement approach (AMA) allows banks to develop their own model for assessing the regulatory capital that covers their yearly operational risk exposure within a confidence interval of 99.9%. Most of the literature on operational risk modeling focuses either on methods based on actual loss data, the so-called loss distribution approach (LDA) [CHA 08, CHA 06, CRU 02, FRA 01], or on application of Bayesian techniques to combine loss-based models and scenario analysis [ALE 03, FIG 07, LAM 07]. However, studies focusing on scenario analysis on a stand-alone basis are more scarce, except for [ALD 06, AND 04, SBA 03] and [STE 06].

The Basel committee released its consultative paper on operational risk in 2001. Since then, banks have started designing and developing their own internal model to measure their exposure to operational risk just as they began implementing consistent and comprehensive operational risk loss data collection processes. The application of AMA is in principle open to any proprietary model, but methodologies have converged over the years and standards have appeared. The result is that most AMA models can now be classified into two categories:

– *Loss distribution approaches*:

The LDA is a parametric technique primarily based on past-observed internal loss data (potentially enriched with external data). Based on concepts used in actuarial models, the LDA consists of separately estimating a frequency distribution for the occurrence of operational losses and a severity distribution for the economic impact of the individual losses.

– *Scenario-based approaches*:

Scenario-based AMA shares with LDA the idea of combining two dimensions (frequency and severity) to calculate the aggregate loss distribution used to derive the operational VaR. It differs, however, from LDA in that estimation of both distributions builds on experts' opinion regarding various scenarios.

Based on their activities and their control environment, banks build scenarios describing potential adverse events actualizing the operational risks identified as relevant. Then experts are asked to give opinions on probability of occurrence (i.e. frequency) and potential economic impact should the events occur (i.e. severity).

9.5.1.2. *Experts' opinions*

To ensure compliance of model with regulatory requirements, banks associate LDA models with scenario-based experts' opinions. The operational risk manager decides who should serve as "experts" to assess the various scenarios. In most banks, scenario analysis is carried out by department or business lines. The operational risk manager asks the head of each business line to provide a list of staff members with sufficient skills, experience and expertise to take part in the scenario analysis exercise. Internal risk governance implies that the head of a business line has the ultimate responsibility for managing operational risk in the daily activities of the unit and for ensuring that a sound and efficient control environment is in place. As a result, this person will probably be requested to review, validate or approve results of the estimation process. Often workshops are held, with all experts including the head of business line attending. Participants discuss and debate to obtain a final common estimate [PET 09].

Before opinions can be combined, they must be elicited and expressed in some quantified form, which is the root of the third challenge. Indeed, as stated by Hogarth [HOG 75], "man is a selective, sequential information processing system with limited capacity … ill-suited for assessing probability distributions". Unfortunately, many of the solutions to combine opinions require that each individual's opinion to be encoded as a subjective probability distribution.

The problems related to obtaining probability measures by experts and combination of opinions from several experts has been extensively studied by statisticians over the last decades. Good reviews of these topics can be found in [GAR 05] for statistical methods used, [DAN 04] for the psychological aspects, [CLE 07, GEN 86] for mathematical aggregation of opinions and [PLO 93] for behavioral aggregation of opinions.

9.5.1.3. *Total quality management*

Total quality management (TQM) has been defined as management of activities, results and decisions for quality throughout the organization. TQM in the financial industry would mean managing all aspects of finance business to achieve business objectives, including profitable growth. TQM implies managing the process to deliver acceptable process output or the product. That would be ensured through quality inspection, control and assurance technique.

TQM involves planning the output, carrying out the activities and controlling the output within established specification limits. TQM works well in the absence of true global competition, where customer expectations are moderate. In terms of process yields, they could be upto around 95%. Due to excessive verification activities, appraisal cost increase resulting in a high cost of quality. Process expectations are more driven by the process capability rather than the customer's needs.

Today, customer expectations are very high, and in order to achieve excellence, we must establish clear targets. The targets are driven by the customer expectations. In order to learn customer expectations, Kano's model has been a powerful method where customer demands are classified into three categories: assumed, spoken and desired. We can think of these three types of customer requirements as minimal, paid for and wished for. Only when customers get what they want, in addition to the minimal and paid for, will suppliers' performance be favored [GUP 09].

9.5.1.4. *Process of excellence (4P model)*

The 4P model of process management developed in 2006 is a great way to achieve excellence.

The four P_s (prepare, perform, perfect and progress) offer a better implementation of process thinking than the typical plan of do, check and act:

Prepare implies doing homework or setting up a process to achieve target performance. For example, if a process to distribute dividends must be designed, preparation must include getting all the information required; developing a system for scheduling, printing, enveloping and mailing; an error-free and streamlined process flow; and defining skills and identifying the right personnel to perform. Preparation is a critical element of managing a process for excellence. Without good preparation, errors occur and target performance is missed. *Perform* implies doing things well, instead of just doing it. During the perform aspect, critical process steps must be identified, measured and monitored against specified target values. *Perfect* represents the evaluating performance against the specified targets. Initially, aiming for a target performance may appear to be a difficult task; however, the process must be designed through inputs (good preparation) and activities (perform) such that the output lands at or close to the target value (perfect). Keeping close to target performance keeps the process output away from the lower and upper specification limits, resulting in less failures and thus lower cost. One of main benefits of implementing the 4P model is the attitude, changing from "acceptability" to "excellence". The excellent process output will lead to better profit margins than the acceptable process output due to reduced cost of appraisals [GUP 09].

The 4P model has also proven to be helpful in identifying measures of effectiveness at the process level and system level. The measures of effectiveness can be established at the input, in-process or output stages of a process. For example, for the mortgage approval process, the measures of effectiveness could be financial strength of the borrower, timely verification of borrower's records at the input level, compliance to establish activities or regulatory requirements prior to approving the mortgage at the process level and payment schedule compliance at the output level.

9.5.1.5. *Six Sigma*

According to documents at Motorola, where Six Sigma was first used, "Six Sigma is our 5-year goal to approach the standard of zero defects, and be best-in-class in everything we do". Accordingly, we can define Six Sigma as an approach to achieve virtual perfection fast, and be the best in class in everything. A tactical definition based on statistical analysis, Six Sigma can be defined as having the process capability twice as good as required. At Motorola, Six Sigma was originally defined as a measure of the goodness of products and services. Higher sigma means better quality of a product or service, and lower sigma means poor quality of a product or service. The original Six Sigma initiative included leadership drive, the Six Steps to Six Sigma methodology and related measurements [GUP 09].

The six steps are as follows:

1) *Define* your products or services.

2) *Identify* your customers and their critical needs.

3) *Identify* your needs and resources.

4) *Map* your process.

5) *Remove* non-value-added activities and use error-free methods.

6) *Measure* the sigma level and continue to improve the process if the sigma level is less than six.

The statistical definition focuses on tactics and tools, while the original definition focuses on the intent and methodology of Six Sigma. The intent of Six Sigma is to achieve a rapid significant improvement by using the commonsensical DMAIC (define, measure, analyze, improve and control) methodology.

The Basel committee and rating agencies have acknowledged Six Sigma as a best practice framework in operational risk management. Providing these Six Sigma black belts with a Lean perspective would be even better. Lean is the popular name for a philosophy that strives to eliminate waste of all types. It was developed by the Toyota Corporation and came to the United States and European Union as Just-In-Time manufacturing; it has now evolved to be applied beyond manufacturing [TAR 09].

9.5.1.6. *The role of the rating agencies*

Rating agencies such as Moody's, Fitch, and Standard and Poors have published various white papers and standards stating what they will look for in a risk-managed organization.

Referring to [TAR 09], rating agencies include the following elements that are applicable across all organizations:

– a risk management committee and working groups with an enterprise-wide charter, which possesses the needed training, expertise, resources and time to do its job;

– a risk identification process that is enterprise-wide, independently reviewed and audited on a periodic basis (the frequency typically mandated by external auditors may not be adequate for areas of high risk);

– assurances that the risk committee and risk managers communicate on a regular basis beyond the reporting of risks (this would be greatly facilitated by a risk committee reporting to the board of directors);

– a risk-weighted approval process for new products and strategies (we provide an example of how this can work in the next section);

– an ongoing effort to diversify risk on an enterprise-wide basis. (the goal is to prevent an overconcentration of risk in any one area that could jeopardize the health or very existence of the organization);

– a centralized and dedicated risk management organization that is staffed with the appropriate subject matter experts and has the charter to remain independent from those taking the risks. This organization would be charted to identify, communicate and audit all risks without fear of retaliation (this process clearly failed in most of the leading financial services organizations as risk managers were ignored or punished for raising concerns over the subprime market).

9.5.2. *Quantitative methods*

9.5.2.1. *Operational VAR*

The concept of VAR was developed by J.P. Morgan in the 1990s as an overall market risk measure. VAR measures the maximum estimated loss in the market value of a portfolio over a specified time horizon with a specified confidence level. This methodology has been adopted for use to quantify operational risk under the AMA of Basel II, which requires losses over a 1-year time horizon at a 99% confidence level.

9.5.2.2. *Multifactor causal models*

These types of models attempt to explain operational losses with control factors as illustrated in the following equation:

$$Y_t = \alpha + \beta_{1t} X_{1t} + \ldots + \beta_{nt} X_{nt} + \varepsilon_t$$

where Y_t represents the operational loss dollar amount in a particular business line and/or event type, $X(s)$ represent the process drivers and α and $\beta_i(s)$ are the estimated parameters measuring the impact of the process driver on the loss amount.

9.5.2.3. *Regime switching models*

There are two basic approaches taken in the switching models: thresholds and Markov. The threshold models are generally used when the model's state is believed to follow the observed value of a variable in relation to some threshold. The number of consecutive months of negative growth could be used as the threshold. The Markov models are used when the variable that determines the model's state is assumed to follow a Markov process.

The Markov switching model is illustrated as:

$$Y_t = X_t \tilde{b}_1 \quad S_t = 1$$

$$X_t \tilde{b}_2 \quad S_t = 2$$

where S_t is the state variable that depends on time and is unobservable. The process determining the state of the model is assumed to follow a Markov process. The probability of moving from state i to state j is determined by the Markov chain:

$$P(S_{t+1} = j \mid S_t = i) = p_{j,i}$$

Consider the company that has experienced a great deal of difficulty in application change management. To assess the financial impact of the decision, management can model the operational losses before and after outsourcing the application change management function.

Operational risks susceptible to regime shifts will have time varying parameters. More interesting and challenging situations arise when the regime shifts are not single.

9.5.2.4. *Discriminant analysis*

Discriminant analysis is a statistical technique for classifying observations into predefined categories. The methodology can be applied to quantitative or ranked qualitative data such as qualitative data from audits and Six Sigma failure analyses. The model parameters are estimated based on a data set for which the categorization of each observation is known.

The discriminant function L can be written as:

$$L=c+b_1x_1+b_2x_2+...+b_nx_n$$

where c is the constant, b_i are the discriminate coefficients and x are the predictor variables. The linear discriminate function can be used to predict the class of a new observation with an unknown categorization. For a situation with two categories, two discriminate functions, L1 and L2, are estimated.

$$L_1=c_1+b_{1,1}x_1+b_{1,2}x_2+...+b_{1,n}x_n$$

$$L_2=c_2+b_{2,1}x_1+b_{2,2}x_2+...+b_{2,n}x_n$$

9.5.2.5. *Agent-based modeling*

Agent-based modeling (ABM) and simulation has been used since the 1990s in the social sciences to develop new theories and to provide evidence for existing theories. It is a method currently used to study complex systems such as corporations and the stock market. These complex systems cannot be modeled through analytical expressions. ABM models a system as groups of autonomous interacting decision-making entities called agents. Each agent is governed by a set of rules that it applies based on the circumstances of the agent. The end result is a distributed decision-making process.

ABM can be used to understand and measure the operational risk of a company through modeling the business processes. They modeled employees as interacting agents. Using historical data on losses and errors, the researchers modeled several common mistakes, such as confusing local currency with the euro. Through the modeling they were able to discover under what circumstances these common errors led to catastrophic losses. ABM was able to uncover vulnerabilities in the business processes of the bank [CER 09].

9.5.2.6. *Bayesian networks*

A Bayesian network (BN) is a graphical model. It reflects the states of the process modeled and integrates the probabilistic relationships between the variables. BNs facilitate modeling cause and effect relationships in complex inference networks. These models can be driven by empirical data and can handle missing data by incorporating expert opinion [CER 09].

9.6. Board responsibilities in risk management

The board sets the strategic direction, appoints management, establishes operational policies and, most importantly, takes responsibility for ensuring the soundness of a bank. The board is answerable to depositors and shareholders for the lawful, informed, efficient and able administration of the institution. The members of the board usually delegate the day-to-day management of banking to officers and employees, but board members are responsible for the consequences of unsound or imprudent policies and practices concerning lending, investing, protecting against internal fraud, or any other banking activity [VAN 08].

One of the most important functions of independent directors should therefore be to avoid economic and legal mistakes that could threaten the life of the bank. When problems are discovered by internal controls or external auditors, they should be brought to the immediate attention of the board of directors. The most important duty of the board is to ensure that the management team has the necessary skills, knowledge, experience and sense of judgment to manage the bank's affairs in a sound and responsible manner. The management team should be directly accountable to the board, and this relationship should be supported by robust structures.

An effective board should have a sound understanding of the nature of the bank's business activities and associated risks. It should take reasonable steps to ensure that management has established strong systems to monitor and control those risks. Even if members of the board are not experts in banking risks and risk management systems, they should ensure that such expertise is available and that the risk management system undergoes appropriate reviews by suitably qualified professionals. The board should take timely actions to ensure a level of capitalization that reasonably matches the economic and business environment of the bank as well as its business and risk profile. Moreover the board should ensure that the bank has adequate internal audit arrangements in place and that risk management systems are applied properly at all times. The board should also ensure that the banking laws and regulations applicable to a bank's business are followed. It should take all reasonable steps to ensure that the information in the bank's disclosure statements is transparent and accurate and that adequate procedures are in place, including external audits or other reviews, where appropriate, to ensure that the information disclosed is not false or misleading [VAN 08]. Now it is easy to understand the causes of failure of banks, it is hidden in their board and explains by the deficiencies in board and senior management.

9.7. Manager responsibilities in risk management

The board and management need to support one another, but each one has its own distinct role and responsibilities to fulfill. The chief executive officer CEO and the management team should run the bank's day-to-day activities in compliance with board policies, laws and regulations, and should be supported by a sound system of internal controls. Although the board should leave day-to-day operations to management, it should retain overall control. The dictation of a board's actions by management indicates that the board is not fulfilling its responsibilities, ultimately to the detriment of the institution.

Management should provide directors with the information they need to meet their responsibilities and should respond quickly and fully to board requests. In addition, management should use its expertise to generate new and innovative ideas and recommendations for consideration by the board. A bank should have adequate policies in place to increase the accountability of its managers. The duties and responsibilities of a bank's senior management include appointment to middle-level management positions of persons with adequate professional skills, experience and integrity; the establishment of adequate performance incentives and personnel management systems; and staff training. Management should ensure that the bank has an adequate management information system and that the information is transparent, timely, accurate and complete.

Management's role in identifying, appraising, pricing and managing financial risk is described well by the Basel Committee on Banking Supervision. The Basel Committee has stated that any corporation that uses new financial instruments has a critical need for all levels of management to acquire knowledge and understanding of their inherent risks and to adapt internal accounting systems to ensure adequate control. Risk management should be an integral part of the day-to-day activities of each and every line manager in order to ascertain that risk management systems are applied properly and that procedures are followed. Management should also ensure that the bank has adequate internal controls, including appropriate audit arrangements, because risk management often fails as a result of an ineffective decision-making process and weak controls, not of unanticipated or extraordinary risks [VAN 08].

9.8. Islamic banking risk management

Since its inception, IFSB has issued many standards, guiding principles and technical note for the Islamic financial services industry. In our case, we will concentrate on risk management (IFSB-1).

9.8.1. *IFSB principles of credit risk management*

PRINCIPLE 9.1.– Islamic financial institutions shall have in place a strategy for financing, using the various Islamic instruments in compliance with Shariah, whereby they recognize the potential credit exposures that may arise at different stages of the various financing agreements.

PRINCIPLE 9.2.– Islamic financial institutions shall carry out a due diligence review in respect of counterparties prior to deciding on the choice of an appropriate Islamic financing instrument.

PRINCIPLE 9.3.– Islamic financial institutions shall have in place appropriate methodologies for measuring and reporting the credit risk exposures arising under each Islamic financing instrument.

PRINCIPLE 9.4.– Islamic financial institutions shall have in place Shariah-compliant credit risk mitigating techniques appropriate for each Islamic financing instrument.

9.8.2. *IFSB principles of liquidity risk management*

PRINCIPLE 9.5.– Islamic financial institutions shall have in place a liquidity management framework (including reporting) taking into account separately and on an overall basis their liquidity exposures in respect of each category of current accounts, unrestricted investment accounts and restricted investment accounts.

PRINCIPLE 9.6.– Islamic financial institutions shall undertake liquidity risk commensurate with their ability to have sufficient recourse to Shariah-compliant funds to mitigate such risk.

The liquidity management policies of a bank normally comprise a decision-making structure, an approach to funding and liquidity operations, a set of limits to liquidity risk exposure, and a set of procedures for planning liquidity under alternative scenarios, including crisis situations [VAN 08].

9.8.3. *FSB principle of market risk management*

Market risk is the risk that a bank may experience loss due to unfavorable movements in market prices [VAN 08].

PRINCIPLE 9.7.– Islamic financial institutions shall have in place an appropriate framework for market risk management (including reporting) in respect of all assets held, including those that do not have a ready market or are exposed to high price volatility.

9.8.4. *Operational risk management*

Van Greuning and Iqbal [VAN 08] noted that Islamic banks are perceived to be more exposed to operational risks associated with the failure of controls, procedures, information technology systems and analytical models.

Operational risk is considered high on the list of risk exposures for Islamic banks. A survey conducted by Khan and Ahmed [KHA 01] shows that the managers of Islamic banks perceive operational risk as the most critical risk after *markup risk*. The survey finds that operational risk is lower in the fixed-income contracts of murabahah (cost plus sales) and ijarah (leasing) and higher in the deferred sales contracts of salaam (agriculture) and istisnah (manufacturing). The relatively higher rankings of the instruments indicate that banks find these contracts complex and difficult to implement.

The three methods of measuring operational risk proposed in Basel II would have to be adapted considerably if they were to apply to Islamic banks. The use of gross income as the basic indicator of operational risk could be misleading in Islamic banks, insofar as the large volume of transactions in commodities and the use of structured finance raise operational exposures that are not captured by gross income. In contrast, the standardized approach that allows for different business lines would be better suited, but it would have to be adapted to the needs of Islamic banks. In particular, agency services under mudarabah and commodity inventory management need to be considered explicitly.

10

Corporate Governance and Risk-Taking

Risk-taking has been widely debated in financial literature since the 1980s. Several theoreticians, mainly Bowman [BOW 80], Tversky and Kahneman [TVE 81], MacCrimmon and Wehrung [MAC 86], March and Shapira [MAR 87] and Bromiley [BRO 91] have shed some light onto this issue. Nowadays, further to the scandals of Enron, Worldcom, Global Crossing and other well-known companies, it is managerial risk-taking that has been specifically emphasized. Indeed, it is worth pointing out the determinants of managerial risk-taking. The downfall of these big enterprises has been largely explained by the weakness of the systems of governance. In this vein, Healy and Palepu [HEA 03] asserted that the main reason behind these bankruptcies is the dangerous and even deceitful strategies of management for the benefit of leaders and hence the renewal of public interest for governance problems whose background is so classic. In the same way, Kose *et al.* [KOS 05] appreciated the quality of investors' protection by the capacity to influence the investment choices of the manager and rationalize his risk-taking.

10.1. Board of supervisors and risk-taking

The board of supervisors is a very important mechanism in governance, according to Jensen and Meckling [JEN 76]. The shareholders elect the supervisors to control the management and drive the firm's strategy, which would incite managers to incur more risks and undertake riskier projects in order to enhance the value of the company. Moreover, Wiseman and Gomez-Mejia [WIS 98] attested that a strong custody from the board of supervisors leads to objectives that are hard to reach, stimulating managerial risk-taking. Morellec and Smith [MOR 05] have already sustained the hypothesis that the board of supervisors can influence managerial risk-taking. According to them, the board of supervisors cannot dictate the investment policy as the relative decisions are neither verifiable nor contractual, although they are observable.

Nevertheless, both financial strategy and managerial risk-taking are observable and contractual. The board of supervisors can therefore influence such decisions and even threaten the manager when he shows his lack of either diligence or responsibility. However, Charléty [CHA 06] considered that the board efficiency is often controversial since the supervisors are not always chosen for their expertise and competence nor remunerated according to the performance achieved. Similarly, Healy and Palepu [HEA 03] signaled that some supervisors at Enron were conscious of the risky and abusive behavior of some managers and even reached the true information not released in reports, but did not declare it. It seems then relevant to discern the impact of the board of supervisors on managerial risk-taking according to its composition, its size and its chairmanship.

Firstly, Fama and Jensen [FAM 83] considered that the existence of external supervisors, who are outside the firm, increases the viability of the board and reduces the probability of collision for the expropriation of shareholders' wealth by the manager. Short *et al.* [SHO 99] noted that independent supervisors assure the mission of strategic consultants and controllers for the manager and approach managerial decisions with objectivity. Therefore, the manager must be careful to take prudent and rational measures in terms of risk-return.

Furthermore, Borokhovich *et al.* [BOR 04] showed that firms whose boards essentially consist of external supervisors usually undertake risky projects but above all afford the most sophisticated instruments to manage and control risks. Beasley *et al.* [BEA 05] also put in evidence that the supervisors' independence increases the efficiency and the perspicacity of the board. That is why they asserted that such a board positively influences managerial risk-taking and guarantees its conditions of success. Likewise, Hossain *et al.* [HOS 00] advanced that the presence of internal administrators, employees of the enterprise, provides the manager with more discretion and enables him to have an opportunist behavior through either under investing or undertaking too risky projects. They are often incited to enhance the manager's career without worrying about the firm performance as their careers are also tied to the manager's performance.

However, Buckley and Van Der Nat [BUC 03] and Dionne and Triki [DIO 04] found that the presence of external supervisors is meaningless. According to them, such supervisors do not stimulate managerial risk-taking because either they do not have the required profile and necessary training or they do not know how to manage risk or even do not arrange worthwhile information. Healy and Palepu [HEY 03] also attested that although most members of the Enron board were independent, they were inefficient in their mission. Thus, it seems that external supervisors are supposed to stimulate managerial risk-taking but this is not always true.

The size of the board of supervisors can also have an impact on managerial risk-taking. Adams and Mehran [ADA 03] revealed that large board firms usually recorded higher performances associated with higher managerial risk-taking. They also found that small-board firms can be easily manipulated and influenced by managers. In the same vein, Blanchard and Dionne [BLA 04] suggested that as the number of supervisors increases, the more developed and sophisticated the instruments used to hedge, which justifies a more intensive managerial risk-taking. However, Lipton and Lorsh [LIP 92] noted that even though the board capacities increase with its size, this advantage would be counterbalanced by inherent additional costs due to the lack of coordination and synchronization of efforts. The process of exchange of information and decision-making becomes more difficult and slow. In addition, Wiseman and Gomez-Mejia [WIS 98] stipulated that by increasing the number of supervisors, criteria proposed to appreciate managerial behavior diversify and become more ambiguous. The manager then becomes indecisive and confused and hence risk averse and prudent. Thus, managerial risk-taking seems to be reduced by the enlargement of the board size.

10.2. Regulation: supervision and risk-taking

The role of law in protecting investors' interests was initially put in evidence with Jensen and Meckling's study [JEN 76]. So, the regulations can play an important role in aligning the attitudes of managers toward the risk with those of shareholders. La Porta *et al.* [LA 02] asserted that public authorities often impose strict enough rules so as to supervise managerial decisions and restrict their discretionary behaviors. They added that the role of public authorities proved to be more prevailing and eminent in developing countries that are characterized by a weak protection of shareholders' rights. They noted that the State shareholding in such countries becomes more significant and is usually conjugated in an intensive intervention of government, as an attempt to protect these shareholders. Besides, La Porta *et al.* [LA 02] proposed to allocate the task of protecting and developing the shareholders' rights to benevolent delegates. Moreover, Walker *et al.* [WAL 02] attested that several legal and judicial reforms have been taken in public corporations further to different financial scandals. Shareholders including the State require henceforth more mastery and control of any risk that the firm may face so as to preserve the firm's value and improve it perpetually.

Maguire and Albright [MAG 05] also assigned to the law a relevant and effective role in controlling managerial risk-taking. The manager fears being criticized or convicted by a court in full public view and even losing his or her job in case of serious mistakes resulting from his audacious and adventurous behavior. Such a measure is supposed to restrict managerial latitude and force managers to follow rational strategies presenting an attractive report in terms of return-risk. Furthermore, Maguire and Albright [MAG 05] outlined the role of the media in cultivating this culture of risk aversion and thus dissuading managers from undertaking risky opportunities, and this through the various reports and enquiries condemning the adverse events and the abusive behaviors of managers.

In the same way, Gebauer and Fleisch [GEB 07] put in evidence the role of law and legislation in turning out managers from risky projects. Although managers are convinced of the advantages of risk-taking, they often estimate that political and social costs that may occur are much more noteworthy than latent gains. They are thus dissuaded from incurring risky projects. The managers are also afraid of losing their power and their authority and then show their reticence toward all new strategy susceptible to increase the potential of risk.

However, Kose *et al.* [KOS 05] showed that systems favoring shareholders' protection incite managers to invest in risky and profitable projects so as to accelerate the economic growth. Kose *et al.* [KOS 05] appreciated the vigor of laws by the level of shareholders' protection. It is according to this vigor that the manager will either give up risky projects capable of increasing the firm's value and drain deferred and enormous incomes or avoid such projects to protect his immediate and small profits. In fact, the consumption cost of small profits increases, while the optimal satisfaction level of the manager decreases. They also proposed to design benevolent agents to protect and develop shareholders' rights and showed the incontestable weight of social groups on managerial risk-taking.

Beasley *et al.* [BEA 05] clarified that managerial risk-taking must not be led in the same way as the legal setting varies through activities. According to them, bankers are the pioneers in managerial risk-taking because of the last international reforms introduced by "Basel II, 2004". It seems that legislation wholly discourages managers from incurring risks, but also punishes them when they do not maximize the firm's value. Its impact on managerial risk-taking is then confused and it depends on the specificity of the business itself.

Fernandez and Gonzalez [FER 05] consider the same time span for a sample of listed banks and provide evidence, suggesting that in countries with low accounting and auditing requirements more power on official supervisory authorities may reduce risk-taking behavior from the perspectives of managers. Moreover, they indicate that higher restrictions on bank activities can diminish the probability of a banking crisis.

The role of a bank's supervisory authority is moving away from monitoring compliance with banking laws and prudential regulations. A more appropriate mission statement today would be "to create a regulatory and legal environment in which the quality and effectiveness of bank risk management can be optimized in order to contribute to a sound and reliable banking system". The task of bank supervision becomes monitoring, evaluating and, when necessary, strengthening the risk management process that is undertaken by banks. However, the supervisory authority is only one of the many contributors to a stable banking system. Other players are also responsible for managing risk, and prudential regulations increasingly stress the accountability of top-level management. Recognizing the high cost of voluminous reporting requirements without corresponding benefits, many countries are moving toward a system of reporting that encourages and enables supervisors to rely more extensively on external auditors in the ordinary course of business, subject to having a clear understanding of their role in the risk management [VAN 08].

Recently, EY analysis [EY 16] has explained the major hurdles faced by financial institutions in the GCC in their digital transformation. It mentions that a limited technology support, including the burden of IT legacy and application complexity resulting from duplicated functions, point-to-point interfaces and heterogeneous and outdated technologies, is slowing down the deployment of digital services (see Figure 10.1).

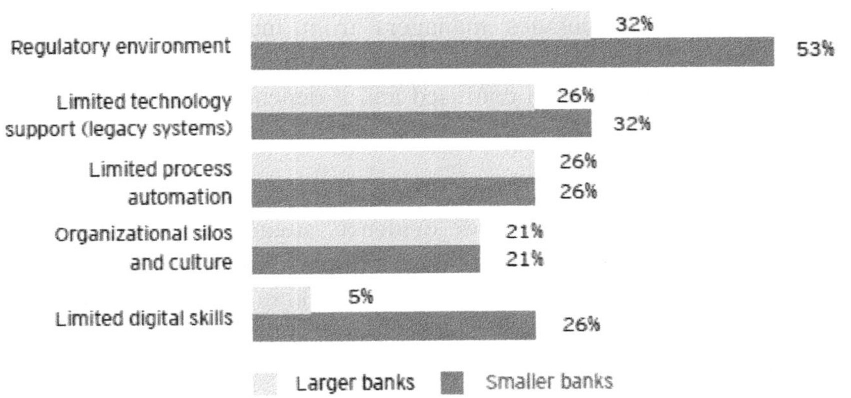

Figure 10.1. *Islamic banks and regulations (source: EY analysis [EY 16])*

The EY report [EY 16] explains that a GCC central bank vice governor said “Banks should not see regulators as an inhibitor of innovation, but as a partner in helping to develop digital banking in a secured way”. “We only focus on security to protect the financial health of our residents and, as soon as it is demonstrated that a function is secured and that it is supported by an appropriate legal framework, such as electronic signature, we don’t analyze the relevance any further to approve it”.“ Unfortunately, we have often had to reject some requests in the past that were insufficiently developed and demonstrated”.

Therefore, to increase IT agility, EY [EY 16] recommends to (1) upgrade core banking system to gain access to out-of-the-box digital functionality and technology; (2) rationalize the application portfolio, modernize IT architecture (middleware, Service Oriented Architecture (SOA), Business Process Management (BPM)) and eliminate point-to-point interfaces, upgrade the IT operating model to gain agility and enable a faster time to market for new evolutions and hire and acquire digital talents.

10.3. Ownership and risk-taking

Jensen and Meckling [JEN 76] advanced that property dispersal dissuades shareholders from exercising an active control upon the manager that lets the latter behave against the shareholders' interests mainly when he perceives risk-taking differently. In the same way, Shavell [SHA 79] presumed that firms whose capital is detained by majority shareholders often undertake risky projects and that it is this category of shareholders who incite the manager to adopt such a strategy. The main reason is to improve the firm's profitability and hence shareholders' wealth.

Besides, Shleifer and Vishny [SHL 86] and Holderness and Sheehan [HOL 88] showed that property concentration allows the shareholders to more efficiently control the managerial decisions and compel them to work in their favor. Indeed, a scattered-property structure increases costs and necessary efforts to influence managerial decisions. The pressure of shareholders on managers is then less efficient. Thus, Gadhoum [GAD 99] confirmed that the property concentration has a significant impact on managerial entrenchment and the manager is therefore obliged to maximize his risk-taking in order to enhance the value of the firm, otherwise he will be fired and replaced.

Similarly, Beck and Levine [BEC 02] and Beck *et al.* [BEC 03] attributed to this type of property an eminent role in the protection of outside shareholders' rights against the abuses of managers particularly when they adopt too risky businesses without worrying about the threatening effects that can occur. Pritsker [PRI 05] suggested in this respect that the presence of majority shareholders modulates the strategic choices of management in favor of firm value maximization and therefore reduces the conflicts inherent to managerial risk-taking that may arise.

Charléty [CHA 06] showed that "small" shareholders, individually, are not incited to play an active role, which seems too expensive compared with potential profits which are proportional to their participations in the capital. On the other hand, a "big" shareholder (or an association) may be interested in looking for any worthwhile information that might improve the value of his stocks. The managerial risk-taking then proves to be stimulated by a concentrated-structure capital. Also, the shareholding category may influence the managerial behavior. Smith and Stulz [SMI 85] and Pearce and Zahra [PEA 92] sustained that institutional investors are better aware and more competent than other shareholders. Furthermore, this category of shareholders can afford more efficient tools and professional means to actively control the management. They can even rent financial expertise services in order to appreciate the investments' value and judge their opportunity in terms of risk-return. Likewise, Wright *et al.* [WRI 96] advanced that institutional shareholders, because of their expertise and their outside diversified portfolios, usually incite the manager to undertake riskier projects so as to maximize the firm's value and hence shareholders' wealth. Wright *et al.* [WRI 96] also showed that institutional shareholders deeply influence managerial risk-taking and positively stimulate it.

Dionne and Triki [DIO 04] approved this hypothesis, but specified that only institutional shareholders detaining more than 5% of the capital are powerful enough to decrease the costs of information asymmetry and oblige the manager to adopt a measured risk strategy to optimize the firm value. Nevertheless, Davis *et al.* [DAV 05] showed a negative impact of block shareholders who would rather align their interests with those of managers in order not to gamble their welfare. Besides, Davis *et al.* [DAV 05] advanced that such shareholders consider that it is strategically more appropriate to cooperate with the manager. We therefore expect that the presence of institutional shareholders will wholly induce managerial risk-taking.

Laeven and Levine [LAE 09] show that private ownership by banks is related to their risk-taking. In studying the financial crisis, Fahlenbrach and Stulz [FAH 09] conclude that high levels of insider ownership (the classic correction to the principal/agent incentive alignment problem) did not lead the banks to take excessive risk. Bank CEOs suffered large losses during the crisis, indicating that while executives maintained well-aligned equity ownership stakes they may have misunderstood the accretion of risk occurring within the banking system.

In contrast, Bebchuk and Spamann [BEB 09] argue that the principal–agent conflict between bank owners and managers has been effectively externalized to the taxpayers, and that compensation structures strongly determine the risk preferences of managers. Perhaps bank CEOs directed their firms into projects and business that shareholders valued and for which the CEOs were justly compensated. If so, managerial interests were properly aligned with the risk appetites of their common shareholders.

10.4. Audit committee and risk-taking

Following Van Greuning and Bratanovic [VAN 09], the audit committee and the internal auditors are regarded as an extension of the board's risk management policy function and risk-taking behavior. The modern internal auditors should describe their task as providing assurance regarding the bank's corporate governance, control systems and risk management processes. Assurance can be achieved only through an understanding and analysis of the key risk indicators driving the individual processes making up each business line. Although the audit committee play a valuable role in assisting management in identifying and addressing risk areas, the prime responsibility for risk management cannot be abdicated to them, but rather should be integrated into all levels of management.

10.5. Incentive pay and risk-taking

The use of incentive pay in banking is widely believed to have motivated excessive risk-taking and, thus, to have acted as a contributory factor to the recent financial crisis (e.g. [BEB 09]).

In the banking industry, the use of stock options in executive compensation has become so widespread over the last decade that the contractual risk-taking incentives for CEOs at large US banks are now higher than at non-financial firms [DE 10].

Acrey *et al.* [ACR 11] investigate the relationship between CEO compensation and bank default risk predictors to determine if short-term incentives can explain recent excesses in bank risk. They find only modest evidence that CEO compensation structures promote significant firm-specific heterogeneity in bank risk measures or risky activities.

The non-financial literature finds that higher CEO Vegas lead to riskier investment choices and bind corporate resources to riskier activities [COL 06, GUA 99, NAM 03, RAJ 02]. For the banking industry, De Young *et al.* [DE 10] and Mehran and Rosenberg [MEH 07] show that high-Vega banks engage in riskier types of activities. By contrast, Fahlenbrach and Stulz [FAH 11] do not find that CEO Vegas explain the performance of bank stocks (i.e. previous managerial risk-taking) during the recent financial crisis.

Conclusion

Financial and economic crises are manifestations of a number of structural reasons why banking stability and corporate governance have become more important for economic development and the well-being of the real economy. Becht *et al.* [BEC 02] identified five reasons why corporate governance has become so prominent in the past two decades: (1) the world-wide privatization wave, (2) pension fund reform and growth of private savings, (3) the takeover wave of the 1980s, (4) deregulation and integration of capital markets and (5) crises. Despite the general focus on the topic of corporate governance, very little attention has been paid to the corporate governance of banks. Unlike corporations, banks have special features; this singularity makes their corporate governance mechanisms different and operate in a unique way. Most research on corporate governance has been concerned with the resolution of those collective problems caused by the separation between management and control. This book explains banking corporate governance, performance and risk-taking by conventional banks and Islamic banks. We note that Islamic bank may use the same governance mechanisms as a conventional bank, in addition to the Shariah supervisory boards (SSB), the Shariah review unit, the Islamic International Rating Agency (IIRA) and the Islamic Financial Services Board (IFSB) as the main mechanisms of monitoring the Islamic banking system. However, unlike the conventional system, Islamic banking is based on the active participation of public policy institutions, regulatory and supervisory authorities and Shariah authorities, which checks consistence with Islamic law (*Shariah*) principles and is guided by Islamic economics. It is worth recalling that banking governance effects performance and risk-taking. Therefore, performance measurement is an assessment of an organization's performance, including the measures of productivity, effectiveness, quality and timeliness. Hence, classical methods (e.g. ratio analysis, income statement analysis, market value added, cash flow statement, variance analysis, standard costing, etc.) and modern methods are used. Performance is the outcome of many interlinking factors where corporate governance is the only possible element within the whole set of performance drivers. Good banking governance has long been considered a crucial role for stakeholders in the business environment. Moreover, risk-taking has been widely debated in the financial literature; further to financial scandals, managerial risk-taking has been specifically emphasized. Indeed, it becomes worth pointing out the different banking risk exposures (e.g. market risk, liquidity risk, credit risk, operational risk, etc.). We conclude that all banks are exposed to the same risks. In addition, Islamic banks are exposed to Shariah risk, which is related to the structure and functioning of Shariah boards at the institutional and systemic level. Regarding risk management, many tools are used to reduce risk-taking (e.g. asset–liability management, financial derivatives, Basel principles, risk-adjusted return on capital, market value at risk (VAR), Monte Carlo method, beta method, minimizing credit risk, assessing the default risk and the credit VAR). For operational risk management, quantitative and qualitative methods are proposed. Moreover, the IFSB has issued many guiding principles and technical notes for the Islamic financial services industry in order to reduce risk-taking. We conclude that there are similar determinants of performance and risk-taking for both conventional banks and Islamic banks. This similarity is due to the fact that all banks operate in the same institutional environment, they face the same risks – except operational issues generated by SSB – and they use the same tools in managing their assets and liabilities. However, there are significant differences between conventional and Islamic banks because the latter provide Shariah compliant finance and have SSB. The key differentiation between conventional banks and Islamic banks in terms of governance is the ethical underpinning and the existence of SSB in Islamic banking. Working under the guidance of the SSB and the management of Islamic banks has provided the opportunity of raising operational issues with Shariah scholars who can examine them in the light of Islamic rules and principles and give specific rulings.

Bibliography

[AAO 99] AAOIFI, Statement on the purpose and calculation of the capital adequacy ratio for Islamic banks, Accounting and Auditing Organization for Islamic Financial Institutions (AAOIFI), Bahrain, 1999.

[ABD 09] ABDULLAH H., VALENTINE B., "Fundamental and ethics theories of corporate governance", *Middle Eastern Finance and Economics*, vol. 4, pp. 88–96, 2009.

[ABU 09] ABU-TAPANJEH A.M., "Corporate governance from the Islamic perspective: a comparative analysis with OECD principles", *Critical Perspectives on Accounting*, vol. 20, pp. 556–557, 2009.

[ADA 01] ADAMS R.H., Nonfarm income, inequality, and poverty in rural Egypt and Jordan, Policy Research Working paper no. 2572, The World Bank, 2001.

[ADA 03] ADAMS R.H., MEHRAN H., "Is corporate governance different for bank holding companies?", *Economic Policy Review*, vol. 9, pp. 123–142, 2003.

[ADA 04] ADAMS R.B., MEHRAN H., Board structure, banking firm performance and the bank holding company organizational form, Working paper, The Federal Reserve Bank of New York, 2004.

[ADA 05] ADAMS R.B., MEHRAN H., Board structure and banking firm performance, EFA Moscow Meetings, 2005.

[ADA 10] ADAMS R.B., HERMALIN B.E., WEISBACH M.S., "The role of boards of directors in corporate governance: a conceptual framework and survey", *Journal of Economic Literature*, vol. 48, pp. 58–107, 2010.

[AGA 90] AGRAWAL A., MANDELKER G., "Large shareholders and the monitoring of managers, the case of antitakeover charter amendment", *Journal of Financial and Quantitative Analysis*, vol. 25, pp. 143–167, 1990.

[AGY 73] AGYRIS C., "Some limits of rational man organizational theory", *Public Administration Review*, vol. 33, pp. 253–267, 1973.

[AKE 16] AKEB H., LEVY A., "Market efficiency and behavioral finance, non risk-correlated returns on antipodal study markets in 2000–2014", *Journal of Research in Management Sciences*, no. 112, 2016.

[AL 00] AL-RIFAI T., KHAN A., "The role of venture capital in contemporary Islamic finance", *Proceedings of the Fourth Harvard University Forum on Islamic Finance: Islamic Finance: The Task Ahead*, Cambridge, Massachusetts, 2000.

[ALC 72] ALCHIAN A.A., DEMSETZ H., "Production, information costs, and economic organization", *American Economic Review*, vol. 62, pp. 777–795, 1972.

[ALE 08] ALEXANDRU C.G., LAURENTIU R.M., The assessment of banking performances indicators of performance in bank area, MPRA Paper No. 11600, 2008.

[ALI 07] ALI A., CHEN T., RADHAKRISHNAN S., "Corporate disclosures by family firms", *Journal of Accounting and Economics*, vol. 44, pp. 238–286, 2007

[ALL 99] ALLEN D.W., "Transaction costs", in BOUCKAERT B., DE GEEST G. (eds), *The Encyclopedia of Law & Economics – Vol. 1*, Edward Elgar, Cheltenham, 1999.

[AMI 81] AMIHUD Y., LEV B., "Risk reduction as a managerial motive for conglomerate mergers", *Bell Journal of Economics,* vol. 12, pp. 605–617, 1981.

[AND 03] ANDERSON R.C., REEB D.M., "Founding family ownership and firm performance: Evidence from S&P 500", *Journal of Finance*, vol. 58, no. 3, pp. 1301–1328, 2003.

[AND 04] ANDERSON C.W., CAMPBELL T.L., "Corporate governance of Japanese banks", *Journal of Corporate Finance*, vol. 10, no. 3, 2004.

[AND 05] ANDRES P., AZOFRA V., LOPES F.J., "Corporate boards in OECD countries: size, composition, compensation, functioning and effectiveness", *Corporate Governance and International Review*, vol. 13, no. 3, pp. 377–397, 2005.

[AOK 90] AOKI M., "Toward an economic model of the Japanese firm", *Journal of Economic Literature*, vol. 28, pp. 1–27, 1990.

[AOK 94] AOKI M., "Monitoring characteristics of the main bank system: an analitical developmental view", in AOKI M., PATRICK H. (eds), *The Japanese Main Bank System: Its Relevance for Developing and Transforming Economies*, Oxford University Press, 1994.

[AOK 95] AOKI M., KIM H.K., "Corporate governance in transitional economies: insider control and the role of banks", Working paper, The World Bank, Washington D.C., 1995.

[ARN 10] ARNAUD A., "The French licensing authority faced with globalization of Islamic finance", in KHAN M.F., PORZIO M. (eds), *Islamic Banking and Finance in the European Union: A Challenge*, Edward Elgar, Cheltenham , 2010.

[ARO 10a] AROSA B., ITURRALDE T., MASEDA A., "Ownership structure and firm performance in non-listed firms: evidence from Spain", *Journal of Family Business Strategy*, vol. 1, pp. 88–96, 2010.

[ARO 10b] AROSA B., ITTURRALDE T., MASEDA A., "Outsiders on the board of directors and firm performance: evidence from Spanish non-listed family firms", *Journal of Family Business Strategy*, vol. 1, pp. 236–245, 2010.

[ARO 10c] AROURI M., LEVY A., NGUYEN KHUONG D., "ROE and value creation under IAS/IFRS: evidence of discordance from French firms," *European Financial and Accounting Journal*, vol. 3, pp. 84–112, 2010.

[ATK 97] ATKINSON A.A., WATERHOUSE J.H., WELLS R.B., "A stakeholder approach to strategic performance management", *Sloan Management Review,* Spring, 1997.

[BAE 01] BAE S.C., NOH S., "Multinational corporations versus domestic corporations: a comparative study of R&D investment activities", *Journal of Multinational Financial Management*, vol. 11, pp. 89–104, 2001.

[BAK 07] BAKER M., WURGLER J., Investor sentiment in the stock market, NBER Working paper no. 13189, June 2007.

[BAR 02a] BARTH J.R., NOLLE D.E., YAGO G., "A cross-country analysis of the bank supervisory framework and bank performance", *Financial Markets, Institutions & Instruments*, vol. 12, pp. 67–120 2002.

[BAR 02b] BARTH J.R., CAPRIO G., LEVINE R., "Bank regulation and supervision: what works best?", *Journal of Financial Intermediation*, vol. 13 pp. 5–248, 2002.

[BAR 13] BARTH J.R., CAPRIO G., LEVINE R., Bank regulation and supervision in 180 countries from 1999 to 2011, NBER Working paper no. 18733, National Bureau of Economic Research, 2013.

[BAU 08] BAUER R., FRIJNS B., OTTEN R. *et al.*, "The impact of corporate governance on corporate performance: evidence from Japan", *Pacific-Basin Finance Journal*, vol. 16, pp. 236–251, 2008.

[BAY 90] BAYSINGER B., HOSKISSON R.E., "The composition of boards of directors of strategic control: effects on corporate strategy", *Academy of Management Review*, vol. 15, no. 1, pp. 72–87, 1990.

[BEC 02] BECHT M., BOLTON P., RÖELL A., Corporate governance and control, ECGI, Finance working paper no. 02/2002 (updated in 2005), 2002.

[BEC 11] BECHT M., BOLTON P., RÖELL A., "Why bank governance is different", *Oxford Review of Economic Policy,* vol. 27, no. 3, pp. 437–463, 2011.

[BEC 06] BECK T., DEMIRGUC-KUNT A., LEVINE R., "Bank concentration, competition and crises: first results", *Journal of Banking and Finance*, vol. 30, pp. 1581–1603, 2006.

[BEC 13] BECK T., DEMIRGUC-KUNT A., MERROUCHE O., "Islamic vs. conventional banking: business model, efficiency and stability", *Journal of Banking and Finance*, vol. 37, pp. 433–447, 2013.

[BEL 12] BELTRATTI A., STULZ R.M., "The credit crisis around the globe: Why did some banks perform better?", *Journal of Financial Economics*, vol. 105, pp. 1–17, 2012.

[BEN 12] BEN BOUHENI F., BELLALAH M., *Islamic Banking & Risk Management: Problems of Islamic Banks and Recommandations*, Lambert Academic Publishing, 2012.

[BEN 13a] BEN BOUHENI F., "L'impact de la régulation et de la supervision sur la rentabilité bancaire", *La Revue du FINANCIER*, vol. 35, pp. 52–66, 2013.

[BEN 13b] BEN BOUHENI F., "The effects of supervision on banking performance: European evidence", *International Conference: Governance & Control in Finance & Banking: a New Paradigm for Risk & Performance*, Paris, France, April 18–19, 2013.

[BEN 14a] BEN BOUHENI F., "Banking regulation and supervision: can it enhance stability of banks in Europe?", *Journal of Financial Economic Policy,* vol. 30, pp. 1655–1670, 2014.

[BEN 14b] BEN BOUHENI. F., Banking governance: Islamic banks vs. conventional banks, lecture at Hanken Centre For Corporate Governance, Finland, 26th February, available at: https://www.shs.fi/banking-governance-islamic-banks-vs-conventional-banks-262-1630-1800, 2014.

[BEN 15a] BEN BOUHENI F., "Agent-based models of financial markets: the agents' behaviors", Zurich University, Switzerland, 2015.

[BEN 15b] BEN BOUHENI F., AMMI C., "Banking governance: what's special about Islamic banks?", *Journal of Applied Business Research*, vol. 31, no. 4, pp. 1621–1630, 2015.

[BEN 02] BENNEDSEN M., FELDMANN S.E., "Lobbying and legislative organization, the effect of the vote of confidence procedure", *Business and Politics*, vol. 4, pp. 1–18, 2002.

[BEN 10] BENSIMHON L., LEVY A., "The origin of stock-market crashes: proposal for a mimetic model using behavioral assumptions and an analysis of legal mimicry", *International Journal Of Business*, vol. 15, no. 3, pp. 289–306, 2010.

[BER 94] BERGLÖF E., VON THADDEN L., "Short-term vs. long-term interests: a model of capital structure with multiple investor", *Quarterly Journal of Economics*, vol. 109, pp. 1055–1084, 1994.

[BER 04] BERGLÖF E., CLAESSENS., "Enforcement and corporate governance", Working paper no. 3409, World Bank Policy Research, 2004.

[BER 14] BERK J., DE MARZO P., *Corporate Finance: The Core*, Global Edition, Pearson, 2014.

[BER 32] BERLE A., MEANS C., *The Modern Corporation and Private Property*, Macmillan, 1932.

[BER 88] BERLINER C., BRIMSON J.A., *Cost Management for Today's Advanced manufacturing: The CAM-I Conceptual Design*, Harvard Business School Press, 1988.

[BER 03] BERTRAND M., MULLAINATHAN S., "Enjoying the quiet life? Corporate governance and managerial preferences", *Journal of Political Economy*, vol. 111, pp. 1043–1075, 2003.

[BET 93] BETHEL J.E., LIEBESKIND J., "The effect of ownership structure on corporate restructuring", *Strategic Management Journal*, vol. 14, pp. 15–31, 1993.

[BHI 08] BHIMANI A., "Making corporate governance count: the fusion of ethics and economic rationality", *Journal of Management and Governance*, vol. 12, pp. 135–147, 2008.

[BHI 12] BIAZZO S., GARENGO P., *Performance Measurement with the Balanced Scorecar: A Practical Approach to Implementation within SMEs*, Springer, 2012.

[BLA 04] BLACK B., JANG H., KIM W., Does corporate governance affect firm market value? Evidence from Korea, Working paper, Stanford University, 2004.

[BOC 04] BOCCI, F., "Defining performance measurement. A comment", *Perspectives on Performance*, vol. 3, pp. 20–21, 2004.

[BOL 95] BOLTON P., "Privatization, and the separation of ownership and control: lessons from Chinese enterprise reform", *Economics of Transition*, vol. 3, no. 1, pp. 1–12, 1995.

[BOL 96] BOLTON P., SCHARFSTEIN D.S., "Optimal debt structure and the number of creditors", *Journal of Political Economy*, vol. 104, pp. 1–25, 1996.

[BOO 93] BOOT A., THAKOR A., "Security design," *Journal of Finance*, American Finance Association, vol. 48, no. 4, pp. 1349–78, 1993.

[BOU 00] BOURNE M.C.S., MILLS J.F., WILCOX M. *et al.*, "Designing, implementing and updating performance measurement systems", *International Journal of Production & Operations Management*, vol. 20, no. 7, pp. 754–71, 2000.

[BOY 86] BOYD J.H., PRESCOTT., "Financial intermediary-coalitions", *Journal of Economic Theory*, vol. 38, no. 2, pp. 211–232, 1986.

[BRA 07] BRAENDLE U.C., KOSTYUK A.N., "Developments in corporate governance", VirtusInterpress, 2007.

[BRA 68] BRAINARD W.C., TOBIN J., "Pitfalls in financial model-building", *American Economic Review*, vol. 58, pp. 99–122, 1968.

[BRE 06] BRENNAN N., "Boards of directors and firm performance: is there an expectations gap?", *Corporate Governance: An International Review*, vol. 14, no. 6, pp. 577–593, 2006.

[BRI 88] BRICKLEY J.A., LEASE, R.C., SMITH C.W., "Ownership structure and voting on antitakeover amendments", *Journal of Financial Economics*, vol. 20, pp. 267–291, 1988.

[BRO 06] BROWN L.D., CAYLOR M.L., "Corporate governance and firm valuation", *Journal of Accounting and Public Policy*, vol. 25, pp. 409–434, 2006.

[BUA 08] BUANG A.H., "Appreciation of Shariah principles in property management in contemporary Malaysia", *Jurnal Syariah*, vol. 16, pp. 555–566, 2008.

[BUR 10] BURKIA A.A., AHMED S., "Bank governance changes in Pakistan: Is there a performance effect?", *Journal of Economics and Business*, vol. 62, pp. 129–146, 2010.

[CAL 91] CALOMIRIS C.W., KAHN C.M., "The role of demandable debt in structuring optimal banking arrangements", *American Economic Review*, vol. 81, pp. 497–513, 1991.

[CAP 02] CAPIRO G., LEVINE R., "Corporate governance of banks: concepts and international observations", presented in the Global Corporate Governance Forum Research Network Meeting, April 5, 2002.

[CAP 07] CAPRIO G., LEAVEN L., LEVINE R., "Governance and bank valuation", *Journal of Financial Intermediation*, vol. 16, no. 4, pp. 584–617, 2007

[CHA 92] CHANG C., "Capital structure as an optimal contract between employees and investors", *Journal of Finance*, vol. 47, pp. 1141–1158, 1992.

[CHA 09] CHAPRA U., "The global financial crisis: can Islamic finance help?", *New Horizon*, issue 170, Institute of Islamic Banking and Insurance, 2009.

[CHA 10] CHAPRA U., Global perspective on Islamic finance, LSE–Harvard Public Lecture on Islamic Finance, February 24, 2010.

[CHE 98a] CHEMLA G., "L'impact de la négociation et des prises de contrôle sur l'ampleur de l'effet de cliquet", *Annales d'Économie et de Statistique*, no. 54, pp. 157–17, 1998.

[CHE 98b] CHEN C.R., STEINER T.L., WHYTE A.M., "Risk-taking behavior and management ownership in depository institutions", *Journal of Financial Research*, vol. 21, no. 1, pp. 1–16, 1998.

[CHE 03] CHEN H., VOLPE R.P., "Gender differences in personal financial literacy among college students", *Financial Services Review*, vol. 11, pp. 289–30, 2003.

[CHH 09] CHHAOCHHARIA V., LUC LAEVEN L., "Corporate governance norms and practices", *J. Finan. Intermediation*, vol. 18, pp. 405–431, 2009.

[CHI 93] CHISHTI S.U., "Relative stability of interest-free economy", *Journal of Research in Islamic Economics*, vol. 3, no. 1, pp. 3–12, 1993.

[CHO 07] CHOI J., PARK S.W., TOO S.S., "The value of outside directors: evidence of corporate governance reform in Korea", *Journal of Financial and Quantitative Analysis*, vol. 42, pp. 941–962, 2007.

[CIA 01] CIANCANELLI, P., REYES-GONZALEZ J.A., Corporate governance in banking: A conceptual framework, Working paper no. 253714, SSRN, 2001.

[CLA 03] CLAESSENS S., Corporate governance and development, report, The International Bank for Reconstruction and Development, 2003.

[CLA 02] CLAESSENS S., DJANKOV S, FAN J. *et al.*, "Disentangling the incentive and entrenchment effects of large shareholdings", *Journal of Finance*, vol. 57, pp. 2741–2771, 2002.

[CLA 12] CLAESSENS S., YURTOGLU B., "Corporate governance in emerging markets: a survey", *Emerging Markets Review*, vol. 15, pp. 1–33, 2012.

[CLA 04] CLARKE G.R., "Effect of enterprise ownership and foreign competition on internet diffusion in the transition economies", *Comparative Economic Studies*, vol. 46, no. 2, pp. 341–370, 2004.

[CLA 95] CLARKSON M.B.E., "A stakeholder framework for analyzing and evaluating corporate social performance", *The Academy of Management Review*, vol. 20, no. 1, pp. 92–117, 1995.

[COA 37] COASE R.H., "The nature of the firm", *Economica*, vol. 4, pp. 386–405, 1937.

[COL 01] COLES J.W., MCWILLIAMS V.B., SEN N., "An examination of the relationship of governance mechanisms to performance", *Journal of Management*, vol. 27, no. 1, pp. 23–50, 2001.

[COL 06] COLES JL., HERTZEL M., KALPATHY S,. "Earning management around employee stock options reissues", *Journal of Accounting and Economics*, vol. 41, pp. 173–200, 2006.

[COO 08] COOKE D.T., *The Wiley Guide to Managing Projects*, John Wiley & Sons, 2008.

[COR 06] CORE J.E., GUAY W.R., VERDI R.S., "Agency problems of excess endowment holdings in not-for-profit firms", *Journal of Accounting and Economics*, vol. 41, pp. 307–333, 2006.

[COR 07] CORNETT A.J. MARCUS A.S., HASSAN T. *et al.*, "The impact of institutional ownership on corporate operating performance", *Journal of Banking and Finance*, no. 31, pp. 1771–1794, 2007.

[COR 11] CORNETT M.M., MCNUTT J.J., STRAHAN P.E. *et al.*, "Liquidity risk management and credit supply in the financial crisis", *Journal of Financial Economics*, vol. 101, pp. 297–312, 2011.

[DAI 03] DAILY C., DALTO D., CANNELLA A., "Corporate governance: decades of dialogue and data", *Academy of Management Review*, vol. 28, no. 3, pp. 371–82, 2003.

[DAN 90] DANTHINE A., BAGUETTE Y., LEDUC G. *et al.*, "The OSI 95 connection-mode transport service – the enhanced QoS", *4th IFIP Conf. on High Performance Networking*, 1990.

[DAS 04] DAS A., GHOSH S., "Corporate governance in banking system: An empirical investigation", *Economic and Political Weekly*, vol. 39, pp. 1263–1266, 2004.

[DAV 97] DAVIS, DONALD R., WEINSTEIN, *et al.*, "Using international and Japanese regional data to determine when the factor abundance theory of trade works", *American Economic Review*, vol. 87, no. 3, pp. 421–46, 1997.

[DAY 84] DAYTON K.N., "Corporate governance: The other side of the coin", *Harvard Business Review*, 1984.

[DE 95] DE BONDT F.M.W., THALER R.H., "Financial decision making in markets and firms: A behavioural perspective", *Handbooks in Operations Research and Management Science*, vol. 9, pp. 385–410, 1995.

[DE 08] DE ANDRES P., VALLELADO E., "Corporate governance in banking: The role of the board of directors", *Journal of Banking & Finance*, vol. 32, pp. 2570–2580, 2008.

[DE 01] DE TONI A., TONCHIA S., "Performance measurement system: Mode characteristics and measures", *International Journal of Operations & Productions Management*, vol. 21, nos. 1–2, pp. 46–70, 2001.

[DE 05] DE WAAL A., "Briefing: Darfur, Sudan: prospects for peace", *African Affairs*, vol. 104, pp. 127–35, 2005.

[DEA 85] DEANGELO H., DEANGELO L., "Managerial ownership of voting rights: a study of public corporations with dual classes of common stock", *Journal of Financial Economics*, vol. 14, pp. 33–69, 1985.

[DEL 10] DELGADO-GARCÍA J.B. *et al.*, "The impact of ownership structure on corporate reputation: evidence from Spain", *Corporate Governance: An International Review*, vol. 18, no. 6, pp. 540–556, 2010.

[DEM 85] DEMSETZ H., LEHN K., "The structure of corporate ownership: causes and consequences", *Journal of Political Economy*, vol. 93, pp. 1155–1177, 1985.

[DEM 01] DEMSETZ H., VILLALONGA B., "Ownership structure and corporate performance", *Journal of Corporate Finance*, vol. 7, no. 3, pp. 209–233, 2001.

[DEM 83] DEMSETZ H., "The structure of ownership and the theory of the firm", *Journal of Law and Economics*, vol. 26, pp. 375–390, 1983.

[DEW 95] DEWATRIPONT M., MASKIN E., "Contractual contingencies and renegotiation", *Rand Journal of Economics*, vol. 26, pp. 704–719, 1995.

[DEW 94] DEWATRIPONT M., TIROLE J., "A theory of debt and equity: diversity of securities and manager shareholder congruence", *Quarterly Journal of Economics*, vol. 109, pp. 1027–1054, 1994.

[DIA 83] DIAMOND D.W., DYBVIG P.H., "Bank runs, deposit insurance, and liquidity", *Journal of Political Economy*, vol. 91, pp. 401–419, 1983.

[DIA 84] DIAMOND D.W., "Financial intermediation and delegated monitoring", *Review of Economic Studies*, vol. 51, pp. 393–414, 1984.

[DIA 91] DIAMOND D.W., "Monitoring and reputation: the choice between bank loans and directly placed debt", *Journal of Political Economy*, vol. 99, pp. 689–721, 1991.

[DIA 93] DIAMOND D.W., "Bank loan maturity and priority when borrowers can refinance", in MAYER C., VIVES X. (eds), *Capital Markets and Financial Intermediation*, Cambridge University Press, 1993.

[DIA 01a] DIAMOND D.W., RAJAN R.G., "Liquidity risk, liquidity creation, and financial fragility: A theory of banking", *Journal of Political Economy*, pp. 109, 287–327, 2001.

[DIA 01b] DIAMOND D.W., RAJAN G.R., "Banks and liquidity", *The American Economic Review, Papers and Proceedings of the Hundred Thirteenth Annual Meeting of the American Economic Association*, vol. 91, no. 2, pp. 422–425, 2001.

[DIX 90] DIXON J.R., NANNI A.J., VOLLMANN T.E., *The New Performance Challenge: Measuring Operations for World-class Competition*, Business One Irwin, Homewood, IL, 1990.

[DJA 08] DJANKOV S., LA PORTA R., LOPEZ-DE-SILANES F. *et al.*, "The law and economics of self-dealing", *Journal of Financial Economics*, vol. 88, pp. 430–465, 2008.

[DJE 06] DJELIC M-L., SAHLIN-ANDERSSON K., "Introduction: A world of governance: The rise of transnational regulation" in DJELIC M-L., SAHLIN-ANDERSSON K. (eds), *Transnational Governance*, Cambridge University Press, 2006.

[DON 95] DONALDSON T., PRESTON L.E., "The stakeholders theory of corporation: concepts, evidence and implications", *Academy of Management Review*, vol. 20, no. 1, pp. 65–91, 1995.

[DON 91] DONALDSON L., DAVIS J.H., "Stewardship theory or agency theory: CEO governance and shareholder returns", *Australian Journal of Management*, vol. 16, pp. 49–65, 1991.

[DOU 99] DOUGLAS G., ALLEN F., *Comparing Financial Systems*, The MIT Press, Cambridge, MA, 1999.

[DUN 98] DUNLAVY, C.A., "Corporate governance in late 19th century Europe and the U.S.: the case of shareholder voting rights", in HOPT K.J., KANDA H., ROE M.J. *et al.* (eds.), *Comparative Corporate Governance: The State of the Art and Emerging Research*, Oxford University Press, Oxford, 1998.

[DUR 02] DURNEY A., HAN E.K, "Explaining differencies in the quality of governance among companies", in CHEW D.H., GILLAN S.L. (eds), *Global Corporate Governance*, Columbia University Press, 2002.

[DUS 06] DUSUKI A.W., "Corporate governance and stakeholder management of islamic financial institutions", *National Seminar in Islamic Banking and Finance*, Nilai, 20–30 August, 2006.

[EEL 60] EELLS R.S., *The Meaning of Modern Business: an Introduction to the Philosophy of Large Corporate Enterprise*, Columbia University Press, 1960.

[EIS 76] EISENBERG M.A., *The Structure of the Corporation: A Legal Analysis*, Little, Brown and Company, 1976.

[EIS 98] EISENBERG T., SUNDGREN S., WELLS M.T., "Larger board size and decreasing firm value in small firms", *Journal of Financial Economics*, vol. 48, pp. 35–54, 1998.

[EL 05] EL-GAMAL A.M., Islamic Bank corporate governance and regulation: A call for mutualization, report, Rice University, 2005.

[ERK 10] ERKENS D., HUNG M., MATOS P., "Corporate governance in the 2007–2008 financial crisis: Evidence from financial institutions worldwide", *J Corp Financ*, vol. 18, no. 2, pp. 389–411, 2010.

[FAH 11] FAHLENBRACH R., STULZ R.M., "Bank CEO incentives and the credit crisis", *Journal of Financial Economics*, vol. 99, pp. 11–26, 2011.

[FAM 83] FAMA E.F., JENSEN M.C., "Separation of ownership and control", *Journal of Law and Economics*, vol. 26, no. 2, pp. 301–325, 1983.

[FAM 73] FAMA E.F., MACBETH J.D., "Risk, returns, and equilibrium: Empirical tests", *Journal of Political Economy*, vol. 99, no. 2, pp. 385–415, 1973.

[FAM 85] FAMA E.F., "What's different about banks?", *Journal of Monetary Economics*, vol. 15, pp. 29–39, 1985.

[FAM 80] FAMA E.F., "Agency problems and the theory of the firm", *The Journal of Political Economy*, vol. 88, no. 2, pp. 288–307, 1980.

[FAM 83] FAMA E.F., JENSEN M.C., "Agency problems and residual claims", *Journal of Law & Economics*, vol. 26, pp. 327–350, 1983.

[FLA 94] FLANNERY M.J., "Corporate finances, market discipline, and bank supervision", *Proceedings no. 37*, Federal Reserve Bank of Chicago, 1994.

[FLA 04] FLANNERY M.J., KWAN S.H., NIMALENDRAN M., "Market evidence on the opaqueness of banking firms' assets", *Journal of Financial Economics*, vol. 71, no. 3, pp. 419–460, 2004.

[FRA 90] FRANKS J., MAYER C., "Capital markets and corporate control: A study of France, Germany and the UK", *Economic Policy*, vol. 4, no. 10, pp. 189–231, 1990.

[FRA 94] FRANKS J., MAYER, C., The ownership and control of German corporations, Working paper, London Business School and University of Oxford, 1994

[FRE 99] FREEMAN E.R., "Divergent stakeholder theory", *Academy of Management Review*, vol. 24, no. 2, pp. 233–236, 1999.

[FRE 84] FREEMAN E.R., *Strategic Management: A Stakeholder Approach*, Pitman, 1984.

[FRE 02] FREMONT O., CAPAUL M., The state of corporate governance: experience from country assessments, report, The World Bank, 2002.

[FUR 01] FURFINE C., The interbank market during a crisis, *BIS Working Papers*, no. 99, 2001.

[GAD 06] GADHOUM Y., GUEYIÉ J.P., CHAHLOUL M., "Le conseil d'administration dans la gouvernance des entreprises nord-américaines", *Gestion*, vol. 23, 2006.

[GAF 07] GAFFIKIN M., Accounting theory and practice: the ethical dimension, Working paper, Faculty of Business – Accounting & Finance, University of Wollongong, 2007.

[GER 73] GERGEN K.J., "Social psychology as history", *Journal of Personality and Social Psychology*, vol. 26, pp. 309–320, 1973.

[GER 11] GERVAIS O., KOLET I., LALONDE R., "A larger slice of a growing pie: the role of emerging Asia in forecasting commodity prices", *Money Affairs*, vol. 23, no. 1, pp. 75–95, 2011.

[GIB 93] GIBB J., Benchmarking Conference, Auckland, New Zealand, December 1995.

[GIN 11] GINGLINGER E., MEGGINSON W., WAXIN T., "Employee ownership, board representation, and corporate financial policies", *Journal of Corporate Finance*, vol. 17, pp. 868–887, 2011.

[GOO 95] GOODHART C., SCHOENMAKER D., "Should the functions of monetary policy and banking supervision be separated?", *Oxford Economic Papers*, vol. 47, no. 4, pp. 539–560, 1995.

[GOR 98] GORTON G., WINTON A., "Banking in transition economies: does efficiency require instability?", *Journal of Money, Credit, and Banking*, vol. 30, no. 3, pp. 621–650, 1998.

[GOR 00] GORTON G., SCHMID F.A., "Universal banking and the performance of German firms", *Journal of Financial Economics*, vol. 58, nos. 1–2, pp. 29–80, 2000.

[GOR 02] GORTON G., WINTON A., Financial Intermediation, *NBER Working Paper Series*, no. 8928, 2002.

[GRA 06b] GRAIS W., PELLEGRINI M., Corporate governance in institutions offering Islamic financial services: issues and options, World Bank Policy Paper No. 4052, 2006.

[GRE 98] GREATBANKS R., BOADEN R., "Can SMEs afford to measure performance?", *Proceedings of the Performance Measurement – Theory and Practice Conference*, Cambridge, pp. 14–17, 1998.

[GRE 10] GREEN S., "Global perspective on Islamic finance", LSE–Harvard Public Lecture on Islamic Finance, 24 February 2010.

[GRO 80] GROSSMAN S., HART O., "Takeover bids, the free-rider problem and the theory of the corporation", *Bell Journal of Economics*, vol. 11, pp. 42–64, 1980.

[GRO 86] GROSSMAN S., SANFORD J., OLIVER D. *et al.*, "The costs and benefits of ownership: A theory of vertical and lateral integration", *Journal of Political Economy*, vol. 94, no. 4, pp. 691–71, 1986.

[GUA 99] GUAY W., "The impact of derivatives on firm risk: an empirical examination of new derivatives users", *Journal of Accounting Economics*, vol. 26, pp. 319–362, 1999.

[GUI 06] GUISO L., SAPIENZA P., ZINGALES L., "The cost of banking regulation", *NBER Working Paper Series*, no. 12501, 2006.

[GUP 11] GUPTA S, JAIN P.K., YADAV S., "Generating financial flexibility and financial performance through disinvestment: A comparative study of disinvested and non- disinvested public sector enterprise in India", *Global Journal of Flexible Systems Management*, vol. 12, pp. 1–2, 2011.

[HAM 01] HAMAT M., "Accounting system, needs for accounting standards and the implications of Islamic banking on the current tax laws", *Conference of Managing and Implementing Dual Banking System*, Kuala Lumpur, 2001.

[HAN 03] HANSON R.C., SONG M.H., "Long-term performance of diversting firms and the effect of managerial ownership", *JEAF*, vol. 27, pp. 321–336, 2003.

[HAR 13] HARRISON W.T., HORNGREN C.T., THOMAS C.W., *Financial Accounting*, Pearson, 2013.

[HAR 83] HART O., "Monopolistic competition in the spirit of chamberlain: a general model", STICERD - Theoretical Economics Paper Series no. 82, LSE, 1983.

[HAR 85] HART O., "Imperfect competition in general equilibrium: an overview of recent work", in ARROW K., HONKAPOHJA S. (eds), *Frontiers of Economics*, Blackwell, Oxford, 1985.

[HAR 89] HART O., "An economist's perspective on the theory of the firm", *Columbia Law Review*, vol. 89, no. 7, pp. 1757–1774, 1989.

[HAR 90] HART O., MOORE J., "Property rights and the nature of the firm", *Journal of Political Economy*, vol. 98, no. 6, pp. 1119–1158, 1990.

[HAR 95] HART O., MOORE J., "Debt and seniority: An analysis of the role of hard claims in constraining management", *American Economic Review*, vol. 85, no. 3, pp. 567–85, 1995.

[HAS 01] HASAN Z., "The 1997-98 financial crisis in Malaysia: causes, response", *Islamic Economic Studies*, vol. 9, no. 2, 2002.

[HAS 09] HASAN Z., "Corporate governance: western and Islamic perspectives", *International Review of Business Research Papers*, vol. 5, no. 1, pp. 277–29, 2009.

[HAS 86] HASANUZZAMAN S.M., "Definition of Islamic economics", *Journal for Research in Islamic Economics*, vol. 1, no. 2, pp. 51–53, 1986.

[HAU 89] HAUBRICH J.G., "Financial intermediation: delegated monitoring and long-term relationships", *Journal of Banking and Finance*, vol. 13, no. 1, pp. 9–20, 1989.

[HAW 96] HAWLEY J.P., WILLIAMS A.T., Corporate governance in the United States: the rise of fiduciary capitalism, Working paper, Saint Mary's College of California, School of Economics and Business Administration, 1996.

[HEF 05] HEFFERNAN S, *Modern Banking*, John Wiley & Sons, 2005.

[HER 03] HERMALIN B.E., WEISBACH, M.S., "Boards of directors as an endogenously determined institution: a survey of the economic literature", *Federal Reserve Bank of New York Economic Policy Review*, vol. 9, pp. 7–26, 2003.

[HIL 00] HILLMAN A.J., CANNELLA JR A.A., PAETZOLD R.L., "The resource dependence role of corporate directors: strategic adaptation of board composition in response to environmental change", *Journal of Management Studies*, vol. 37, no. 2, pp. 235–255, 2000.

[HIR 12] HIRSHLEIFER D., LOW A., HONG TEOH S., "Are overconfident CEOs better innovators?", *Journal of Finance*, vol. 67, no. 4, pp. 1457–1498, 2012.

[HOL 79] HOLMSTROM B., "Moral hazard and observability", *The Bell Journal of Economics*, vol. 10, no. 1, pp. 74–91, 1979.

[HOL 82] HOLMSTROM B., "Moral hazard in teams", *The Bell Journal of Economics*, vol. 13, no. 2, pp. 324–340, 1982.

[HOL 94] HOLMSTROM B., MILGROM P., "The firm as an incentive system", *American Economic Review*, vol. 84, no. 4, pp. 972–91, 1994.

[HOL 99] HOLMSTROM B., "Managerial incentive problems – a dynamic perspective", *Review of Economic Studies*, vol. 66, no. 1, pp. 169–182, 1999.

[HOO 03] HOOKER J., Why business ethics?, Working paper, Carnegie Mellon University, 2003.

[HUA 11] HUANG H.-H., CHAN M.-L., HUANG I. *et al.*, "Stock price volatility and overreaction in a political crisis: The effects of corporate governance and performance", *Pacific-Basin Finance Journal*, vol. 19, pp. 1–20, 2011.

[HUB 95] HUBBARD R.G., PALIA D., "Executive pay and performance evidence from the U.S. banking industry", *Journal of Financial Economics*, vol. 39, no. 1, pp. 105–130, 1995.

[HUS 01] HUSON M., PARRINO R., STARKS L., "International monitoring mechanisms and CEO turnover, a long term perspective", *Journal of Finance,* vol. 56, pp. 2265–2297, 2001.

[IFS 05b] ISLAMIC FINANCIAL SERVICES BOARD (IFSB), Guiding principles of risk management for institutions (other than insurance institutions) offering only Islamic financial services, Draft 1, IFSB, Kuala Lumpur, Malaysia, 2005.

[IMF 04] INTERNATIONAL MONETARY FUND (IMF), Compilation guide for Financial soundness indicators, Washington, DC, 2004.

[IQB 99] IQBAL Z., MIRAKHOR A., "Progress and challenges of Islamic banking", *Thunderbird International Business Review*, vol. 41, nos. 4–5, pp. 381–405, 1999.

[IQB 02] IQBAL Z., MIRAKHOR A., "Development of Islamic financial institutions and challenges ahead", in SIMON A. RIFAAT A.K. (eds), *Islamic Finance: Growth and Innovation*, Euromoney Books, 2002.

[IQB 04] IQBAL Z., MIRAKHOR A., "A stakeholders model of corporate governance of firm in islamic economic system", *Islamic Economic Studies*, vol. 11, pp. 43–63, 2004.

[IQB 05a] IQBAL Z., "Impact of consolidation on islamic financial services industry", *2nd International Conference on Challenges Facing the Islamic Financial Services Industry*, Tehran, Iran, 6–7 April, 2005.

[IQB 05b] IQBAL Z., TSUBOTA H., "Emerging Islamic markets", *The Euromoney International Debt Capital Markets Handbook*, London: Euromoney Publishing, 2005.

[IQB 07] IQBAL Z., MIRAKHOR A., *Introduction to Islamic Finance: Theory and Practice*, John Wiley & Sons, 2007.

[JAB 06] JABBARI A.N., "Capital adequacy standard for institutions offering Islamic financial services", *Islamic Financial Services Board 2nd International Research Conference on Islamic Banking: Risk Management, Regulation & Supervision,* Kuala Lumpur, 7–8 February, 2006.

[JEN 76] JENSEN M.C., MECKLING W., "Theory of the firm: managerial behavior, agency costs and capital structure", *Journal of Financial Economics*, vol. 3, pp. 305–360, 1976.

[JEN 83] JENSEN M., RUBACK R.S., "The market for corporate control: The scientific evidence", *Journal of Financial Economics*, vol. 11, nos. 1–4, pp. 5–50, 1983.

[JEN 86] JENSEN M.C., "Agency cost of free cash flow, corporate finance, and takeovers", *American Economic Review*, vol. 76, no. 2, 1986.

[JEN 90] JENSEN M.C., MURPHY K.J., "Performance pay and top-management incentives", *Journal of Political Economy*, vol. 98, pp. 225–264, 1990.

[JEN 93] JENSEN M.C., "The modern industrial revolution, exit, and the failure of internal control systems", *The Journal of Finance*, vol. 48, no. 3, pp. 831–880, 1993.

[JOH 98] JOHN K., SENBET L., "Corporate governance and board effectiveness", *Journal of Banking and Finance*, vol. 22, no. 4, pp. 371–403, 1998.

[JOH 96] JOHNSON J.L., DAILY C.M., ELLSTRAND A.E., "Board of directors: A review and research agenda", *Journal of Management*, vol. 22, pp. 409–438, 1996.

[JOH 00] JOHNSON S., LAPORTA R., LOPEZ-DE-SILANES F. *et al.*, "Tunneling", *The American Economic Review*, vol. 90, no. 2, pp. 22–27, 2000.

[JON 00] JONES S.D., SCHILLING D.J. *Measuring Team Performance*, Jossey-Bass, San Francisco, CA, 2000.

[JOR 04] JORDANA J., FAUR L.D. (eds.), *The Politics of Regulation: Institutions and Regulatory Reforms for the Governance Age*, Edward Elgar, 2004.

[KAH 99] KAHF M., "Islamic Banks at the threshold of the third Millennium", *Thunderbird International Business Review*, vol. 41, nos. 4–5, pp. 445–60, 1999.

[KAN 12a] KANG Y.-S., KIM B.-Y., "Ownership structure and firm performance: Evidence from the Chinese corporate reform", *China Economic Review*, 2012.

[KAN 12b] KANG Y.-S., KIM J.M., GUOJUN Ch. *et al.*, *Sources of Value Gains in Minority Equity Investments by Private Equity Funds: Evidence from Block Share Acquisitions*. Asian Finance Association Conference, Taipei, Taiwan, July 2012.

[KAP 92] KAPLAN R.S., NORTON D.P., "The balanced scorecard – measures that drive performance", *Harvard Business Review*, vol. January-February, pp. 71–79, 1992.

[KAP 96] KAPLAN R.S., NORTON D.P., "Using the balanced scorecard as a strategic management system", *Harvard Business Review*, vol. January-February, pp. 75–85, 1996.

[KAP 01] KAPLAN R.S., NORTON D. P., *The Strategy-focused Organization,* Harvard Business School Press, 2001.

[KEA 93] KEASEY K., WRIGHT M., "Issues in corporate accountability and governance", *Accounting and Business Research*, vol. 23, pp. 291–303, 1993.

[KEE 89] KEEGAN D.P., EILER R.G., JONES C.R., "Are your performance measures obsolete?", *Management Accounting*, pp. 45–50, June 1989.

[KES 86] KESNER I., DALTON D., "Boards of directors and the checks and (im)balances of corporate governance, *Business Horizons*, vol. 29, no. 5, pp. 17–23, 1986.

[KHA 87] KHAN M.F., "Islamic interest-free banking: a theoretical analysis", in KHAN, M. (ed.), *Theoretical Studies in Islamic Banking and Finance*, IRIS Books, 1987.

[KHA 94] KHAN M.F., "Comparative economics of some Islamic financing techniques", *Islamic Economic Studies*, vol. 2, pp. 81–102, 1994.

[KHO 04] KHORSHID A., *Islamic Insurance: A Modern Approach to Islamic Banking*, Routledge Curzon, 2004.

[KIN 93] KING R.G., LEVINE R., "Finance and growth: Schumpeter might be right", *The Quarterly Journal of Economics*, vol. 108, no. 3. pp. 717–737, 1993.

[KIN 08] KINKKI S., "Minority protection and dividend policy in Finland", *European Financial Management*, vol. 14, no. 3, pp 470–502, 2008.

[KLA 04] KLAPPER L., LOVE I., "Corporate governance, investor protection, and performance in emerging markets", *Journal of Corporate Finance*, vol. 10, no. 5, pp. 703–723, 2004.

[KNO 86] KNOEBER C., "Golden parachutes, shark repellents and hostile tender offers", *American Economy Review*, vol. 77, pp. 155–167, 1986.

[KOB 02] KOBRIN J.S., "Economic governance in an electronically networked global economy", in HALL R.B., BIERSTEKER T.J. (eds), *The Emergence of Private Authority in Global Governance*, Cambridge University Press, 2002.

[KOP 08] KOPPARUPU S.K., IONNASIS A., *Financial Risk Management for Islamic Banking and Finance*, Palgrave Macmillan, 2008.

[KOS 98] KOSE J., SENBET L.W., "Corporate governance and board effectiveness", *Journal of Banking & Finance*, vol. 22, pp. 371–403, 1998.

[LA 98] LA PORTA R., LOPEZ-DE-SILANES F., SHLEIFER A. *et al.*, "Law and finance", *Journal of Political Economy*, vol. 106, pp. 1113–1155, 1998.

[LA 99] LA PORTA R., LOPEZ-DE-SILANES F., SHLEIFER A. *et al.*, "Corporate ownership around the world", *Journal of Finance*, vol. 54, pp. 471–517, 1999.

[LA 00] LA PORTA R., LOPEZ-DE-SILANES F., SHLEIFER A. *et al.*, "Investor protection and corporate valuation", *Journal of Financial Economics*, vol. 57, pp. 1147–1170, 2000.

[LA 02] LA PORTA R., LOPEZ-DE-SILANES F., SHLEIFER A., "Government ownership of banks", *Journal of Finance*, vol. 57, pp. 265–301, 2002.

[LAN 89] LANG L.H.P., LITZENBERGER R.H., "Dividend announcements", *The Journal of Financial Economics*, vol. 24, p. 181–191, 1989.

[LAR 11] LARCKER D.F., ORMAZABAL G., TAYLOR D.J., "The market reaction to corporate governance regulation", *Journal of Financial Economics*, vol. 101, pp. 431–448, 2011.

[LAU 02] LAUSTEN M., "CEO turnover, firm performance and corporate governance: Empirical evidence on Danish firms", *International Journal of Industrial Organization,* vol. 20, no. 3, pp. 391–414, 2002.

[LEF 08] LEFORT F., URZÚA F., "Board independence, firm performance and ownership concentration: evidence from Chile", *Journal of Business Research*, vol. 61, pp. 615–622, 2008.

[LEL 11] LEL U., "Currency hedging and corporate governance: A cross-country analysis", *Journal of Corporate Finance*, vol. 18, pp. 221–237, 2011.

[LEM 03] LEMMON M.L., LINS K.V., "Ownership structure, corporate governance, and firm value: evidence from the East Asian financial crisis", *Journal of Finance*, vol. 58, pp. 1445–1468, 2003.

[LEV 97] LEVINE R., "Financial development and economic growth: Views and agenda", *Journal of Economic Literature*, vol. 35, pp. 688–726, 1997.

[LEV 04] LEVINE R., The corporate governance of banks: a concise discussion of concepts and evidence, Working paper no. 3404, World Bank Policy Research, 2004.

[LEV 05] LEVINE R., "Finance and Growth: Theory and Evidence", in *Handbook of Economic Growth,* PHILIPPE A., STEVEN N. (eds), Elsevier, 2005.

[LEV 12] LEVY A., *Islamic Finance, Toward a Humanist Finance* (in Arabic), Gualino Lextenso Editions, 2012.

[LEV 15a] LEVY A., REZGUI H., "Structuring risk and solvency ratio Basel, adaptation to Islamic finance, a study of the ratio of the IFSB to a bank of Bahrain", *AFC Congress*, Montreal, Canada, 2015.

[LEV 15b] LEVY A., REZGUI H., "When international finance revalues the human in its governance, the case of Islamic finance and its ethical Committees, an application to the Bahrain Islamic Bank", in *Normative Dynamics: Arbitrate, Negotiate Instead of Standard in Organizations*, EMS Editor, 2015.

[LEV 16] LEVY A., *Islamic Finance, Authorized and Prohibited Financial Transactions* (in Arabic), Crossroads, Casablanca, Morocco, 2016.

[LEW 01] LEWIS M., "Dumb and getting dumber", *Credit Union Magazine*, Savingteen Supplement, January 2001.

[LIN 09] LIN C., YUE M., SU D., "Corporate governance and firm efficiency: evidence from china's publicly listed firms", *Managerial and Decision Economics*, vol. 30, pp. 193–209, 2009.

[LIN 11] LIN C., YUE M., MALATESTA P., "Ownership structure and the cost of corporate borrowing", *Journal of Financial Economics*, vol. 100, pp. 1–23, 2011.

[LIN 65] LINTER J., "The valuation of risk assets and the selection of risky investments in stock portfolios and capital budget", *The Review of Economics and Statistics,* vol. 47, no. 1, pp. 13–37, February 1965.

[LIP 92] LIPTON M., LORSCH J., A modest Proposal for Corporate Governance, *Business Lawyer*, vol. 48, no. 1, pp. 59–77, 1992.

[LIP 92] LIPTON M., LORSCH J.W., "A modest proposal for improved corporate governance", *Business Lawyer*, vol. 48, pp. 59–77, 1992.

[LIU 08] LIU Y., TAFFER R., "Damned out of their own mouths: CEO overconfidence on M&A decision making and its impact on firm performance", Working paper, University of Edinburgh, 2008.

[LLE 01] LLEWELLYN C., *Listrik. Mengenal Limu Energi*, Grolier International Inc., London, 2001.

[LOC 94] LOCKAMY A., COX J.F., *Reengineering Performance Measurement: How to Align Systems to Improve Processes, Products, and Profits*, Irwin Professional Pub, 1994.

[LOR 11] LORENZO C., CROCI E., DEL GIUDICE A., "Ownership structure, family control, and acquisition decisions", *Journal of Corporate Finance*, vol. 17, pp. 1636–1657, 2011.

[LYN 91] LYNCH R.L., CROSS K.F., *Measure Up – The Essential Guide to Measuring Business Performance*, Mandarin, London, 1991.

[MAC 71] MACE M.L., *Directors: Myth and Reality*, Harvard Business School Press, Boston, 1971.

[MAC 03] MACEY J., O'HARA M., "The corporate governance of banks", *FRBNY Economic Policy Review*, April, pp. 91-107, 2003.

[MAK 94] MAK Y.T., ROUSH M.L., "Flexible budgeting and variance analysis in an activity-based costing environment", *Accounting Horizons*, vol. 8, pp. 93–103, 1994

[MAL 05] MALMENDIER U., TATE G., "CEO overconfidence and corporate investment", *Journal of Finance*, vol. 60, pp. 2661–2700, 2005.

[MAL 08] MALMENDIER U., TATE G., "Who makes acquisitions? CEO overconfidence and the market's reaction", *Journal of Financial Economics*, vol. 89, pp. 20–43, 2008.

[MAS 91] MASKELL B.H., *Performance Measurement for World Class Manufacturing Model for American Companies*, Productivity Press, 1991.

[MAY 98] MAYER C., "New issues in corporate finance", *European Economic Review*, vol. 32, pp. 1167–1183, 1998.

[MCA 02] MCADAM R., BAILIE B., "Business performance measures and alignment impact on strategy-the role of business improvement models", *International Journal of Operations and Production Management*, vol. 22, nos. 9–10, pp. 972–996, 2002.

[MCC 90] MCCONNELL J., SERVAES H., "Additional evidence on equity ownership and corporate value", *Journal of Financial Economics*, vol. 27, no. 2, pp. 595–612, 1990.

[MCM 08] MCMILLEN M.J.T., "*Shariah*-compliant project finance: an overview including structures", *Journal of Islamic Economics*, October 2008.

[MEE 95] MEEKING A., "Unlocking the potential of performance measurement: a guide to pratical implementation", *Public Money Management*, vol. 15, pp. 5–12, 1995.

[MER 87] MERTON R.C., "A Simple Model of capital market equilibrium with Incomplete Information", *Journal of Finance*, vol. 42, pp. 483–510, 1987.

[MET 05] METAWIE M., GILMAN M., "Problems with the implementation of performance measurement systems in the public sector where performance is linked to pay: a literature review drawn from the UK", *3rd Conference on Performance Measurements and Management Control*, Nice, 2005.

[MEU 01] MEULBROEK L.K., "The efficiency of equity-linked compensation: Understanding the full cost of awarding executive stock options", *Financial Management*, vol. 30, no. 2, pp. 5–44, 2001.

[MIL 63] MILGRAM S., "Behavioral study of obedience", *Journal of Abnormal and Social Psychology*, vol. 67, pp. 371–378, 1963.

[MIL 74] MILGRAM S., *Obedience to Authority: An Experimental View*, Harper and Row, 1974.

[MIN 10] MINTON B.A., JÉRÔME P.A. ROHAN W. *et al.*, "Board composition, risk taking and value: Evidence from financial firms", *SSRN Electronic Journal*, available at: https://www.eurofidai.org/Taillard_2010.pdf, 2010.

[MIR 76] MIRRLEES J.A., "Optimal tax theory: A synthesis", *Journal of Public Economics*, vol. 6, no. 4, pp. 327–358, 1976.

[MIT 02] MITTON T., "A cross-firm analysis of the impact of corporate governance on the East Asian financial crisis", *Journal of Financial Economics*, vol. 64, no. 2, pp. 215–241, 2002.

[MOL 15] MOLLAH S., ZAMAN M., "Shari'ah supervision, corporate governance and performance: Conventional vs. Islamic banks", *Journal of Banking & Finance*, vol. 58, pp. 418–435, 2015.

[MOR 07] MORCK R., "Behavioral finance in corporate governance – independent directors, non-executive chairs, and the importance of the devil's advocate", NBER Working paper no. 10644, 2007.

[MOR 02] MORGAN D., "Risk competence and adventure tourists: applying the adventure experience paradigm to white-water rafters", *Leisure*, vol. 26, nos. 1–2, pp. 107-127, 2002.

[MOS 93] MOSENG B., BREDRUP H., "A methodology for industrial studies of productivity performance", *Production Planning & Control*, vol. 4, no. 3, pp. 198–206, 1993.

[MOU 02] MOULLIN M., *Delivering Excellence in Health and Social Care: Quality Excellence and Performance Measurement*, Open University Press, 2002.

[MOU 05] MOULLIN M., "Performance measurement definitions: linking performance measurement and organisational excellence", *International Journal of Health Care Quality Assurance*, vol. 20, pp. 181–183, 2005.

[MUE 06] MUELLER E., SPITZ-OENER A., "Managerial ownership and company performance in german small and medium-sized private enterprises", *German Economic Review*, vol. 7, no. 5, pp. 233–247, 2016.

[MUN 07] MUNIANDY B., "CEO duality, audit committee effectiveness and audit risks: a study of Malaysian market", *Managerial Auditing Journal*, vol. 22 , no. 7, pp. 716–728, 2007.

[MYE 77] MYERS S.C., "Determinants of corporate borrowing", *Journal of Financial Economics*, vol. 5, pp. 147–175, 1977.

[NAM 04] NAM S.-W., Corporate governance of banks: Review of issues, Report, Asian Development Bank Institute, 2004.

[NAN 92] NANNI A.J., DIXON J.R., VOLLMAN T.E., "Integrated performance measurement: management accounting to support the new manufacturing realities", *Journal of Management Accounting Research*, vol. 4, pp. 1–19, 1992.

[NEE 94] NEELY A.D., MILLS J.F., RICHARDS A.H. *et al.*, "Realising strategy through measurement", *International Journal Oper. Prod. Man.*, vol. 14, pp. 140–152, 1994.

[NEE 02a] NEELY A.D., ADAMS C., KENNERLEY M., *The Performance Prism- The Scorecard for Measuring and Managing Business Success*, Pearson Education, 2002

[NEE 02b] NEELY A.D., MILLS J.F., RICHARDS A.H. *et al.*, *Getting the Measure of Your Business*, Cambridge University Press, 2002.

[NEE 02c] NEELY A.D., *Business Performance Measurement: Theory and Practice,* Cambridge University Press, 2002.

[NIC 97] NICKELL S.J., "Unemployment and labor market rigidities: Europe vs North America", *Journal of Economic Perspectives*, vol. 11, no. 3, pp. 55–74, 1997.

[OCA 94] OCASIO W., "Political dynamics and the circulation of power: CEO succession in U.S. industrial corporations, 1960–1990", *Administrative Science Quarterly*, vol. 39, pp. 285–312, 1994.

[OCO 11] O'CONNELL V., CRAMER N., "The relationship between firms performances characteristic in Ireland", *European Management Journal*, vol. 28, pp. 387–399, 2011.

[OEC 16] OECD (Organization for Economic Co-Operation and Development), G20/OECD Principles of Corporate Governance 2015, Report, March 2016.

[OZD 11] OZDEMIRA O., UPNEJA A., "Board structure and CEO compensation: Evidence from U.S. lodging industry", *International Journal of Hospitality Management*, vol. 31, pp. 856–863, 2011.

[PAR 04] PAREDES T.A., "Too much pay, too much deference: Behavioral corporate finance, CEOs, and corporate governance", *Florida State University Law Review*, vol. 32, p. 673, 2004.

[PAR 97] PARRINO J.D., "Spin-offs and wealth transfer: The Marriot case", *Journal of Financial Economics*, vol. 43, pp. 241–274, 1997.

[PAR 94] PARTOVI F., "Determining what to benchmark: an analytic hierarchy process approach", *International Journal of Operations and Production Management*, vol. 14, no. 6, pp. 25–39, 1994.

[PAS 00] PASS C., LOWES B., DAVIES L. (eds), *Collins Dictionary of Economics*, Collins, 2000.

[PEA 05] PEASNELL K.V., POPE P.F., YOUNG S., "Board monitoring and earnings management: do outside directors influence abnormal accruals?", *Journal of Business Finance & Accounting*, vol. 32, pp. 1311–46, 2005.

[PLE 12] PLENBORG T., PETERSEN C., *Financial Statement Analysis: Valuation-Credit Analysis- Executive Compensation*, Pearson Education, 2012.

[PLI 15] PLIHON D., La régulation financière doit dépasser les frontières, available at: www.humanite.fr/dominique-plihon-la-regulation-financiere-doit-depasser-les-frontieres-565187, 2015.

[POL 07] POLO A., "Corporate governance of banks: the current state of the debate", MPRA Paper No. 2325, 2007.

[PRA 05] PRATT D., *The Challenge of Islam: Encounters in Interfaith Dialogue*, Ashgate Publishing Limited, 2005.

[PRI 11] PRICE R., ROMA F.J., ROUNTREE B., "The impact of governance reform on performance and transparency", *Journal of Financial Economics 99*, 2011.

[PRO 97a] PROWSE S.D., "Institutional investment patterns and corporate financial behavior in the U.S. and Japan", *Journal of Financial Economics*, vol. 27, pp. 43–66, 1997.

[PRO 97b] PROWSE S.D., "Corporate control in commercial banks", *Journal of Financial Research*, vol. 20, no. 4, pp. 509–527, 1997.

[RAJ 92] RAJAN G.R., "Insiders and outsiders: The choice between informed and arm's-length debt", *Journal of Finance*, vol. 47, no. 4, pp. 1367–1400, 1992.

[REC 89] RECHNER P., DALTON D., "The impact of CEO as board chairperson on corporate governance: evidence vs rhetoric", *Academy of Management Executive*, vol. 3, pp. 141–143, 1989.

[ROB 00] ROBERTS, J., VAN DEN STEEN E., Shareholder interests, human capital investments and corporate governance, Working paper no. 1631, Stanford University Graduate School of Business, 2000.

[ROE 94] ROE M., The institutions of corporate governance, Discussion Paper No. 488, Harvard John M. Olin Discussion Paper Series, 1994.

[ROS 73] ROSS S.A., "The economic theory of agency: the principal's problem", *American Economic Review*, vol. 63, no. 2, pp. 134–139, 1973.

[ROT 08] ROTHBARD M.N., *The Mystery of Banking*, The Ludwig von Mises Institute, 2008.

[RUG 83] RUGGIE J., "Continuity and transformation in the world polity: toward a neorealist synthesis", *World Politics*, vol. 35, pp. 261–285, 1983.

[SAF 09] SAFIEDDINE A., "Islamic financial institutions and corporate governance: New insights for agency theory", *Corporate Governance: An International Review*, vol. 17, pp. 142–158, 2009.

[SAI 08] SAITO O., *Hikaku Keizai hatten ron (Comparative Economic Development Theory)*, Iwanami Shoten, 2008.

[SAN 07] SANTIAGO-CASTRO M., BROWN C.J., "Ownership structure and minority rights: A Latin American view", *Journal of Economics and Business*, vol. 59, pp. 430–442, 2007.

[SAN 97] SANTOMERO A., "The theory of financial intermediation", *Journal of Banking and Finance*, vol. 21, pp. 1461–1485, 1997.

[SCH 88] SCHARFSTEIN D., "The disciplinary role of takeovers", *Review of Economic Studies*, vol. 55, pp. 185–199, 1988.

[SCH 99] SCHNEIDERMAN A., "Why balanced scorecards fail", *Journal of Strategy Performance Measure*, vol. 6, pp. 6–1, 1999.

[SCH 95] SCHNITZER M., "Breach of trust in takeovers and the corporate charter", *Journal of Industrial Economics*, vol. 43, no. 3, pp. 229–260, 1995.

[SEW 05] SEWELL W., *Logics of History: Social Theory and Social Transformation*, The University of Chicago Press, Chicago, 2005.

[SHA 09] SHANMUGAM B., ZAHARI Z.R., "A primer on Islamic finance", *Research Foundation Publications, CFA Institute*, November, pp. 1–121, 2009.

[SHA 74] SHAPIRO A., "Exchange rate changes, innovation and the value of the multinational corporation", *Journal of Finance*, vol. 30, pp. 485–502, 1974.

[SHA 04] SHARMA P., "An overview of the field of family business studies: Current status and directions for the future", *Family Business Review*, vol. 17, pp. 1–36, 2004.

[SHI 03] SHILLER R., "From efficient markets theory to behavioral finance", *The Journal of Economic Perspectives*, vol. 17, no. 1, pp. 83–104, 2003.

[SHL 86a] SHLEIFER A., VISHNY R.W., "Greenmail, white knights, and shareholder's interest", *Rand Journal of Economics*, vol. 17, pp. 293–309, 1986.

[SHL 86b] SHLEIFER A., VISHNY R.W., "Large shareholders and corporate control", *Journal of Political Economy*, vol. 94, pp. 461–488, 1986.

[SHL 88] SHLEIFER A., SUMMERS L., "Breach of trust in hostile takeovers", in AUERBACH A.J. (ed.), *Corporate Takeovers: Causes and Consequence*, University of Chicago Press, Chicago, 1988.

[SHL 89] SHLEIFER A., VISHNY R.W., "Management entrenchment: The case of manager-specific investments", *Journal of Financial Economics*, vol. 25, pp. 123–140, 1989.

[SHL 94] SHLEIFER A., VISHNY R.W., "Politicians and firms", *Quarterly Journal of Economics*, vol. 109, pp. 995–1025, 1994.

[SHL 97] SHLEIFER A., VISHNY R.W., "A survey of corporate governance", *Journal of Finance*, vol. 52, pp. 737–783, 1997.

[SHL 99] SHLEIFER A., "Family firms", *Journal of Finance*, vol. 58, no. 5, pp. 2173–207, 1999.

[SIA 06] SIAS R.W., STARKS L.T., "Changes in institutional ownership and stock returns: assessment and methodology", *The Journal of Business*, vol. 79, no. 6, pp. 2869–2910, 2006.

[SID 04] SIDDIQI M.N., "Wealth of Muslim nations", available at: www.siddiqi.com/mns/, 2004.

[SID 07] SIDDIQI M.N., "An approach to Islamic economics", available at: www.siddiqi.com/mns/, 2007.

[SIG 01] SIGLER K.J., PORTERFIELD R., "CEO compensation: Its link to bank performance", *American Business Review*, vol. 19, pp. 110–114, 2001.

[SIM 99] SIMPSON W.G., GLEASON A.E., "Board structure, ownership, and financial distress in banking firms", *International Review of Economics and Finance*, vol. 8, pp. 281–292, 1999.

[SIM 02] SIMPSON W.G., KOHERS T., "The link between corporate social and financial performance", *Journal of Business Ethics*, vol. 35, pp. 97–109, 2002.

[SIN 86] SINK P.E., "Performance and productivity measurement: the art of developing creative score boards", *Industrial Engineer*, pp. 86–90, January 1986.

[SIN 89] SINK D.S., TUTTLE T.C., *Planning and Measurement in Your Organization of the Future*, Industrial Engineering and Management Press, 1989.

[SKI 71a] SKINNER W., "The decline, fall and renewal of manufacturing", *Industrial Engineering*, pp. 32–38, October 1971.

[SKI 71b] SKINNER W., "The anachronistic factory", *Harvard Business Review*, vol. 49, pp. 61–70, 1971.

[SOI 98] SOIT N., *Measuring Business Performance*, Profile Books, London, 1998.

[STA 95] STAVINS R.N., "Transaction costs and tradeable permits", *Journal of Environmental Economics and Management*, vol. 29, no. 2, pp. 133–148, 1995.

[STE 98] STERNBERG E., *Corporate Governance: Accountability in the Marketplace*, Institute of Economic Affairs, London, 1998.

[STI 75] STIGLITZ J.E., "The theory of "screening", education, and distribution of income", *American Economic Review*, vol. 65, pp. 283–300, 1975.

[SUN 04] SUNDARAM A.K., INKPEN A.C., "Stakeholder theory: the corporate objective revisited", *Organization Science*, vol. 15, no. 3, pp. 370–371, 2004.

[THO 00] THOMSEN S., PEDERSEN T., "Ownership structure and economic performance in the largest European countries", *Strategy Management Journal*, vol. 21, pp. 689–705, 2000.

[THO 06] THOMSEN S., PEDERSEN T., KVIST H.K., "Blockholder ownership: Effects on firm value in market and control based governance systems", *Journal of Corporate Finance*, vol. 2, pp. 246–269, 2006.

[THO 16] THOMSON R., Canada Islamic finance: Outlook 2016, Report, Toronto Financial Services Alliance and Islamic Finance Gateway, 2016.

[TOB 69] TOBIN J., "A general equilibrium approach to monetary theory", *Journal of Money, Credit and Banking*, vol. 1, no. 1, pp. 15–29, 1969.

[USM 98] USMANI M.T., *An Introduction to Islamic Finance*, Idarutul Ma'arif, Karachi,1998.

[VAN 08] VAN GREUNING H., IQBAL Z., *Risk Analysis for Islamic Banks*, The World Bank, 2008

[VAN 09] VAN GREUNING H., BRATANOVIC, S., Analyzing and managing banking risk: a framework for assessing corporate governance and financial risk management, Document No. 20043, The World Bank, 2009

[VEN 86] VENKATRAMAN N., RAMANUJAM V., "Measurement of business performance in strategy research: A comparison of approaches, *Academy of Management Review*, vol. 11, pp. 801–814, 1986.

[VIS 09] VISSER H., *Islamic Finance: Principles And Practice*, Edward Elgar, 2009.

[WEI 88] WEISBACH M.S., "Outside directors and CEO turnover", *Journal of Financial Economics*, vol. 20, pp. 431–460, 1988.

[WEL 98] WELLS M.T., "Larger board size and decreasing firm value in small firms", *Journal of Financial Economics*, vol. 48, no. 1, pp. 35–54, 1998.

[WES 99] WESTPHAL J.D., "Collaboration in the boardroom: Behavioral and performance consequences of CEO board social ties", *Academy of Management Journal*, vol. 42, no. 1, pp. 7–24, 1999.

[WES 06] WESTPHAL J.D., STERN I., "The other pathway to the boardroom: Interpersonal influence behavior as a substitute for elite credentials and majority status in obtaining board appointments", *Administrative Science Quarterly*, vol. 51, pp. 169–204, 2006.

[WES 07] WESTPHAL J.D., STERN I., "Flattery will get you everywhere (especially if you are a male Caucasian): How ingratiation, boardroom behavior, and demographic minority status affect additional board appointments at U.S. companies", *Academy of Management Journal*, vol. 50, pp. 267–288, 2007.

[WHE 03] WHEELER D., COLBERT B., FREEMAN R.E., "Focusing on value: reconciling corporate social responsibility, sustanibility and a stakeholder approach in a network world", *Journal of General Management*, vol. 28, pp. 1–28, 2003.

[WIL 83] WILLIAMSON O.E., "Technology and the organization of work: A reply to Jones", *Journal of Economic Behavior & Organization*, vol. 4, no. 1, pp. 57–62, 1983.

[WIL 96] WILLIAMSON O., *The Mechanisms of Governance*, Oxford University Press, Oxford, 1996.

[WRI 96] WRIGHT P., STEPHEN P., FERRIS P. *et al.*, "Impact of corporate insider, blockholder, and institutional equity ownership on firm risk taking", *Academy of Management Journal*, vol. 39, pp. 441–463, 1996.

[WRI 05] WRIGHT M., LOCKETT A. "Resources, capabilities, risk capital and the creation of university spin-out companies", *Research Policy*, vol. 34, no. 7, pp. 1043–1057, 2005.

[YAQ 00] YAQOUBI M., "The modern religion", *Q News: The Muslim Magazine*, issue 326, January 2000.

[YEH 07] YEH Y.H., LEE T.S., SHU P.G., "The agency problems embedded in firm's equity investment", *Journal of Business Ethics*, vol. 79, pp. 151–166, 2008.

[YER 96] YERMACK D., "Good timing: CEO stock option awards and company news announcements", *Journal of Finance*, vol. 52, pp. 449–476, 1996.

[YIX 11] YIXIANG T., *The Econometrics of Financial Markets*, Chinese Market Press, 2011.

[YUN 07] YUNIS H., *Legal Risks and Good Governance for the Islamic Finance Industry*, Taylor Wessing, 2007.

[ZAH 01] ZAHER T., HASSAN M.K., "A comparative literature survey of Islamic finance and banking", *Financial Markets, Institutions and Instrument*, vol. 10, no. 4, pp. 155–199, 2001.

[ZEN 91] ZENDER J.F., "Optimal financial instruments", *The Journal of Finance*, vol. 64, no. 5, 1991.

[ZER 80] ZERBE R.O., "The problem of social cost in retrospect", *Research in Law and Economics*, vol. 2, pp. 83–102, 1980.

[ZIG 98] ZIGON J., *How to Measure Employee Performance*, Zigon Performance Group, 1998.

[ZIN 94] ZINGALES L., "The value of the voting right: a study of the Milan stock exchange experience", *Review of Financial Studies*, vol. 7, pp. 125–148, 1994.

[ZIN 98] ZINGALES. L., "Corporate governance", in NEWMAN, P. (ed.), *The New Palgrave Dictionary of Economics and the Law*, Palgrave Macmillan, 1998.

[ZUL 09] ZULKIFLI H., "Corporate governance: Western and Islamic perspectives", *International Review of Business Research Papers*, vol. 5 no. 1, pp. 277–29, 2009.

Glossary

The most common terms in Islamic finance.

Al ajr	Commission fees or remuneration for services billed.
Al Rahn	Agreement under which an asset is used as collateral for a debt. The guarantee can be used in case of failure.
Al Wadia	Resale of goods at a discount to the originally quoted price.
Amana or Amanah	(Reliability, loyalty, honesty). The term refers to escrows. A person may hold property for the account of others, sometimes under a contract.
Arboum	Deposit paid at the signing of a contract. If the buyer fails the seller retains the deposit.
Baï	Contract, commercial, etc.
Baï al-arboun	Sales contract under which a deposit is made in advance in partial settlement of the price of raw materials purchased. This deposit is kept if the buyer does not meet its obligations.
Bai al Dayn	Debt financing: provision of financial resources for the production, trade and services in the form of sale/purchase of business documents. The *bai al dayn* is a short-term facility with a maturity not exceeding one year. Only documents representing debts arising from business transactions in good faith can be negotiated.
Baï as salamm or Salam	Acquisition by the Islamic Bank of property on behalf of a client and then resale it pays in installments. This is a leaseback in conventional finance. Contract for the pre-payment for goods delivered subsequently. No sale is possible if the goods did not exist at the time the contract but this type of sale, which is an exception, is permitted provided that the goods are defined and the delivery date. This type of sale

	generally on physical assets, excluding gold and silver, which are considered monetary values.
Baï bithaman ajil	Sales contract with deferred payment of goods. The bank buys capital goods or goods requested by the customer and then sells it at an agreed price, with a profit margin. The customer can pay in installments over a set period, or in a single payment. This contract is similar to Murabaha contract but with deferred payment.
Baï mouajal	Acquisition by the Islamic Bank of property on behalf of a client and then resale it for deferred payment. This is a term sale in conventional finance. Specifically this contract provides for the sale of goods with deferred payment. The bank or money lessor buys the goods (assets) on behalf of the company. The bank then sells the goods to the customer at an agreed price, plus a profit margin. The company can pay the total balance at an agreed future date or make payments over a set period. This contract is similar to murabaha contract in the sense that it is also a credit sale.
Baitul mal	Cash.
Card hassan	Interest free but cost coverage by the borrower. In conventional finance would be called a mutual loan.
Darura	Principle that "necessity knows no law" which allows to adapt the old requirements to the needs of the 21st Century.
Fatwa	Opinion, answer a religious decree Ulema (expert Sunna) or a committee of Shariah, guardians of the strict observance of Sharia.
Fiqh	Islamic jurisprudence for the religious life and practice. This is an important source of the economy and Islamic finance.
Gharar	(Risky, uncertain) This is one of three fundamental prohibitions in Islamic finance, with riba and maysir. Gharar is a complex concept that covers certain types of uncertainty or contingency related to a contract. The Gharar ban often serves as a basis for criticism of conventional financial practices such as short selling, speculation and derivatives.
Hadit	Oral transmission that complements the writings of the Koran. Tradition relating to deeds, words and attitudes of the Prophet.
Halal	Authorized.
Haram	Forbidden (*Harem* comes from the same root).
Hawala	Trade bill (of exchange, promissory note, check or draft). The debtor transfers the responsibility for payment of its debt to a third party who is himself his debtor. The responsibility for payment and ultimate responsibility to a third party. The hawala allows the settlement of international accounts by accounting transfers. It removes a great extent the need for physical transfer of cash.

Ijara Agreement under which the bank buys an item for a customer and then leases it for a specified period.

Ijara wa ictina Agreement under which the bank buys an item for a customer and then leases it under finance leases for a specific period but the customer has the option to acquire the property at the end of the contract. It's a classic leasing finance mode.

Ijma Consensus. Generally understood that Ulema specialist field.

Ijtihad Comments and interpretations of Sharia.

Istina Progressive Funding: purchase agreement of property with progressive payment of the price as and when the property is built. Akin to outsourcing.

Jou halal Price stipulated for the supply of a service. This term is sometimes used in a technical sense in the model of Islamic banking.

Koran (Read) contains writings as chapters (suras) and verses (ayats) of Revelation.

Maysir Prohibited pure chance. One of three fundamental prohibitions in Islamic finance, with riba and Gharar. In a game of chance one wins and the other loses. But if everyone wins or loses together or by good fortune that a bettor wins a lot but in case of bad draw he owes nothing is tolerated. The maysir is the basis for rejection of speculation, derivatives, conventional insurance and non real economy.

Moucharaca From *Chirca*, which means participation or association. This is an equity investment, where profit sharing is proportional to the amount invested. The moucharics therefore participate in the capital and management. It is a kind of co-financing. It is a form of risk capital.

Moudaraba Investment Partnership where capital is fully contributed by the bank rab-el-mal and project management is provided by the other mudarib the rass-el-mal. The profit is distributed out of contract in a breakdown previously set but the losses are supported only by the investor.

Moudarib Partner manager, entrepreneur in a mudaraba.

Mourabaha Installment sale contract where a party makes a contribution in industry (competence, intangible assets, etc.) and the other financial capital contribution.
This allows to acquire property without a loan bearing interest. Widely used in micro credit.

Ouléma Expert to take position to judge whether a transaction is legal or not, based on Sharia.

Rab-al-mal A person who invests capital in a mudaraba contract.

Riba Increase, addition. This is one of the fundamental prohibitions in Islamic finance, with gharar and maysir.

	Predetermined fixed interest charged whatever the result of the project. All rates of return without risk or guaranteed a loan or investment reports to the riba. There is talk of wear but this is a misnomer because it would make lawful interest served at the normal rate.
Salam	Deferred delivery contract, but paid in advance.
Sanii	Subcontractor in a Istisna contract.
Sharia	Literally order, prescribe. All laws and rules from the Quran and Sunna, body of law in Islam.
Sharia Board	*Religious Compliance Committee*, composed of Islamic scholars, advising on compliance with Shariah Islamic financial institutions for their activities, operations or financial arrangements.
Soukouk	Specific obligations that the investor finances a tangible asset side or not, as participation, investment certificates, the cash flows will be stable over a period. The Sukuk is a commercial paper which gives the investor the underlying part ownership and income attached. Funds are transferred to an ad hoc company which makes investments and collects revenues and then transfers to investors who enjoy the usufruct of these assets in proportion to their investment. They usually bear the risk of the issuer's credit rather than the actual risk of the assets held by special purpose entity. The sukuk are rated and graded on the target market but it is not mandatory. The Sukuk are typically issued by companies, some financial institutions and states (Bahrain, Malaysia, Pakistan, etc.).
Souna	Literally custom or usage. Which restores all the words and deeds of the Prophet's life. All the customs of Muslims. It complements the Koran.
Tacafoul	Islamic Sharia-compliant insurance, so to mutual or cooperative form with pooling of funds. In tacafoul system, members are both insurers and insured. Traditional insurance is prohibited in Islam because it contains several prohibited items such as Haram gharar and riba.
Tawarouc	Reverse *murabaha.*
Wad	Pledge.
Wadiah	Contractual arrangement deposit account management or savings.
Zacat	Tax on property of individuals based on charity or wealth. This is one of the 5 pillars of Islam.

Index

L, M, N

O, P, Q, R

S, T, U, V

Other titles from

ISTE

in

Innovation, Entrepreneurship and Management

2016

BARBAROUX Pierre, ATTOUR Amel, SCHENK Eric
Knowledge Management and Innovation (Smart Innovation Set – Volume 6)

BOUTILLIER Sophie, CARRÉ Denis, LEVRATTO Nadine
Entrepreneurial Ecosystems (Smart Innovation Set – Volume 2)

GALLAUD Delphine, LAPERCHE Blandine
Circular Economy, Industrial Ecology and Short Supply Chains (Smart Innovation Set – Volume 4)

GUERRIER Claudine
Security and Privacy in the Digital Era (Innovation and Technology Set – Volume 1)

MEGHOUAR HICHAM
Corporate Takeover Targets

MONINO Jean-Louis, SEDKAOUI Soraya
Big Data, Open Data and Data Development (Smart Innovation Set – Volume 3)

MOREL Laure, LE ROUX Serge
Fab Labs: Innovative User (Smart Innovation Set – Volume 5)

2015

CASADELLA Vanessa, LIU Zeting, DIMITRI Uzunidis
Innovation Capabilities and Economic Development in Open Economies (Smart Innovation Set – Volume 1)

CORSI Patrick, MORIN Dominique
Sequencing Apple's DNA

CORSI Patrick, NEAU Erwan
Innovation Capability Maturity Model

FAIVRE-TAVIGNOT Bénédicte
Social Business and Base of the Pyramid

GODÉ Cécile
Team Coordination in Extreme Environments

MAILLARD Pierre
Competitive Quality and Innovation

MASSOTTE Pierre, CORSI Patrick
Operationalizing Sustainability

MASSOTTE Pierre, CORSI Patrick
Sustainability Calling

2014

DUBÉ Jean, LEGROS Diègo
Spatial Econometrics Using Microdata

LESCA Humbert, LESCA Nicolas
Strategic Decisions and Weak Signals

2013

HABART-CORLOSQUET Marine, JANSSEN Jacques, MANCA Raimondo
VaR Methodology for Non-Gaussian Finance

2012

DAL PONT Jean-Pierre
Process Engineering and Industrial Management

MAILLARD Pierre
Competitive Quality Strategies

POMEROL Jean-Charles
Decision-Making and Action

SZYLAR Christian
UCITS Handbook

2011

LESCA Nicolas
Environmental Scanning and Sustainable Development

LESCA Nicolas, LESCA Humbert
Weak Signals for Strategic Intelligence: Anticipation Tool for Managers

MERCIER-LAURENT Eunika
Innovation Ecosystems

2010

SZYLAR Christian
Risk Management under UCITS III/IV

2009

COHEN Corine
Business Intelligence

ZANINETTI Jean-Marc
Sustainable Development in the USA

2008

CORSI Patrick, DULIEU Mike
The Marketing of Technology Intensive Products and Services

DZEVER Sam, JAUSSAUD Jacques, ANDREOSSO Bernadette
Evolving Corporate Structures and Cultures in Asia / Impact of Globalization

2007

AMMI Chantal
Global Consumer Behavior

2006

BOUGHZALA Imed, ERMINE Jean-Louis
Trends in Enterprise Knowledge Management

CORSI Patrick *et al.*
Innovation Engineering: the Power of Intangible Networks

Printed and bound by CPI Group (UK) Ltd, Croydon, CR0 4YY

15/09/2026

14962342-0003